OUT OF SRI LANKA

To the People of Sri Lanka

OUT OF SRI LANKA

TAMIL, SINHALA & ENGLISH POETRY
FROM SRI LANKA & ITS DIASPORAS

EDITED BY
VIDYAN RAVINTHIRAN,
SENI SENEVIRATNE
SHASH TREVETT

BLOODAXE BOOKS

ISBN: 978 1 78037 673 8

First published 2023 by
Bloodaxe Books Ltd,
Eastburn,
South Park,
Hexham,
Northumberland NE46 1BS.

www.bloodaxebooks.com
For further information about Bloodaxe titles
please visit our website and join our mailing list
or write to the above address for a catalogue.

Supported using public funding by
ARTS COUNCIL
ENGLAND

Cover design: Neil Astley & Pamela Robertson-Pearce.

Printed in Great Britain by Bell & Bain Limited, Glasgow, Scotland, on
acid-free paper sourced from mills with FSC chain of custody certification.

CONTENTS

E = written in English
S = translated from Sinhala
T = translated from Tamil

Richard de Zoysa (1958–90) E

INTRODUCTION

Already I begin with a stutter, unable to find a proper name adequate to the geography I wish to invoke. *Sri* (auspicious, blessed, holy) *Lanka* invokes a natural unity, an island-nation, in this instance one that also claims divine authorisation through its adoption of the Sinhala character, *Sri*, in its title. The introduction of this character on the licence plates of cars and buses sparked waves of protest in the Tamil areas of the country in the 1950s, almost 20 years before *Sri Lanka* replaced the colonial name Ceylon in 1972. But this already gets me too far into the story. *Ceylon, Lanka, Eelam* (and a whole prior genealogy of names: *Taprobane, Serendib*, where man alone is vile, etc.) are all too partial, too fraught, too freighted with bad history. As a poor compromise, I hit on *Lanka*, *Illangai* in Tamil, as distinguished from the separatist homeland, *Eelam*, sought by the Liberation Tigers of Tamil Eelam…

SUVENDRINI PERERA

As the first true anthology of Sri Lankan *and* diasporic poetry, this book affirms a national literature that has never been adequately read and studied. It is also, however, a transnational endeavour. Given Sri Lanka's history of multiple colonisation – by the Portuguese, the Dutch, and the British – as well as waves of both forced and voluntary migration out of the country, its literatures must be understood globally. This challenges literary marketing and literary history, which separate, for example, 'British Asian' or 'Asian-American' poetries from the 'postcolonial literature' of the Global South. But it affirms the work of scholars – this is Harshana Rambukwella, analysing the politics and poetics of Sinhala nationalism – who have tried to incorporate Sri Lanka 'into regional and global networks… a move that in its own way undermines nationalist assumptions about the past.'

Many poets in this anthology fled during the civil war and refuse to identify as 'Sri Lankan'; others remain endangered; while these poems were collated in the pandemic years of 2020-22, Sri Lanka underwent nothing short of a revolution, following economic crisis.

In what sometimes felt like a terrifying reprise of the country's brutal history – and, at other times, like a breath of fresh air, the start of something better – politicians were forced out of their positions and their homes, and organised protests combined with outright rioting, in events bursting suddenly on a Western media-scape otherwise preoccupied with the war in Ukraine.

On 9 July 2022, the front pages of the *Guardian* and BBC web-sites, and of Reddit, showed thousands – Buddhists, Hindus and Muslims in solidarity – storming the residence of the President, Gotabaya Rajapaksa. Labelled a war criminal by the UN (with two cases pending against him in the US), he and his brother Mahinda Rajapaksa aren't only responsible for corruption, cronyism and mismanagement of the economy, but for the detainment and murder of innocents during the civil war, and countless suppressive acts against minority Tamils and Muslims. Yes, by 2022, there was no fuel, food, and people died for want of medical supplies; schools closed, daily power outages lasted for hours, trishaws (tuk-tuks) sat in vast, snake-like, torpefied queues for days on end, seeking petrol – and inflation reached a crazy fifty percent. Yet as the families of the disappeared (snatched off the street, detained without trial, raped, killed, internally displaced) continue to insist, the protest movement has raged since the end of the civil war in 2009, and is really a matter of life and death. Sri Lanka has the second highest number of enforced disappearances of all the world's nations: his-tories of the civil war, such as Rohini Mohan's *The Seasons of Trouble*, Gordon Weiss's *The Cage*, and Frances Harrison's *Still Counting the Dead*, are must-reads for anyone who considers them-selves an informed world citizen.

Tear-gassed and fired on with water cannon (police beat jour-nalists on the scene savagely, firing live rounds into crowds) a unified people, chanting 'Go Home Gota' – urging him to step down and return to the US – temporarily repossessed the colonial mansion Rajapaksa didn't even live in, but within whose walls mil-lions of rupees were discovered squirrelled away. Amazed by the luxurious lifestyle of their President – such a comparison with their own struggles! – ordinary people leapt joyously into his swimming pool, took selfies on his immaculately manicured lawn, and slept in his dozens of regally-appointed beds. 'Occupy Temple Trees': the building became a communal soup kitchen and library. Pictures of protesters show them watering the plants, sweeping up; two women try out the President's gym equipment. Rajapaksa, having escaped by air to Singapore, via the Maldives, agreed to resign.

This was before the government upped their emergency measures, threw the protesters out, and made a former Prime Minister, Ranil Wickremesinghe – felt to be in cahoots with the Rajapakasas – the new President. It remains to be seen if the country will change for the better after all.

The economic crisis had worsened for months: why were these events so rarely covered in the UK and US news? On Reddit, confused Americans related these images – of a radical uprising, against a dynasty that used bribes and assassinations and media and social media blackouts to maintain power – to the venal assault of Trump supporters on the Capitol. Reading these posts, we began – as one often does, online – to feel addictively angry, and, as Sri Lankans, both misunderstood and unseen. We reconsidered what this anthology might achieve. As editors, we agree with the Indian poet and essayist, Adil Jussawalla – he was talking about the bombing of the Babri Masjid in 1992 – that poems splurged onto the page or webpage right after the event aren't usually *good* poems (which require time for reflection): we haven't rushed to include anything on the events of summer 2022.

Yet the time is right – the moment is now – for the world to know Sri Lanka better: its beauty and its pain. Seeing Sri Lankans of different stripes unify in civil disobedience (the government fruitlessly stirred up lies about Muslims, to shatter the protest along identity lines) confirmed our decision to, in this anthology, not segregate Anglophone, Sinhala and Tamil poems, but stick to an alphabetical ordering that creates serendipitous connections. Let us affirm this book's cosmopolitan agenda: its mixture, too, of styles and places and times of writing. Poetries from different subject-positions find in this book, we hope, a way of living alongside each other. Concentrating on work published after Independence in 1948, we have occasionally ignored this boundary, to acknowledge a longer history of poetic modernism. Recovering from archives works long out of print, we also put a call out for new poems being written today. Some have never been published before.

This anthology represents a human rights intervention, it is – discussing a country afflicted with amnesia, in denial of its past – a matter of putting things on record. Tamil poets in particular write a poetry of witness; these works reshape our understanding of the poetics of atrocity, and of trauma (the tsunami of December 2004, which killed almost 40,000 Sri Lankans and displaced a million more, also looms large). But since poetries of the Global South, and post-colonial poetry, is often read reductively – not as art – let us also insist on the multiple creativities on show here, often in poems that simultaneously challenge and pleasure the reader. We recognise as

21

anthologists, selecting and discarding poems, that the application of Anglo-American literary standards – by a trio of poets based, now, in the UK and the US – to global literatures, even those to which one is personally tied, raises questions. But the refusal of Anglo-American audiences to grapple seriously with 'world poetry' *as poetry* is a tremendous oversight. It is in the aesthetic realm that the claims of otherness, disturbing the reader out of their centrally-heated reverie, may be strongly felt. There are poems in this anthology whose accents of sentiment and accusation, whose vehemences of yearning and mourning, as well as technicalities of diction, rhythm, imagery and lineation, may jar with sensibilities shaped (straitened) by creative writing workshops and mainstream review culture. There are also poems to immediately delight anyone eager to explore poetry from beyond their shores, but unsure where to begin. Lovers of poetry will, we hope, enjoy these works employing both traditional and open forms; we've concrete poems, spoken-word provocations, and experimental, post-lyric hybrids of verse and prose.

*

Modern English poetry in Sri Lanka originated with George Keyt; Tamil, with Mahakavi; and Sinhala, with Siri Gunasinghe. These poetries developed parallel to each other, their lines rarely touching – astonishing, in an island smaller in size than Scotland. (The exception would be those bilingual poets who wrote in both Sinhala and English: for more on this, see the discussion below of Sinhala poetry.) Even though Anglophone poets were influenced, to a certain extent, by the folk tales and ballads of their linguistic community, there is more Wordsworth and Matthew Arnold than Lal Hegoda in Yasmine Gooneratne's poetry. As Tamil and Sinhala poets made sense of the new reality of life beyond colonial subjugation, there was no interaction between the two, no cross-pollination.

Yet Rambukwella argues this was to be expected, since there was no pan-Sri Lankan identity prior to colonisation: following Independence, no existing framework could be reverted to. The island was unified under a single ruler only in 1815, when the British conquered the kingdom of Kandy, the last pocket of resistance to European rule. Although the British claimed rule over the whole island, they relied on ethnic predicates and 'communal representation': the colonial census hardened pre-existing identity-categories, until 'elite politicians from various communities perceived themselves as representatives of a particular ethno-religious group rather than as members of an overarching nation.' Post-Independence, these ethnically 'homogenous and eventually conflictual identities' were exploited by political parties to such an extent that Sri Lankans are still searching today, for a mode of life transcending (in particular) the boundaries separating Sinhala from Tamil, and Buddhist from Hindu.

The hope expressed by this book's juxtaposition of wildly different poets must therefore be tempered, by a recognition of dividing lines whose force has not diminished. It feels necessary, in what follows, to explain to the reader the genealogies of Tamil, Sinhala, and English poetry in siloed terms.

*

Tamil poetry

Tamil poetry in Sri Lanka has a long history linked with South India. Eelattu Poothanthevanar wrote in the Sangam period – between 100 BC and AD 300 – in the courts of Madurai in South India. Sangam literature is the cornerstone of Tamil literature in both countries: religious and political in nature, it is governed by strict forms. Tamil poetics did not change for a long time: poets responded to colonialism, the spread of Christianity, and European incursions on Tamil society and culture with a poetics still derived from the Sangam era. Only in the last 80 years has Tamil poetry from Sri Lanka changed in a revolutionary manner. Following Independence in 1948, poets had to make sense of a new post-colonial reality, and also contend with the rise of Sinhala national-ism. While fiction and drama took longer to adjust, poetry from each of the Tamil regions of Sri Lanka – the North, the East and the Hill Country – seemed to revel in the possibilities.

The 1940s saw the emergence of the *marumalarchi* (renaissance) writers, including Mahakavi, Mugugaiyan and Neelavanan. Mahakavi published his first collection in 1951, using Jaffna speech-sounds to break free of South Indian styles. Though a traditionalist with little time for free verse, he created a modern diction, and, by establish-ing Kavi Arangus (places where poets read publicly) nurtured the next generation. These younger poets, including Ponnambalam, M.A. Nuhman and Shanmugam Sivalingam, were Marxist, opposed caste-divisions, and championed the downtrodden.

The UNP government elected in 1977 'promised', writes Jennifer Hyndman, 'to create a just and free society that included Tamil-speaking people'; it also opened the country's 'markets to unbridled capitalist development and export-oriented industrialisation'. Just four years later, Jaffna Public Library was burnt to the ground by Sinhalese arsonists aided by police and politicians. Over ninety thousand irrecoverable ancient documents were lost, many written on palm leaves (it is said that Tamil letters evolved their round and flowing shape, so the pen wouldn't tear those delicate leaves). In July 1983, thousands of Tamils were attacked, many were killed, and their homes and business were looted and set aflame. Once again, the police were in cahoots, providing lists of Tamil families and Tamil businesses to target. Comparable with the *Kristallnacht* or 'Night of Broken Glass' in Nazi Germany – the German-Sri Lankan, Jewish poet Anne Ranasinghe lived through both, and wrote a poem about it – Black July was an attempt at genocide. It drastically reshaped Sri Lankan Tamil poetry, both for those who remained, and for a growing community of ex-pats and refugees.

The events of 1983 started the civil war. Two seminal anthologies were published: *Maranathul Valvom* (We Live Amidst Death) in 1984, in which a new generation of poets, including Cheran, Jeyapalan and Solaikkili, created a poetry of witness; and *Sollaatha Sethigal* (Unspoken Words), collecting the poetry of ten Tamil women – the first book of this kind – which came out in 1986. Urvasi, Chelvi and Sivaramani wrote of families shattered, rape, murder, and changing gender roles in Tamil society. In 2012 the poet and academic M.A. Nuhman (see page 249) wrote that 'poetry in a time of ethnic conflict plays two different roles. On the one hand it promotes the ideologies of ethnicity, nationalism and violence. On the other hand, it exposes the ugly nature of these ideologies and calls for the meaningful reconstruction of human values and unity.' Selecting from Tamil poets who catalogued the trauma and dislocation of the civil war years, we focus the latter, not the former.

The civil war also saw the emergence of a distinctive Muslim Tamil poetics, from the people formerly known as the 'Ceylon Moors' who lived in the Tamil-speaking North and East of the country. Although they were initially supportive of the liberation struggle, relations between the LTTE (Liberation Tigers of Tamil Eelam) and the Muslim community deteriorated in the late 1980s, leading to ethnic cleansing by the LTTE of Muslims living in the Tamil areas they controlled. Almost seventy thousand Muslims were forcibly evacuated from the North, others were brutally killed. Poets including Rashmy, Anar and Alari memorialise this suffering.

Tamil poetry, ever since the Sangam period, has prioritised *thinai*: a concept of landscape. The traditional five landscapes – *Kurunji* (hill country), *Neithal* (coastal), *Mullai* (forest), *Marutam* (pastoral) and *Palai* (desert) – frame cultural, economic, ecological and emotional realities. The Indian Tamil poet, scholar and translator, A.K. Ramanujan describes *thinai* as both a place and a mood. When the civil war began in 1983, this poetics of location started to fragment. As people moved – through choice or necessity – to new spaces, experiences of exile and trauma drastically altered old notions of the exterior and the interior. Literature had to adapt: Tamil poets, including those of the diaspora, began to write about loss and cultural realignment, working within a tradition where exile or banishment from one's homeland was seen as the ultimate punishment. The new Tamil poetry therefore built on the legacies of the past: it articulated unprecedented horrors, yet through a poetics of landscape now estranged into a nightmare of dislocation.

Tamil poets know that their works will provide the only record of crimes never investigated, and often covered up, by the state. They resist the neo-colonialism of the Sinhala government, that has erased Tamil history and culture from Sri Lanka's actual and mental topographies. The building of Viharas in the north, the renaming of streets and road signs with Sinhala script placed prominently above the Tamil; the involvement of the military in Tamil schools to 're-educate' children – poetry counteracts these erasures. Most importantly, Tamil poems are monuments constructed out of words and rhythms, for those barred by the government from mourning their dead, whether they be civilians or LTTE combatants. Physical memorials are bulldozed by the authorities, religious ceremonies and remembrance services are not permitted. This is why Ahilan writes, in 'Semmani 03':

> I am building them a memorial
> not with stones
> or with water,
> but with the sounds flowing in the air
> which follow me incessantly.

>> (tr. from Tamil by Shash Trevett)

It is the poets and their translators who have become guardians of a Tamil history unrecognised by the Sri Lankan government. This heartbreaking poetry of trauma coming out of Tamil Sri Lanka needs to be read and discussed, so that the world can never again say, they did not know.

*

Sinhala poetry

'The year 1956,' writes D.C.R.A. Goonetilleke, presented a 'watershed in Sri Lankan history,' when the Sinhala Only act was passed, making it the official language: a decision further minoritising Tamils (the Gal Oya riots occurred that year), and leading to agonised reflection on the part of English speakers:

> A national dress with all that it symbolises, replaced the top hat and coat-tails, and English was displaced from its pre-eminent position as the official language and the medium of instruction in schools and universities. English was relegated to the status of a second language, despite the regrets of the English-educated classes. But it was not properly treated as a second language; it was neglected for two decades and even reviled. Paradoxically, it was in this context that literature in English by Sri Lankans came into prominence. Faced with the loss or at least a significant diminution of their privileges, the English-educated became more aware of themselves and the social, cultural, and literary context in which they lived.
>
> 'Sri Lankan Poetry in English: Getting Beyond the Colonial Heritage', *ARIEL: A Review of International English Literature*, 21.3 (July 1990): 39-53, p.40.

Since many in this anthology wrote (write) in both Sinhala and English, the long-term effects of this situation can occasionally be felt in both poetries, and some poetry in English may be – as Yasmine Gooneratne observes – deeply influenced by Sinhala, and even Tamil and Sanskrit, poetics:

> Sinhala folk poetry, which uses laconic understatement and the briefest possible allusions to a familiar cultural and social context to convey complex personal emotion, was a world unknown to the Ceylonese poet in English until George Keyt published a volume of translations in 1938. Side by side with this feeling for economy in expression that marks the folk tradition, goes a very different mode of writing; elaborate diction and an artistically contrived play of metaphor and simile characterise the courtly and scholarly poetic traditions Ceylonese poets inherit from ancient Sanskrit, Tamil and Sinhala literature. Here form – though not all in all – counts for a good deal, and the rules of decorum are strictly observed.

As such, though Sri Lankan poetry is an 'amalgam' drawing on Western sources, we shouldn't neglect native sources harder – for some readers – to pinpoint:

It is well to be aware, therefore, of the different literary tra-
ditions and the history of cultural conflict that provide a
background to Sri Lanka's modern poetry. The bare, laconic
expression of certain poets may not be derived from a mod-
ern American source; it may be inherited from a rich and
thriving indigenous folk tradition. The markedly rhythmic
and lyrical qualities of some modern Ceylonese verse, even
when at its "freest", may not be caused by a lingering Tenny-
sonian influence; they are natural to a local literary verse form
that was composed not merely to be recited, but to be sung.

'A Perspective On The Poetry of Sri Lanka', *Journal of South
Asian Literature*, 12.1/2 (Fall-Winter 1976): 1-2, p.1.

Some Sinhala poets write in both English and Sinhala, others only
in English – Suwanda Sugunasiri mentions Gooneratne, Ashley
Halpe and Asoka Weerasinghe. What remains to be mapped, then,
is a Sinhala poetics encompassing works written in both that lan-
guage and in English.

Turning to poems in Sinhala, the question of musicality is
unavoidable. Pre-modern South Asia saw poetry and song as the
same thing and even in the 20th century, observes Garrett Field,
'Sinhala songwriters and poets' share the common, 'ancient Indian
term *rasa* (sentiment; emotion evoked in the listener) in discussions
of Sinhala song and poetry'. He explains the evolution of modern
styles out of colonial residues:

Given that Sri Lanka was a British colony like India, it is not a
coincidence that Sinhala poets in the early twentieth century
had come into contact with the same Christian and Victorian
moral beliefs and tended to utilise verse for didacticism and
reform. Their works were as bound up with the Buddhist
revival as were [John] de Silva's theatre songs. The poets of
the early twentieth century are known as the 'first- generation
Colombo poets'. They published in Sinhala-language news-
papers that propagated the revival and disseminated their works
through a wide range of new publications that included
monthly journals, children's journals, and popular journals
devoted exclusively to Sinhala verse. Many were active par-
ticipants in literary societies, especially the All-Ceylon Poets'
Congress, established to propagate Sinhala-language poetry.

*Modernizing Composition: Sinhala Song, Poetry, and Politics in
Twentieth-Century Sri Lanka* (Oakland: University of California
Press, 2017), p.26.

Cultural nationalism saw the formation by Munidasa Cumaratunga
of the *Hela Havula* (Hela Fraternity) in 1941, whose poets, including

Rapiyel Tennakoon and Jayamaha Vellala, argued for, in the words of Rambukwella, the 'autochthonous origins of the Sinhala as a people and their language and culture'. Unlike their predecessors, they embraced ambiguity, symbol, myth, allusion (providing commentaries on their works, when required) and complex forms harking back to pre-modern Sinhala poetries. Gunadasa Amerasekera, controversial for his nativism – tied to his imagery, in both verse and prose, of 'weva, dagoba, yaya – lake, stupa and paddy field' (Rambukwella) – called for a dynamic tradition illuminating (these are Amerasekera's words) the 'real life of the people', absorbing folk styles into verse-portraits of unstained rural cultures.

The real dynamism came from elsewhere. Field observes in the 1950s the simultaneous and interrelated creation of two 'genres of Sinhala song and poetry that had no precedent in Sri Lanka: radio opera and free verse', or *ñisandäs kāvya*, innovated by Siri Gunasinghe. This modernist experiment – occurring alongside those of the Peradeniya School of poets, inspired by Ediriweera Sarachchandra – transformed modern Sinhala poetry. Refusing tired tropes, Gunasinghe introduced into his 'poetry without metre' subject-matter previously unavailable to poets. He was clear in his stance toward earlier works, and toward overseas influences: old-style Sinhala poems provided 'descriptions of beautiful things like flowers, butterflies, the moonlight, rainbows, waterfalls, flowing rivers, and women. OK, that's fine. Yet after reading English poetry I understood the qualities that poetry did not possess.' Jayantha Amerasinghe, who relates the creation of Sinhala free verse to the 'dual mentality' of a society where a 'capitalist mode of production was superimposed on a feudal economy', directs us to Gunasinghe's article, 'A New Note in Contemporary Sinhalese Poetry', published in the *Observer Annual*, and pointing out – in Amerasinghe's paraphrase – 'the severe limitations and weaknesses of Sinhala poetry influenced by the national revivalist movement at that time, and the constrictive archaisms tied to "four line structure and the Samudra gosha metre".'

*

Anglophone poetry

The poetry of the Global South is neglected by postcolonial scholars more interested in fiction, which seems to provide – to apply George Orwell's view of prose – a clear window on historical realities. As Jahan Ramazani explains:

postcolonial criticism is largely grounded in mimetic presup-
positions about literature. But since poetry mediates experience
through a language of exceptional figural and formal density,
it is a less transparent medium by which to recuperate the
history, politics, and sociology of postcolonial societies [...]
While theoretical inquiry is not necessarily inimical to poetry
[...] the genre also demands specifically literary modes of
response and recognition – of figurative devices, generic
codes, stanzaic patterns, prosodic twists, and allusive turns.

The Hybrid Muse: Postcolonial Poetry in English (University of
Chicago Press, 2001), p.4.

When postcolonial poetry is glanced at, it is in terms of the
counter-appropriation of Anglo-American poetic forms, and a
reclamation, twisting, subversion, of the English language itself.
Some Sri Lankan poets have considered this necessary. Lakdasa
Wikkramasinha, for instance – who wrote in both Sinhala and
English – announced:

I have come to realise that I am using the language of the
most despicable and loathsome people on earth; I have no
wish to extend its life and range, enrich its totality.
    To write in English is a form of cultural treason. I have
had for the future to think of a way of circumventing this
treason; I propose to do this by making my writing entirely
immoralist and destructive.

Lustre. Poems (Kandy: Ariya Printing Works, 1965), p. 51.

Yet Suresh Canagarajah observes how 'puzzling' a poetics Wikkra-
masinha actually created: he wrote startlingly rifted, intensely
configured poems in English, and is represented in this anthology
as an Anglophone poet. It is a complex situation.
    Yasmine Gooneratne writes as part of an English-speaking elite,
and Lilamani de Silva critiques her as out of touch ('I am not sure
if a Lankan April can be spoken of as "Spring"', remarks the critic)
but Gooneratne is alert in both her creative and critical writing to
the erasure of native language-practices:

The Sri Lankan reader of English was encouraged to ignore
and ultimately to forget, the literary traditions of monastery,
court and village that had accumulated over centuries among
singers and writers of Sinhala and Tamil. Johnson, Thomson,
Wordsworth, Byron and Tennyson duly claimed their Ceylon-
ese admirers and imitators and later generations were brought
up on the ringing rhetoric of Scott, Macaulay and (later on)

29

Sir Henry Newbolt. The Oxbridge tradition dies hard in Sri
Lanka, as in many other ex-colonial countries, and university
teaching today merely adds the study of Eliot, Yeats, Hopkins
and Lawrence to its earlier preoccupation with the English
Augustans and Romantics, occasionally making gestures in
the direction of Lowell, Frost and John Crowe Ransom.

'A Perspective On The Poetry of Sri Lanka', p.1

Ranjini Obeyesekere writes about an issue of *New Ceylon Writing*
edited by Gooneratne, that the poets in it

> for the most part belong to [...] a class of 'English educated',
> who for that very reason were isolated from the intensity and
> divisive rivalries generated by the language policies introduced
> by governments after 1956. The politics of language, or 'the
> language' issue', as it came to be known, dominated the political
> arena in the sixties [...] Not only did almost every political
> leader, Tamil and Sinhala, of every political colouring, un-
> ashamedly use the language issue as an instrument with which
> to jockey for power, but their short-sighted and constantly
> changing policies produced generations of young people isolated
> into linguistic groups and fed on inflammable political rhetoric.
> By contrast, the 'English-educated' had been part of the carry-
> over of the colonial education system whose one benefit was
> perhaps that it produced generations of Sinhalese and Tamils
> who could communicate with each other and build relation-
> ships that cut across ethnic barriers. Writers from this group,
> therefore, tend to adopt a liberal stance.
>
> *Journal of South Asian Literature*, 22.1 (Winter, Spring 1987),
> pp. 1-5.

Wikkramasinha and Gooneratne focus linguistic conquest, yet claim
the right to write in English in styles tinged by Western forms. The
Sri Lankan and diasporic poet who chooses to write in English
isn't doing so (not the ones included here, anyway) out of self-
hatred, a yearning to be the coloniser, to sound and look white. In
a sense, canonical English poetry – a set of exemplary texts, giving
voice to what was once called universal human nature – came into
being *in* the colonies. Gauri Viswanathan observes that 'as early as
the 1820s, when the classical curriculum still reigned supreme in
England [...] English as the study of culture and not simply the
study of language had already found a secure place in the British
Indian curriculum.' Sri Lankans had every reason to feel alienated
by the English texts foisted on them – but some came to feel that
the language and its literatures weren't anything they needed to

seize or reclaim, but a persisting inheritance.

There was a mid-century shift in how such things were understood. In 1954 (two years before the Sinhala Only Act declared it the official language, and bullies took tar-brushes to signs featuring Tamil or English), Godfrey Goonetilleke argued that Sri Lankan English, 'derivative' and denatured, was no good for literature: 'a large part of our perceptions...and attitudes in our relation with other human beings does not find a natural place in the English spoken by us.' Yet, with the proclamation of the republic of Sri Lanka – no longer Ceylon – in 1972, came the period, writes Rajiva Wijesinha, 'in which writing in English once again became respectable in Sri Lanka, after the denigration in the previous two decades that seemed to be a corollary of the attainment of independence'. It was in this spirit that Gāmini Salgādo, possibly the first person of colour to become a full professor of literature in England (at Exeter), could write of discovering as a child in the works of Shakespeare flora and fauna alien to his own shores – without feeling alienated: 'the lily that grew in the mind may not have been a recognisable botanical specimen but it was truly a plant or flower of light'.

*

Civil war

One accusation levelled at modern Sri Lankan poetry in Sinhala – returning here to Ranjini Obeyesekere's article – is that it has not reckoned with the atrocities of the civil war. Following 'the shattering events of July 1983',

> The ethnic conflict, hitherto but a slowly festering yet subcutaneous sore in the consciousness of the Sinhala people, suddenly erupted. The riots, arson, looting, and killings of those weeks revealed the violent underside of the body politic and left the country reeling. One would expect then a reflection of these issues and their implications in the creative literature of recent years. What is surprising, even disturbing, is that there has been none.

According to this perspective, to discover a *civil war poetics*, we must turn to 'writing in Tamil and English in Sri Lanka'. We have discussed the poetry of witness practised by Tamil poets; the Anglophone poet less directly connected to events must devise their own strategies. The poems of Jean Arasanayagam (who married a Tamil, got booted out of her home, and began writing at this point in a freer, wilder, even unedited way) evince an impulse to fragmentation always in tension with a yearning, to restore those fragments to a possible unity. This phenomenon registers the contested and bitty colonial history of the island, but also her search for a creative response, to the feeling, as she writes, of a country torn, or tearing itself, in two. Her stylistic excesses, her cataloguing garrulity, are in this respect reminiscent of the poetry of Walt Whitman – whose largesse, nearing shapelessness, his pressurised passion, expresses his anxieties about the United States becoming disunited in the 19th century. Other poems, by Sri Lankan and diasporic poets experiencing cither internal or external exile – a feeling, that is, of encryptedness and disconnection – may remind us of how Northern Irish poetry processes a different set of 'Troubles' (Sri Lankans use this word for their conflict too – the Tamil for it is *pirachanai*).

As anthologists of an emerging national and transnational literature attuned to the events and repercussions of the civil war (1983-2009), we had to make difficult decisions? Should poems approaching sheer notation of atrocities be included, if – despite their aesthetic nullity – they have played a central role in how people understand their plight? These are hard questions with no easy answers. We have not included poetry cheerleading violently for one side or the other: boosting, that is, either Sinhala majority governments, or the LTTE 'whose brutal violence', writes Suvendrini Perera, 'was directed not only against the Lankan state and Sinhala civilians, but also at the Tamil and Muslim populations in the areas that it claimed as its homeland'. Selecting poems about the conflict by diasporic writers, we chose those that engaged with mixed feelings of survivor's guilt, separateness, and the understanding that as a person overseas, one must investigate one's own relationship to such material.

*

Eccentric poetries

We cannot claim that this is a full and comprehensive survey of poetry out of Sri Lanka since 1948. But we can say that we have spent the last two years reading everything that was available to us, in the West. Many texts were out of print; works existing only in private libraries in Sri Lanka became inaccessible during the pandemic. Some poets did not respond to our queries. Several writers we wanted to include are absent.

When choosing Tamil and Sinhala poems we were reliant on existing translations, some of which were excellent, some not so good. All too often we found translations which prioritised the literal over the aesthetic. As Walter Benjamin has written, those who merely 'transmit' meaning from one language to another 'cannot transmit anything but information – hence, something inessential'. These 'inessential' translations failed to capture the cadence, the lilt of the original poem; we had to make decisions on whether to include an important poet, poorly translated, or to leave them out of the book. Regrettably in a few cases we opted for the latter, deciding that it was better for the poet to be absent than to have their work represented by a translation which failed to sing. It is our hope that in the future, a commitment to translating Tamil and Sinhala poetry might become a priority in the country, with funding, mentoring and editorial assistance being given to a new generation of translators, who, building on the work of Chelva Kanaganayakam and Lakshmi Holmström, Ranjini Obeyesekere and Lakshmi de Silva (to name but a few), would keep poems from the past relevant to changing times.

Some poets writing in Sri Lanka do so within rich networks, with the feeling of a tradition and how they slot into it, and connections to, in particular, the South Indian literary scene. These poets are regulars at Jaipur, the Kerala Literary Festival, and events in Singapore. But others, perhaps especially those outside the country yet unconnected to resources in the US and UK, write with no reassurance that their work exists in a coherent continuum, that it will be understood or even glancingly read, and, as a result, they manifest a range of anxieties. To delve into Sri Lankan and diasporic poetries is to reckon with the mixed editorial and aesthetic standards associated with self-published works, with presses putting out uncopyedited or otherwise unreliable texts; some poets go off the grid for good, becoming uncontactable, and when (eventually) tracked down, feel so alienated from their work as to prevent its being republished. We must also consider the 'malaise akin to psychic numbing' which the late academic Malathi de Alwis relates to 'several decades of living with unrelenting violence and atrocity', and how it can either annul the creative soul, or be opposed, and survived, by what readers may observe in this anthology as a strong, unexpected current of dark humour. (When, in January 2023, the police deployed water cannon in Jaffna, Tamil protesters started shampooing their hair.) This mode of resilience brings to mind a joke often told in Sri Lanka, following the tsunami – quoted here, since it could be a prose poem in its own right:

The phone rings at a government office in Colombo. An administrator picks up:

'Hello?'

'Yes, this is the earthquake monitoring centre. We wanted to inform you that a T-tsunami will be arriving in approximately 2 hours.'

'A T.Tsunami? Yes yes, we'll make the necessary arrangements to receive T. Tsunami.'

And so it goes that the administrator sends a car to the airport to pick up a Mr T. Tsunami and the car waits for some time. But alas, it seems a Mr T. Tsunami is not coming – at least not by plane. Actually, by this time, the t-tsunami had already arrived – as everybody knew – by sea.

Tsunami in a Time of War: Aid, Activism & Reconstruction in Sri Lanka & Aceh, ed. Malathi de Alwis and Eva-Lotta Hedman (ICES: Colombo, 2009), pp.206-7.

The explosiveness of Sri Lankan history, its cavalcade of events seeming to demand a response, produces a situation where deeply felt and meaningfully shaped poems are often not written by 'poets', as we understand that role as a profession supported by publishers, festivals, and academic institutions. Instead, we find poems written by photographers, government workers, novelists, journalists – people for whom the luxury of considering themselves one of Shelley's unacknowledged legislators of the world was never available, but who were pressed by extraordinary circumstances toward a lyric recognition of complexities otherwise beyond understanding.

At times our relationship as editors, to the poets in this volume, transformed beyond the usual duties of the anthologist, to include mentorship and editorial input. At times we felt somewhat overwhelmed by the importance of the task we had undertaken and the level of work it required but it was a project close to all our hearts. As three writers of Sri Lankan heritage, who grew up in different decades and with different life experiences, we committed ourselves to a process of dialogue and debate that was uplifting, challenging and supportive in equal measure and through which we all had the opportunity for growth, learning and change.

Even when considering poems written by poets who *do* have connections within Western poetry cultures, let's, finally, consider the absence of 'Sri Lankan' from both British and American understandings of what it means to be (South) Asian. In terms of media, literary, and political representation, Sri Lankan and diasporic people are more than minoritised: they are *hyperminoritised*. They are neglected by diversity initiatives, they have no commemorative

34

events dedicated to their histories, their inheritances (both traumatic and cultural) are simply not talked about or understood. Many poems in this book evince a peculiar isolation, peculiar in that it has not even learned to understand itself in terms of the parameters that, for instance, Black writing has evolved to take control of its destiny. We hope this book helps Sri Lankan and diasporic people decide what they want in the 21st century. What alternative can be imagined to identity politics, so Anglo-American in its biases, and neglectful of transnational histories, and – for Sri Lankans – disturbingly reminiscent of violent tribalisms 'back home'?

VIDYAN RAVINTHIRAN
SENI SENEVIRATNE
SHASH TREVETT

AAZHIYAAL

(*b*. 1968)

Aazhiyaal (the pen name of Mathubashini Ragupathy) was born in Trincomalee in Eastern Sri Lanka. She taught English at the Vavuniya Campus, Jaffna University, before moving to Australia in 1997 where she worked for two decades in the IT sector and commercial management in Canberra. Aazhiyaal has published four collections of poetry in Tamil: *Uraththup Pesa* (2000), *Thuvitham* (2006), *Karunaavu* (2013) and *Nedumarangalaai Vazhthal* (2020), the last honoured by Canada's Tamil Literary Garden. Her poems have appeared in anthologies and have been translated into several languages. She in turn has translated Australian Aboriginal poetry into Tamil (*Poovulagaik Kattralum Kettalum*, 2017). Aazhiyaal writes about women's place within patriarchy and uses her work to make sense of the war in Sri Lanka: 'I believe that poetry is the antidote to the present rat-race. It is needed, it is necessary.'

Unheeded Sights

After the rains
the tiled roofs shone
sparklingly clean.
The sky was not yet minded
to become a deeper blue.
The tar roads reminded me
intermittently of rainbows.
From the entire surface of the earth
a fine smoke arose
like the smoke of frankincense, or akil wood,
the earth's scent stroking the nostrils,
fragrant as a melody.

As the army truck coming towards me
drives away,
a little girl transfers her candy-floss
from one hand to the other
raises her right hand up high
and waves her tiny fingers.

And like the sweet surprise
of an answering air-letter
all the soldiers standing in the truck
wave their hands, exactly like her.

The blood that froze in my veins
for an instant, in amazement,
flows again rapidly, asking aloud,
'War? In this land?
Who told you?'

[tr. from Tamil by Lakshmi Holmström]

Manamperi

We have seen it on many mornings
during our frequent travels
at the edges of street fences – or
at the intersection of four roads.

It takes many forms,
shape-shifting into dog, bear or wolf,
eagle, cat or buffalo.

With its lifted leg beside a telegraph post
it stares at me.
It must be many days since that animal slept.

Its eyes speak aloud
of a creature unknown to me.
The avid hunger in those eyes
makes me aware of an unknown tongue.

In distress I walk past,
telling myself that this must be
the violent language that beautiful Manamperi
and our Koneswari heard, recognised.

In the midst of my sleep that night
after the day's frenzied roaming
and its mental anguish
I too recognised
the same, the very same
deeply embedded language of violence.

Beside me, my husband lay,
his breath cooling.

[tr. from Tamil by Lakshmi Holmström]

Manamperi, age 22, was prominent in the left-wing student uprising against the Sri Lankan government in the late 1960s and 70s. In April 1971, she was captured by the Sri Lankan army, raped and killed. Koneswari Selvakumar, a Tamil woman, aged 33, was gang-raped by the Sri Lankan army in her home, in 1997. A grenade was then thrust into her vagina, and fired.

BĀSHANA ABEYWARDANE
(*b*. 1972)

Rohitha Bāshana Abeywardane was a member of the founding editorial board and later editor in chief of the Sinhala alternative weekly newspaper *Hiru*. In 2003, he was one of the activists who organised the Sinhala-Tamil Art Festival. His journalistic commitments brought on threats to his life, and he had to leave Sri Lanka. He continues to publish and coordinates Journalists for Democracy in Sri Lanka, an organisation founded by journalists in exile. Following a stay in the Heinrich Böll House, Langenbroich, Abeywardane took part in the PEN Writers in Exile Program from September 2007 to August 2010. Today, he lives in Germany with his wife.

The Window of the Present

Nightmares, long dead,
peer through the shattered panes of the
window of the present.

The dead of the south, killed on the streets,
with bullet-riddled skulls,
walk once again, through an endless night,

and those of the north drowned in deluges of fire
when rains of steel drench their unforgiving earth,
gaze through the shards of glass empty eyed;

as slaughtering armies, prowl under starless skies,
upholding sovereignty
with blood-soaked hands.

Our past is the last breath of those
countless generations entombed
without seeing the day of freedom.

But who is to say
that even this July a breath of summer's hope, would not
steal through the shattered panes of the window of the present.

[tr. from Sinhala by Prathap de Silva]

PACKIYANATHAN AHILAN
(*b.* 1970)

Born in Jaffna in the north of Sri Lanka, Packiyanathan Ahilan has lived
through the thirty-year civil war. An academic as well as a poet, he has
published three collections of poetry and is Senior Lecturer in Art History at
the University of Jaffna. As well as writing about the visual arts, poetry,
theatre and heritage, he curates art exhibitions and is co-editor of *Reading Sri
Lankan Society and Culture* (Volumes 1 & 2). Ahilan's poetry is sparse and
staccato, like a heartbeat: he is one of the most influential poets writing in
Tamil in Sri Lanka today.

Days in the Bunker III

Good Friday.
The day they nailed you
to the cross.

A scorching wind
blew across the land and the sea.
One or two seagulls
sailed in an immaculate sky.
The wind
howling in the palm trees
spoke of unfathomable terror.
That was the last day of our village.

We fishermen came ashore,
only the waves

returned to the sea.
When the sun fell into the ocean,
we too fell
on our knees
and wept.

And our lament
turned slowly into night.

In the distance
our village was burning
like a body being cremated.

Good Friday.
The day they nailed you
to the cross.

[tr. from Tamil by Sascha Ebeling]

A Poem about Your Village and My Village

1

I do not know.
I do not know if your village
is near the ocean with its wailing waves
or near a forest.
I do not know your roads
made from red earth and
lined with tall jute palms.
I do not know
the birds of your village
that come and sing in springtime.
I do not know
the tiny flowers along the roadsides
that open their eyelids when the rains pour down.
I do not know the stories
you tell during long nights
to the sound of drumbeats
or the ponds in your village
where the moon goes to sleep.

2

Tonight,
when even the wind is full of grief,
you and I know one thing:
Our villages have become
small
or perhaps large
cemeteries.
The sea with its dancing waves
is covered with blood.
All forests with their
trees reaching up to the sky
are filled with scattered flesh
and with the voices of lost souls.
During nights of war
dogs howl, left to themselves,
and all roads and the thousands
of footprints our ancestors left behind
are grown over with grass.
We know all this,
you and I.
We now know about
the flowers that died,
the abandoned lines of poetry,
the moments no one wants to remember.

3

But
do you know
if the burnt grass
still has roots,
or if the abandoned poems
can still be rooted in words?
If, like them, you do not know
whether our ancient flames
are still silently smouldering
deep down in that ocean
covered with blood,
know this today:
They say that
after he had lain in hiding
for a thousand years

one day
the sun rose again.

[tr. from Tamil by Sascha Ebeling]

Corpse No. 182

One garment torn to shreds.
I removed that and found
another, drenched in pus.

One breast was missing.
Stuck to the other breast
there was a small child
that I could not remove.
They were fused into one body.

I cleaned them and noted down:
Corpse No. 182.

[tr. from Tamil by Sascha Ebeling]

Corpse No.183. Newborn No. 02

No vital signs.
Blood covered her like a sari.
Hanging from her womb
by the umbilical cord,
there was a foetus stirring.
I cut the cord.
I shook it, and it started to cry.

I wrote in the register:
Corpse No.183
Newborn No. 02.

[tr. from Tamil by Sascha Ebeling]

ALARI

(*b.* 1976)

Alari is the pen name of Abdul Latif Mohammad Rifaz, a Muslim Tamil who lives in the East of Sri Lanka. He has published five collections: *Poomikkadiyil Vaanam* (2005), *Paravai Pol Sirakadikkum Kadal* (2006), *Ellaa Pookkalum Uthirnthuvidum* (2008), *Thuliallathu Thukal* (2021) and *Perukku* (2022). Sparse in style and formal in diction, Alari's is an important voice, chronicling the experiences of the Muslim community at the hands of the LTTE: in 'A Lifeless Sea' he recounts the murder of fishermen by the Tamil Tigers and examines notions of power and of powerlessness.

When Someone Is Killed

What does it matter if someone is killed?
Won't the blood seep through the soil
to nourish the hibiscus, which will flower
as usual, dotting the green grass?

Won't the flies lurking in lavatory pits
flit, as usual, from one thing to another?
Won't the voices which mourn now
quieten with time?

Of course, the wind, instead of carrying
the scent of jasmine, will bear the pungent
stink of the dead.

Yet, what does it matter if someone is killed?
Except that somewhere soon,
someone else will need to die.

[tr. from Tamil by Shash Trevett]

A Lifeless Sea

As the waves crashed upon the shore,
we discovered their corpses. Their eyes
were wide open, their hands shrunken,
their bodies bearing bullet wounds.

44

That night, without disturbing the foam,
they had cast their lines into the waves
and had waited patiently for the catch.

The night was oppressive, black as charcoal.
What did they feel, those simple people
who had made no demands of those in power?
No, not even for a piece of land.

The rain which had poured like tears
and the coconut trees which stood drooping
bore witness that night
to them begging on their knees.

Without a sound they were shot.
The white sand reddened and turned black.
With the wind beating our heads in despair
we recovered their bodies.

Between the waves and the shore
the sea remained lifeless.

[tr. from Tamil by Shash Trevett]

The Sun Wanders, Searching for Shade

In the beginning of time
the buildings in my village
did not bear fruit, grow or expand.
Only the farmland, the sirissa
and guinea peach trees grew and multiplied.

Yet in three decades there has been
an explosion of fruitfulness.
Stones and soil have copulated
to give birth to walls and roofs,
high rise dwellings, a forest of buildings.

These houses have no front yards
or entrance ways. There are no murungai
trees flowering by the back door.
The wind can find no mango or neem
leaves to gather. There are no branches
for the crows to cry from.

The houses have borne fruit, spreading out
with a sigh. What used to contain two floors
now rise higher and higher, until
they tear at the sky. The coconut trees,
defeated, bend their heads low.

The parrots which had desired
the cashew and the many sparrows,
losing all sense of direction
head towards the open wilderness.
The woodpecker searching for dead trees
breaks into pillars of granite.

The few surviving siris and guinea peach trees
shed their newly formed fruit and the last
of their flowers, and stand in solitude.
The water is drying at their roots.
In a village parched of trees
the sun wanders, searching for shade.

[tr. from Tamil by Shash Trevett]

LIYANAGE AMARAKEERTHI
(*b.* 1968)

Liyanage Amarakeerthi received his primary and secondary education at rural
schools in Kurunegala, before studying at the University of Colombo, and
proceeding to the University of Wisconsin on a Fulbright Scholarship for his
postgraduate studies. After obtaining his PhD in 2004 he taught at Cornell
University. He joined the University of Peradeniya in 2008. He has published
almost twenty books of fiction, poetry and literary theory, winning awards for
both his short stories and his novels. He is also a celebrated translator working
with Sinhala and English.

Once Upon a Foreign Country

'Broken, beautifully broken,'
I thought
on the day Karuna broke away from the Tigers
and I read it on the Net

I wanted to call my friends
and enjoy the news with them
all the Sinhalese who gather to eat rice together
and brag about building the nation

My defeated, guilty
arrogant Sinhala heart.

Broken
My two-year-old son's sleep
was broken
by the clatter of the computer
on the day Karuna broke away

Piggy-backed as usual
while I read the Net
looking over my head
at Karuna's face on the monitor
my son said 'Thatha'

In fact Karuna does look like me
no need of more proof
my wife thinks so too

Another day
when having risen early
I read in the BBC
about the assassination of Kaushalyan
an Eastern Tiger leader
my son was in my lap
still a bit sleepy

'Thatha,' he said
leaning against my heart
looking at Kaushalyan
on the page I was reading

I had to agree with my son
at least to an extent
I looked like Kaushalyan too

To my son's eyes
still not blinded by culture
still not bound by ideology
all three of us look alike
with no mark of ethnicity
carved on our foreheads

At the instant my son gifted me
with the third eye of insight
I saw Karuna, Kaushalyan and myself as one

If I was born in the North or East
if I had to run in that bitter black July
barely evading torches, knives, swords
and the clubs of Sinhala thugs
in ragged clothes, bleeding all over
carrying little brothers and sisters

screaming
but still not awakening the peacefully sleeping
Sinhala political conscience
in Columbo, Galle, Kurunegala,
and sacred Anuradhapura
if I had to grow up
under the world-destroying Ishwara gaze of the Sun God
tied in the chains of ideology
which polish fear with blood
into public opinion
I may well have been copied into Karuna
and tamed into Kaushalyan

Auden said of Yeats
'Mad Ireland hurt him into poetry'
and this mad island
has hurt us all into the heart of madness

Which idiot says
'There is no problem for Tamils
just because they *are* Tamils'
in this great lie that is Dharmadeepa?

But when I read how Kadirgamar's heart
the heart of a man left alone between Sinhala and Tamil
was pierced by a bullet
when he was cleansing himself of the filth
that got to him hanging around with politicians all day
my heart was defeated

I was alone
without my son over my head
or in my lap by my heart

He doesn't like it any more
to look at the computer which shows him
other forms of his father
perhaps knowing by instinct
that it hurts the heart he leans against

I am afraid again
that my conscience might fall asleep
that I hurt reading the Internet
when living in a foreign country

Should I tell my son of the death of Uncle Kadir?
Why should I give him my Lankan sorrow?
No. I will tell him something good
about Lanka, Sinhala and Tamil

Let him sleep happily
in a foreign country

[tr. from Sinhala by the poet]

Will We Find the Strings of the Veena?

(A letter from Peabody Museum, Harvard University)

Dear friend, in many countries
in numerous museums
I have seen great wonders

From a distant past in Africa
from a distant land in Asia
from many a year ago
in America
under layers of ice in Alaska
and layers of dirt in the Indus Valley
I have seen the stuff found

In each of those places and times
there is something that could be called an arrow

Therefore it is OK to call such a place
'the house of bone / the house of thorns'
or katu-ge as we say in Sinhala

But my friend, in this house of wonder
there are other marvels:
everywhere they found something like an arrow
they also found something that can be called a veena

So it is an evil to call this house
just the house of bone or the house of thorns
or katu-ge as we say in Sinhala

In those bygone days
in those distant lands
the dwellers of distant time and space
aadi waasi humans as we say in Sinhala
were amazing humans
who created something called an arrow
and also made something
that could be called a veena

Listen, buddy
one more crazy thing
from the Peabody Museum –
everywhere in the world
this amazing human
made the veena in the shape of a woman's body

Friend, do you remember
when we were lads
we made bows and arrows?

With a piece of coconut branch
and with strings from the stem of a banana leaf
we also made a veena
which looked a bit
like a girl's butt?

Even though we were still kids
we talked about the beauties of women
and now we find
this museum gives a visual frame
to our own boyhood

This is a house of marvels
a museum at Harvard

In any corner of the world
in any distant past
any human being
has played music after shooting arrows

And when shooting arrows
he has shot an arrow
to pierce a heart

He has played the veena to break hearts

My friend, where is our veena
That consoles our arrow-hit hearts?

The strings of the veena
that made sweet sounds
from the shape of a woman's body

Will we ever recover
those strings of a veena
again in Sri Lanka?

[tr. from Sinhala by the poet]

A Poem's Plea

In that invisible place between time and space, allow me to rest.
In that infinitesimal difference between the flower and its fragrance, let me linger.
In the delicate point between poetry and prose, may I pause
Between air and water in that vapour-like vicinity, allow me to live.
In that ephemeral hour between night time and daytime, may I tarry.
In that grey area between home-land and other-land, let me stay.
In that minute space between Us and Them; there, allow me to be.
At that moment of day-break which lies between a poet and his poem, let me
      linger.
This is not mine, but my poem's plea.

[tr. from Sinhala by Vivimarie Vanderpoorten]

PREMINI AMERASINGHE
(*b.* 1933)

Premini Amerasinghe is a consultant radiologist who lives in Kandy. The poems chosen here are from *Kaleidoscope*, published in 2002. Her latest collection, *Tapestry of Verse* (2019), won the State Literary Prize for Poetry. A member of the Wadiyu Writers Group, she has also written several works of fiction: *The Search* (longlisted for the Dublin IMPAC award in 2003), *Sophie's Story* (2004), *Tangled Threads* (shortlisted for the Gratiaen Prize – the Sri Lankan literary award for the best writer in English – in 2009), *The Golden Deer* (2014) and *Footprints* (2021).

The Matrimonial Column

'Well-connected parents
seek for educated daughter...'
'Sinhala Karawa Buddhist mother
seeks for pretty teacher...'
'Roman Catholic mother
seeks a Sober Suitable
Smart Educated Tamil...'
And on and on it goes.

Well connected…
Yes.
By bands of steel,
to custom and convention,
and the brass four-poster
double bed

Dare she
stroll along the corridors of life,
linger in the niches of experience,
explore the unknown forest,
and through a parting of the leaves
be blinded
by a sunburst of awareness?

Dare she
attempt to reach
the shining summit,
risk a downward plunge
into
the dark pit of Despair
or,
would she
prefer
the monotonous rock-free plain
so pleasing to her mother
chosen
with such painstaking care.

A Rustic Scene

The fields spread out
brash green softened by the morning mist
pegged down by knots of trees
blue water hyacinths
clamour for attention
somnolent buffaloes
blink placidly

A cluster of people
impatient children, astride their mothers' hips
eyes which say nothing
surround a smoking body
black as granite
contorted limbs
stick out like branches
wisps of idle conversation
float above the smoke.

INDRAN AMIRTHANAYAGAM

(*b.* 1960)

Indran Amirthanayagam moved with his family to London in 1969, then on to
Hawaii in 1975. Born in Colombo, he lives in the US. His many books include
The Elephants of Reckoning, which won the 1994 Paterson Prize, as well as books
he has written in Spanish, French and Haitian Creole. His translations of
Manuel Ulacia were honoured by the US Mexico Fund for Culture. He received
fellowships from the Foundation for the Contemporary Arts, the New York
Foundation for the Arts, the MacDowell Colony and the 2022 IFLAC World
Poet/Poeta Mundial award. He retires this year from the United States Foreign
Service. Amirthanayagam depicts the civil war viscerally. These poems prize
acts of resistance and with their references to both life and literature in the
US test against the reality of suffering canonical pronouncements, like those
of Shelley, Yeats and Auden, concerning what poetry is able to accomplish.

The Death Tree

In this serene village
Where the tree has grown
For centuries in the square,
The municipality shines
In its colonial mansion,
The amanuensis writes
In his office, and the only
Family of lawyers
Celebrates the birth
Of its latest licentiate.

This village, from anywhere,
Represents the opposite
Of the great cities
Where human beings
Can lose themselves
In self-inventions,
In the fantastic idea
Of living a lasting happiness
Sprouting from the daily
Cultivation of magic
Mushrooms, the poems
That reveal the most intimate
Darknesses of the answer
To the question brought
By the village messenger,

Why did you leave?
Why grow old with strangers'
Friendships, with national
And international questions,
Here we keep
Your umbilical cord,
Here light the candles
Of your tree of death.

Not Much Art

I hear there isn't much art
in the bombing of Jaffna.

Planes fly overhead
and crews pick up
bombs and fling
them down on houses.

On houses, mind you,
no attempt to dig out
guerrillas hiding in bush empires.

No soldier to soldier combat
in the old man on a bicycle
fleeing his burning compound.

I hear from friends
who watch CNN
that a Norwegian crew

made it in and sent
a report for broadcast
in the post-midnight hour,

the scrambly witchy time
when Americans learn
the darknesses of dark lands,

at that hour, even America
is dark, watching the Dark Star
attack its sister or father.

How shall the night end,
drummed? Our eyes punched
        we sleep.

Versed? Blindfolded
        we sleep.

Brush stroked?
        Eyes wide open,
        we sleep.

There isn't much art
in pill-taking
or the whiskey toothbrush

or 500 laps on one foot
to tire it out before working
the other foot to tire that out,

when each minute the heart
arches, and lungs draw
cigarettes, not peace pipes,

when each minute
sons and daughters
raped and murdered

visit the beachhead
of your dreams
bloated and wild-eyed,

and you run
that foot faster
and faster

punch your eyes out
blindfold them
and tear the cloth off,

and in the white dark
fling the balls out
to meet the arriving dreams,

to receive them whole
blood pumped and pumped,
balls soaring
sockets in attendance.

ANAR

(*b.* 1974)

Anar is the pen name of Issath Rehana Mohamed Azeem, a Muslim Tamil poet from Eastern Sri Lanka. Her schooling ended at 16, due both to her orthodox Muslim upbringing and the civil war. Forbidden to write, Anar secretly listened to poetry recitation programmes on an old radio and sent out her poems under pseudonyms. She has published five collections in Tamil and has won numerous awards including Sri Lanka's National Literature Award, Canada's Tamil Literary Garden Poetry Award, and from India, the Aaathmanam Award, the SPARROW Award and Vijay TV's Sigaram Thotta Pengal award which recognises women who are pioneers in their field. Anar writes about the position of women in a patriarchal society, in a language of haunting melancholy alert to numerous perils. One of Tamil Sri Lanka's most famous voices, she transcends the obstacles of her early life and speaks for those who are voiceless or silenced.

Killing a Woman

Here is a battlefield,
a convenient clinic, a silo
of superabundant supply,
a permanent prison.
Here is a woman's body,
a sacrificial slab.

The heart's ache, the pulse
of life, belongs to us both, but
for women it will not take root.

Before my eyes
my murder is happening.

[tr. from Tamil by Hari Rajaledchumy with Fran Lock]

Woman

When the air starts to cool
anticipating rainfall
I morph into leaf-green.

I am a burgeoning treasure,
under the earth.

I am the sky
that has swallowed up
salt from a mutinous sea.

I am a spell
that is both dream
and poison.

I am opposing
poles of a word,
sending its war cry
out into time.

Where could
I hide myself?

[tr. from Tamil by Hari Rajaledchumy with Fran Lock]

Zulaikha

If you have to know – know this:
I grow beyond meanings.

I am the spark
made from striking stones.

I am a lightning streak
that leaps from here to there.

I have redeemed the years of sin.
I have swept aside all obstacles.

A sybil,
who moves mountains like camels.

I wear the light like a dress,
I am moist as a mound of salt.

I have flung my seasons high,
stars of scorn and pride.

I turn eyes into tempests of love.

I am a dream
that yearns to dream.

My body is red molten lava.

I never
chopped hands or fruits
with knives.

I broke the knife with love.

I am she who loves Yusuf
I am Zulaikha.

[tr. from Tamil by Hari Rajaledchumy with Fran Lock]

This poem is inspired by the medieval Islamic love story 'Yusuf and Zulaikha', which retells the love Potiphar's wife felt for Joseph in Egypt.

JEAN ARASANAYAGAM
(1931–2019)

Born to Dutch Burghers in what was then colonial Ceylon, Jean Arasanayagam married a Tamil in 1961 and was kicked out of her home during the anti-Tamil rioting of 1983, an event initiating a sea-change in both her life and her poetics. She is arguably Sri Lanka's major Anglophone poet.

A prolific poet, prose-writer and painter (her poems allude repeatedly to visual art, and the later works seem a style of action-painting in verse), Arasanayagam won multiple awards and received a Doctorate in Letters from Bowdoin College. Her poems – long, digressive, periodically ungrammatical, sometimes poised and weighed, and sometimes blurting and raw – suggest a range of complexities. These can be the complexities of her Burgher ancestry, interlinked with the colonial enterprise, or the sound and fury of civil war.

Wasp

Yes, now I know who I was,
The wasp carrying pellets of earth,
Building up, piling pellet upon pellet
Shaping solid walls.

What was I going to wall in anyway,
Building what all females build
To lay their eggs in,
Sockets of earth no longer empty
And within the tiny mazed chambers
Larval food stores to feed the young

Sting the victim still alive
Drug it insentient
Until the eggs hatch out
To gorge and gorge.

Wasp. Woman,
Woman, wasp
Building with pellet after pellet
Of earth, what all women build,
Fortresses, larders, storage bins,
Little rooms, caverns, mazes, labyrinths,
Prisons,
Tombs,
Wall ourselves in.

The Poet

Creeps into a misthole to vanish
But doesn't.
Walks through the hot sunshine with
Dust between toes,
Is pressed back by huge, green military trucks
Is almost crushed

I watch her
She takes the hem of her garment and
Wipes the sweat off her brow
The thin cotton is damp and stained.

She tells herself,
'I am common
Anonymous like all the others
Here.
No one knows that I have magic
In my brain.'

A Country at War

Why pretend that things have not changed
When they have   planting flowers and exotics
In pretty gardens   the magnolias in full bloom
Golden carp in pools to make poems with –
Excavate the lawns and you'll find weeds
Springing out of skulls and the birds in the trees
That sang at dawn grasp the light
With taloned claws dragging nets and setting
Snares over the sun   now darkness covers the land.

Our emotions are no longer important
Whom we love or loved once or are likely
To love   all these are inconsequential
Our grand passions turned out to be
Romantic malingering merely and the agony
Of non-requital nothing so painful
As this new feeling   we love with the deepest
Passion those who belong wholly to death
Dispense with the partings and the obsequies,
Why mock the sacrifice   make it cheap
With the false trappings of mourning,
It is what they wished   to part with life
To squander breath, minions of mortality.

Language too must change as we do
Become common   our parley is with the
Assassin and the so-called criminals,
We rub shoulders with them in the street
Listen carefully to the argot of their speech
If we are to understand at all
Why the young now carry arms   make
Even defeat a stance that is heroic
Shake hands too   laugh   banter
With the death dealers see them as human
Even with guilt, utter under our breath
'Father forgive them for they know not what they do'
Others take these picnics seriously
Laughter no longer joy-making
Your smile could be your death
End up vomiting blood from the kicks
And blows as the ruptured spleen splits and bursts.

We shuffle a deck of cards
Spell out new words from their symbols
– The ammunition of our defence –
We are desperate but calm
A priest prays   actors go on stage
We prepare for journeys and plan futures
Mornings we wake up hopeful   interpret
With sybillic fervour our dreams
There's a smell of fresh bread baking
From the wood fire ovens   the smoke
Here is not from the incinerators and
At night the rich fireflies shimmer above
The dark hedge   yet we read alarm
In every cry of every insect
And when we sleep we find night dangerous
The dream turns out to be real
You jostle shoulders with them all
In the crowded cells and touch a shaking
Shoulder before the next encounter – the
Thé dansant of death and torture.

This time the explosions did not go off
For the nonce things still stand intact
But it's only a matter of time   the foundation's
Wired perhaps tomorrow the edifice comes down.

And what of the little tailor and his wife
Living in the shanty below the bridge
They had better sew themselves new skins
Or take to cutting shrouds.

Ancestors

It is so easy to say that one's ancestors
Were degenerate or exploiters or that they were
The lazy hoboes of the seaboard smoking their
Long pipes from morning to night their vision swathed
In a haze of tobacco, reeked of gin sipping it
Like mother's milk, their tables laden with dish
After dish of hot spiced Rijstafel and slaves
Supplying the status quo of their household,

Their rubicund wives sallying forth in satin
And velvet to listen to the sermons of the predikanten,
Cooling their foreheads beaded in sweat with palm
Fans and seeing God in his Calvinistic heaven
Dressed in the velvet cloak of the Elders
With a froth of ruffles at his throat and cherubim
Hovering among sober grey clouds with pearls in their
Earlobes while Satan sweated in the underworld
Barebodied like a pagan stoking his roasting fires
Waiting to go back home and dip their fingers
Into the fruitbowls while the mestizo slaves
Tickled their frizzed fringes and eased into
Slippers their kneaded feet sleeping away history
In long trellised dreams of hot afternoons

Yet it is with a kind of wonder
That I gaze at pictures of their flagships
And gallant Indiamen sail billowing
Find that they did not lack courage
Dared venture out on swelling oceans
Setting out from some European port
In kermis season when the canals
Slid along with skaters on iced marble
As the sea heaved unrolling the heavy parchment
Maps measuring the constellations with their
Astrolabes expecting sea monsters and mermaids
To jettison out of spouting fountains of green brine
– Find that although the seafarers rotted of scurvy
And perished of their bloody fluxes, ate beef
Nibbled already by salty maggots, survived;

– Aboard, a motley of wenches trying their luck
In the new lands, maidens from orphanages
To colonise the new territories with their blood
         Their motives were trade and commerce,
         While they watched the stars reeling
         And dolphins disport themselves

Spent their guilders in the sixteenth-century bordels
And stripteases freed from the continence of long
Voyages, they dared as I have not, to risk all,
Unsure even of return to any earthly harbour
Slung their bones on any soil building with fleshly

Bricks their forts and factories, schools and kirks
And cemeteries

Soaked in sea brine bone weary slept in their
Hammocks while the huge obscene shapes of cargo
Rats scuttled in the dark hole with their stench
Of urine and faecal matter –

Had guts, saw land even in mirages and islands
Where spring water gushed through rock and scrawny
Chickens roasted on spits while fruits strange to
Their taste laved the mouth and tongue

Perhaps found strange men with eyes growing
Out of their sides and heads quivering with spiky
Green snakes

Most of this is true, I peer into their households
Their journeys through the voyeurism of history
Find that my eyes look out of those portraits
Of their genealogies

My ancestor was perhaps one of them
Staggering on a heaving deck looking
Forward to the fresh fruitpluck on the island

The hot sweat turning chill in his cloak
Of stained wool, sea chest bouncing on a heave
Of waves looking forward to a rich ring
With gems bright as winking yellow cockerel eyes
Waiting to dip his quill pen into new ink basins
Write the names of his progeny for history

That man, somewhere my ancestor whose name
Intrigues me slumbers in immortality
Since I will not let him die completely
He leaves some record flowing from his Calvinistic
Loins, a whole terrain copulate with what tenacity
The hybrid growth of his seed flowering
Into this strange foliage, nourished by this soil

If I am persistent enough I'll find new facts
To collaborate the evidence of his tenantship

And new roots for his vineyard, cull the harvest
Of his grape black with richness in wineskins of
Plenty, yet I have my times of drouth and then
Famished grasp the clustering fruit that burst
From udders of juice, find the wine sour.

Who was he? Living in some southern maritime
Port, never to go back with the spice cargoes
Or ivory, chank, gems and dyeroot
Engaged perhaps in private trade, found
Somewhere a woman whom he wived, begot
His offspring, named them with the good Dutch
Names which mixed with different bloods
Lost with time their flavour, yet took on
New colour

How many changes of clothes did he have
For that long sea voyage and how many guilders
Clinked in his pouch? Did his wife learn how
To make suikebrod and poffertjes and wafel
The doughcakes rising in the breudher pans
Or did they make do with salt fish and country
Rice washed down with the local brews,
Did she weave lace or coil her hair in braids
Sleeked with coconut oil,
She was a Dutch mevrouw – her name was
Elizabeth de Zeilve, had her own stamboek
Pure Dutch, came from Punta de Galle…

PARVATHI SOLOMONS ARASANAYAGAM
(*b*. 1964)

Daughter of Jean Arasanayagam, Parvathi Solomons Arasanayagam is the author of three works of fiction and four collections of poetry: *Identities* (2007), *The Searcher* (2009), *Cosmic Mirrors* (2014) and *Human Tide* (2015). Her poems record the significant adventures of a literary life (teaching, travelling, giving readings, having writers as family, and writers and activists as friends) in a country where – on the other hand – nothing is certain and events, stances, opinions, are soon lost to history. Her poems walk the line between countering this spirit of oblivion, and conceding the erasures of individual memory.

Identity

She stands at the
Cross-roads of time,
Gazing at a past
Concealed in the thick
Palls of mist.

'I am half-Tamil,'
She tells me
Hesitantly,
Aware of the complexities
Of this war-tenured age,
'My mother's Dutch Burgher,
I am half-Burgher,
I take on my mother's name.'
She gazes at me and
For a moment we share
A similar legacy
Of hybridity and evasion
In this strategied world of
Survival.

I study my own identity
Out of the fragments of
A colonised past,
Remember those chunks
Of Christmas cake
Served in my mother's
Crystal cut-glass dish which
Carried memories of a distant
Past, the rim, edged in gold
Porcelain dishes and amber-hued decanters
While grandfather Solomons
Sipped Scotch whisky or arrack,
Watching the silent road
Turn to the dusk and the
Elderly rickshaw puller wearily
Ambling past grandpa's house
After a tired day's work.

A Familiar Terrain

The fern trees
light brushed and speckled
like wasted paintbrushes
make me feel postdated
in the shimmery air.

I feel weary as I trudge
past former signposts
of another time when
students wanted change,
a new society and
not vain theorems
and empty promises.

Now only ghost-like
branches brush against
my inner vision, as the sky
burns bright yellow
and the heat rises in swirls.

Where are they, those people?
Locked somewhere in private
enclaves, in other lands
that spoke of the past which
is irretrievable in this
endless journey
ending in death and nullity.
That final inevitable
statement which spells
'Finis' to life.

Human Driftwood

For me it is an ever recurring metaphor,
the wayward unplanned casting ashore
from the shipwreck after violent storms.

Sometimes the walls I gaze on are blank
but silence has its own language,
I watch intently the perfection of spider webs
forming on those whitewashed spaces,
delicate yet tensile, feel my own mind
in the filaments of that complex weaving.

A relic from the past from my grandfather's
collection of ancient armoury, a German helmet,
rusted, corroded, tumbled off the head of
a wounded or dead soldier is fixed firmly
on the verandah wall among deer antlers.
Did it once shield a life in those violent times?
Life is made up of endless metaphors.

THIAGARAJAH ARASANAYAGAM
(*b*. 1934)

Thiagarajah Arasanayagam has won many awards for his many books of poetry
and drama, including the State Literary award for the play *The Intruder* in
1986, the Gratiaen Prize for Literature in 2015, and another State Literary
award in 2016, for *Waiting for Kiruba* and *The Interrogator*. The husband of
Jean Arasanayagam and father of Parvati Solomons Arasanayagam, he was also
given the Lifetime Achievement or Sahitya Ratna award by the Cultural
Ministry in 2021.

Kappal Matha – Kayts

Breaking stones, stones,
stones everywhere, in
little heaps, black and
white and silvery grey
glistening in the noonday
sun, crouching over,
hammer in hand, hammering,
reducing rock blocks to pebbles.
Knocking, knocking of
metal against stone
monotonous, repetitious,

old man squatting,
doing hard labour for
no crime done, only
a victim of war.

'My name Peduru, Peduru
Gnanapragasam.' Leaving
aside his work, the dust covered
being shakes itself out of the
debris of rocks and stones and
pebbles in this lonely corner of a
war devastated island where
the impregnable Hammenhiel
from distant time stands
sentinel in an azure sea,
silent witness to the destruction
of a way of life, peaceful and
God-fearing. 'This my wife.'
She emerges out of a doorless,
windowless house, like eyes gouged
out dark hollows, into the hot
brilliant sunlight reflecting
on white sands, a turquoise sea
and roofless ruins that were
once homes to God-fearing seafaring
men now dead or gone to
know not where, but Peduru
continues his life's narration.

'I sell these stones to builders.'
An anomalous dream in a wasteland.
'She cooks for me,' he beams. Three stones,
a few blackened pots, battered,
and a cold hearth in a corner
greets me to the reality I am
searching. A soft wind blows from
Hammenhiel, turning to fiery coals
in the mid-day sun, reminding me
of other turbulent days
of Dutch colonial domination,
and a censuring eye pointed
to this island of Kayts.

'Even Matha could not save us from
volleys of bombarding ships and
those birds of death that hovered
over us dropping fire and pestilence.'
Peduru, in tearful piety beckons
me to rubble and roofless jagged
walls that once the dome aloft
held, but now only a scorching
sun and a clear blue sky for a
dome. 'She saved me', he whispers.
'She? Who?' Confused, this raw hot
sun, my head, 'who?', I ask him.
'Kappal Matha, the Holy Mother.'
Kneeling amongst the debris of
hatred and violence he invokes
the mother, she, that floundering
Portuguese ship caught in turbulent
stormy seas rescued and brought
to even keel, in response to
Captain and crew abandoning
their lives to the miraculously
saving, the mountainous waves
now sheets of tranquillity and
these men on board vowing an
edifice in remembrance of a
Mercy given. 'I worship her, here.'
'In these ruins, abandoned,' I
ask? 'She lives here, amongst these
broken walls and stones, looking
out onto the turquoise sea as
the tiny boats venture out each
day.'

KI. PI. ARAVINDAN
(1953–2015)

Ki. Pi. Aravindan was the pen name of Christopher Francis, born in 1953 in
Delft in the north of Sri Lanka. An early pioneer of the Tamil freedom
struggle, he was one of many poets and intellectuals who rallied to the cause
of Independence during the 1970s. He was imprisoned many times for his

political work and left Sri Lanka in 1991 as a refugee to France. He was a
journalist, a short-story writer as well as a poet, and worked for European
Tamil television. Aravindan published three collections of poetry and edited
three Tamil poetry journals while in France, where he died in 2015 after a
five-year struggle with cancer.

Look at the Sky

To return home after sunset
to light a lamp to dispel the darkness,
to curl in a corner with a belly
relieved by kanji –
these are the true comforts of having a home.

Will we lose this too?

Extinguishing the lamp and burying it in the soil.
Staring desolately at the emptiness outside.
Retreating into the sign of the cross –
these have become the state of our lives.

Will we lose our city too?

The green of the trees carry
the stench of burning.
Voices murmur in suffering, dogs whine.
Yet the young bull escapes the noose,
foaming at the mouth.

In rain gutters, on trees bearing bud,
in schools and temples, everywhere,
our dreams lie shattered.
Mankind finds purpose as humanity
dissolves. Life, clasped so tightly
could slip away easily.
Even so, we can overcome this
if we look at the sky.

[tr. from Tamil by Shash Trevett]

Directions

If you stand facing the rising sun
the West will fall at your back.
The North Wind will embrace you from the left.
The hot wind blowing to your right, is the South Wind.

The North, the South, the hot South-Westerlies,
the East. Each wind-name bears the weight
of each compass points.

With such simple clarity Amma taught me my poles
a long time ago. Now I am rudderless
unable to tell one direction from the next.

Here, the winds don't seem laden with names.

A storm appears – but do storms too have directions?
I stand removed, an outsider
trying to fix my directions. Each time I fail.

What has happened to them? Have they been lost?
My memories tell me that I set out from the North.
But you came from the South, say the unfriendly voices
in this cold land.

I came from somewhere but in which direction
am I travelling now? Those who came from me
raise their voices. Which direction should I face?

Unlike my mother, who taught me so carefully,
I am unable to teach my children.
I do not have her simplicity, her patience.

If only someone would point me in the direction
of the rising sun, tomorrow I will stand facing
the dawn. I will know my compass points.
And I will be able to teach my children.

[tr. from Tamil by Shash Trevett]

The Night Approaches

The night approaches
an unlit, nascent silver
an endless night.
Eyes gnaw at a frenzied sky
ears suck in the darkness outside.
On pale suffering faces
violence spreads its wings.

Tongues of fire lick the ground.
Agni's birds drench the city
with a devastating rain of fire.
As sound and light dissolve
Yama's messengers parade
in the sky. Waves break in disordered lines
and the lowing of cattle fills the temples.
The gods suffocate.
Joined under death's yoke
the roots of our lives hang exposed
to lightning on the flagpole.

[tr. from Tamil by Shash Trevett]

UPEKALA ATHUKORALA
(b. 1986)

Upekala Bhagyanie Athukorala studied at the University of Colombo and the University of Peradeniya. Since elementary school, she has published poems in Sinhala in weekend and daily newspapers. Her collections are *Paratharaya* ('Distance', 2012), *Sankranthiyaka Sanakeli* ('Carnival of Transition', 2015), and *Irthu aga Shesha Path* ('Remnants of the Seasons', 2020). She has won several national awards for her writing and is at present a teacher at a government school in the Western Province.

Snaggle tooth

Oh what you loved most
was my snaggle tooth.
You admired it all the time

74

saying everyone has incisors, canines, molars and pre-molars
but me – I had a snaggle tooth
my nala dhatha was special.

On our wedding day
I kept my lips together before the camera
but it was you who insisted that I smile
and show my nala dhatha.

I remember the days when
we first started seeing each other
you teased me, squeezing my ear,
pinching my cheek, laying your head
on my chest
playfully threatening me
that you will punch me so hard that
I would swallow my teeth.

Who knew your words
'denne dhath deka badata yanna'
would be carried out for real?
Alas that you would really break
my two front teeth.
Even my snaggle tooth is loose now.
Who knew I would have to
'boil rice without my teeth' someday
terrified?

[tr. from Sinhala by Vivimarie Vanderpoorten]

Some Yashodaras

There are some Yashodaras
who journey alone
having had no love great enough
in previous lives
to wish for
in this.

[tr. from Sinhala by Vivimarie Vanderpoorten]

Crazy Woman

Go on, leave me.
Undo the ropes you tied me with
and go where you may.
Allow this dark and ugly woman to
heal, she who tries to soothe
her bruises by applying balm
with a feather.

Don't.
Don't come in search of me.
Don't carelessly flick
the mimosa leaves into closing
they who amidst thorns
fade and awake and fade again.
Allow this coarse
cruel woman you reject
to awaken.

Watch.
Watch from afar,
and behold the momentary miracle of a
falling raindrop
above your head
from the clouds I built
with tear-soaked cotton.

Behold as this crazy woman you rejected
conjures up
an entire sky.

[tr. from Sinhala by Vivimarie Vanderpoorten]

AVVAI

(b. 1965)

Avvai was born in Colombo and grew up in Jaffna, Northern Sri Lanka; she
is a poet, a feminist and an activist. The daughter of Mahakavi and the sister
of Cheran, she came into prominence in the 1980s, is a trained Carnatic

musician and worked as a chemistry teacher. She has published two poetry collections in Tamil (*Ellai Kadatthal*, 1994, and *Ethai Ninainthaluvathum Saathiyamillai*, 2014), and nine feminist plays; and her poetry has been translated into English and anthologised widely. She now lives in Canada.

The Homecoming

The horror of that night
lives with me still.
Uprooted, I fled across the border
like an abandoned bird,
driven to save my life.
Still vivid
the wrenching horror,
after thirteen years.

I am this earth's daughter:
uprooted, my journey began
when this land became a red-dust desert.
But long years have not parted me
from this land.
This earth, this good earth
nurtured me with its honesty, its strength.
I could not leave it:
my life lies mingled with this earth's dreams.

Today I return
in search of a life
once destroyed.
I re-cross the border,
my companion at my side
and my little ones.

Thanks to all the peace talks, et cetera.

Paths and houses are overgrown,
palmyra trees are beheaded,
fields are planted with landmines.
They mourn silently,
wordlessly proclaim past horror,
tragedy, loss.
Nothing here nurtures life.

Where have they all gone,
the fields with their milky smell
of newly ripening grain,
the wind bearing the rustle
of new paddy,
temple bells at daybreak?
Where are the village mornings
filled with rhythmic chanting?
Where is the music of the nathaswaram?
Nothing here nurtures life.

This earth which endured it all
remains a land laid waste.
Is this only red dust
or is it a good earth still?

I know this:
it is no longer possible
to repair a torn root,
re-plant, water, nurture it again.

But what of it?

In our front courtyard
the neem tree has burst into flower
and the children play cricket
under its shade.

This earth is still held fast,
in that delighted time
of childhood games,
entranced.

[tr. from Tamil by Lakshmi Holmström]

The Return

He returned to me
heart turned iron
brain become gun
friend turned foe:

and I was thrown off-guard
all my love and affection
disappearing.

He had shot his friend:
he spoke of bravery
and sacrifice
and weapons,
of killing people across the boundary.

I was silent,
forgetting entirely
about humankind
and liberty.

But now I know
I cannot any longer
be a mother.

Won't he, one day,
believe me to be his enemy
and bury me, too?

[tr. from Tamil by Lakshmi Holmström]

THILAKARATNA KURUVITA BANDARA
(*b*. 1941)

Thilakaratna Kuruvita Bandara has had a celebrated career as a journalist and
as the editor of multiple newspapers: *Dinamina, Silumina, Irudina, Mawbinma*
and *Siyatha*. He also worked as a consultant for the Sri Lanka Broadcasting
Corporation. He has published three books of prose and seven of poetry in
Sinhala, including *Dewiyo Thathigena Maha Polowata Ethi*. A member of the
State Literature Advisory Committee, he has judged the State Literary
Awards, the Swarna Pusthaka Awards, and various film and journalism
awards'.. His own prizes include the Sri Lanka Media Award, the 'Eminent
Media' Awards presented by the Arthasad Sanniwedana Lakshaya Society, the
Suwanda Padma Golden Award and the Kalabushana Award presented by the
Cultural Ministry.

The Gods Alarmed, Descend to Earth

With camphor, incense, sandalwood and offerings of light
drunk with heady perfume, grovelling on the ground
man prays
for grace
to those cloud-dwellers, the countless million gods;

then
bearing on their heads
the pollen-dust off the feet of Armstrong,
moon-conqueror,
the gods descend to earth
and around cries of 'sadhu'
bow low
beseech Man
to spare the Universe.

[tr. from Sinhala by Ranjini Obeyesekere]

A Child's Pestering

Pretty little chicken who rushes to the rubbish heap
The moment I turn to go inside;
What! Are you still asleep?
You get dust and dirt again on your white, downy wings
Run along and play among the flowers.
Wait a minute I'll fetch some grain for you to eat.
There, wake up now and gobble down these grains.
You don't want it? I'll get a fistful of cooked rice
Here, hurry up, eat what I have brought.
Get up or I will poke you with this tiny teeny stick.
There, I see your mother hen coming by.
Look my little chicken there are ants on your small wings
Wait a bit I'll pick them off of you.
What! Not afraid of the cat, even when he sniffs and pats you?
You rascal! Not a sound, pretending to be asleep!
Mother, do come, look, the chicken's still asleep
If you don't wake him up for me I won't come in the house.

[tr. from Sinhala by Ranjini Obeyesekere]

RUWAN BANDUJEEWA

(*b.* 1983)

Ruwan Bandujeewa is an acclaimed writer of Sinhalese contemporary literature. He reached the height of his writing career in 2013 with the publication of his second collection of poetry *Miḷaṅga Mĩvita* (Next Sweet Wines), which won the Vidyodaya Literary Award and Godage National Literary Award for the best collection of poetry published in 2013. The collection is now in its eighth reprint and is one of the best-selling poetry collections in the island. Bandujeewa's poetry is often concerned with neglected people and has a strong sense of place. His works are included in Sinhala Language and Literature textbooks and curricula.

Earthworms

'Dear father,
why don't we attend
the Ploughing Festival?
Even the king is coming
to the field today.
Shouldn't we break this silence
and announce
it is us
who manured this soil
from within the bowels of the earth?'

'Little earthworm son,
a hoe's blade knows not
those who manured the soil
and those who did not.
Therefore, rising into the open air
is not wise.
Drill your way deeper
to the dark depths of mud.
Doing otherwise, my son,
is not advised.'

[tr. from Sinhala by Chamini Kulathunga]

A Tree to its Flowers

Upon counting
the remaining buds
awaiting to blossom,
a tree said
to its flowers

if there be flowers
volunteering to wilt
raise your hand just once
the wind comes

[tr. from Sinhala by Chamini Kulathunga]

A Joy – A Bliss

Rather than joining in creating
yet another scarecrow
decaying into the homefield
is a joy – a bliss to a stick of straw

[tr. from Sinhala by Chamini Kulathunga]

What Answers from the Common Crows?

Even now, in Pettah
on Jam, Bo, Kottamba trees
when eggs crack and the young are hatched
what answers do the common crows have
in reply to their newborn's questions?

Amma leaves early in the morning
the ekel broom balanced on her beak.
With neat ekel sweeps she tidies
flower gardens, vast compounds, public paths.

However much she toils
each new day, the disobedient
decaying leaves fall as usual.
Amma, why don't we relocate
to somewhere with a garden of our own?

Thaththa sells imitation rings
and chains on congested city roads.
His nail-pierced wings fester
and detach themselves, one after the other.
In the evenings we watch
Thaththa's feet swell up alarmingly.
Why can't we have a better life
like the yellow bird or the blue dove?

Even now, in Pettah
On Jam, Bo, Kottamba trees
when eggs crack and the young are hatched
what answers do the common crows have,
in reply to their newborn's questions?

[tr. from Sinhala by Gaya Nagahawatta)

BRIYANTHY

(*b.* 1985)

An emerging poet, Briyanthy Arumaithurai was born and lives in Uduvil, Northern Sri Lanka. Her poems have appeared in Tamil poetry journals and anthologies and have been translated into English for the anthology *Still We Sing: Voices on Violence Against Women* (2021). Influenced by Tamil poets Cheran, Ahilan, Pramil and Anar, amongst others, Briyanthy strives in her poetry to reconcile the contradictions within herself. She writes on issues surrounding gender, the prevailing political conditions and her own responses to them.

Sorrow Created and Sorrow Relieved

On a day dressed in nakedness
They fastened their decay
On a newborn thing, and called it
'I'

They filled my room
With camphor dolls
Dressed in festive clothing
Woven from thick fibres
Of sorrow

Between the night when the stars rose and fell
And the morning when the sun was extinguished
In a day that was mine
In the remains of cinders drunk by the wind
On the edge of a smile washed by tears
They fastened
The sweet dreams of a life meant for me

From a single point
Saturated with illusion
From the poems that caught fire and blazed
Remain
Blackened edges of paper
And the ashes of my feelings

Now
I
Am none of
These

But a few words scattered to the winds.

[tr. from Tamil by Nedra Rodrigo]

S. BOSE
(1975–2007)

S. Bose was a poet, journalist and editor from Kilinochchi in Northern Sri Lanka. He edited and published both the Tamil poetry journal *Nilam* in Sri Lanka and *Thamil Ullagam* in London. A poet deeply influenced by post-modernist writings, he devoured Kafka and Camus, Marquez and Borges in Tamil translation, and was obsessed with the writings of Pramil. He had a troubled childhood, resentful of the strict school system in Sri Lanka where teachers and their canes were seldom separated, and left education at 15 to join the LTTE. He didn't stay for long, finding the authoritarian structures of the group unbearable. Anti-authoritarianism is a thread which runs through most of his writings. Known for being uncompromisingly principled in his journalism, he was an outspoken critic of the Sri Lankan Army and was detained and tortured by them in 2001. Foretelling his death in his poems, he was assassinated at his home in 2007, in front of his seven-year-old son. Attacks against journalists in Sri Lanka reached a high point during the ten-year presidency of Mahinda Rajapaksa (2005-15).

My Life in Books

My life began with a few books:
that there is no rice in the words of a book
became the trouble of our lives.
No one believed in books.
That their lives too emerged from books
was a truth they wouldn't allow
anyone to believe in.

Books contain no food.
Books contain no clothing
nor gold jewellery.
They are the essence
of this troubled life.

When I declared that henceforth
I would live in my books –
that I would sleep in them
that they would consume my heart,
my pyre, the sound of my grief –
Oh God, no one believed me.

Around me, the rooftops are carpeted
with the white feathers of doves.

[tr. from Tamil by Shash Trevett]

from The Veenai

It was my companion, although
it didn't always travel with me.
Oh God.
Before I was confused with old age
before the fear of darkness heated my brain
before the cruelty of war found a home
in the poems written around me –
the veenai glided with its own charming music
and I lived within it.

Yesterday I was like an old man.
I trembled with a fear of the dark.
The poems I wrote in those war filled days
were full of the stench of bones, full of the fear
in the voices of men.
Oh God, I have lost it all.
The veenai's last sounds have faded
in the wind. Apart from the waning moon
there is nothing left.
Now, as the sun breaks through at dawn
so too will stretch out, a poem.

[tr. from Tamil by Shash Trevett]

Now

In that time of convolutions, marked
by the violent weeping of children,
dust-covered legs climb ceaselessly
until time annihilates them.
Tears, sighs and despondency
cloth the disjointed faces of the people.
Dust-bound legs are robbed of their treasure.

Now, the sky is no longer blue.
And angels no longer gain their wings.

Behind the smoke, the dust and the ashes
of remembrance, little children stand begging,
mocking time. While spinning towards them
ferociously, comes a time which will subsume
all dust and ash and smoke.
Life disintegrates in the depths of their eyes.

[tr. from Tamil by Shash Trevett]

SURESH CANAGARAJAH

(*b.* 1957)

A Tamil-born Sri Lankan linguist, (Athelstan) Suresh Canagarajah is the Edwin
Erle Sparks Professor of Applied Linguistics, English, and Asian Studies at
Pennsylvania State University, where he has taught since 2007. He taught at
the University of Jaffna from 1982 to 1984. His research covers World Englishes
and teaching English to speakers of other languages. He is known for his work
on translingualism, linguistic imperialism, and social and political issues in
language education.

Lavannya's Twilight Bike Ride

A damp, prematurely darkening
late October evening –
the shells from Palaly explode near
drowning the monsoon thunder.
A jeep whizzes past with fifteen-year-olds
clutching AK-47s to the battle site,
crushing the jasmines on the wayside.
From the other side hobble tractors
with the mangled remains of fighters.
As they pile the bodies on the ground,
blood mingles with rainwater
streaming along the wheel marks
to revive the roots of the creeper.
In neighbouring campgrounds
camouflaged girls play hopscotch,
their guns resting against palmyras.
Smell of fresh baked bread distracts

as the baker's boy cycles past,
while the six o'clock Marchetti bombers
make the day's last run towards cadre bunkers.
I slow down for mothers listlessly
crossing the road with provisions
to cope with tomorrow's uncertainties.
Business is brisk at the junction-shops
where mudalalies bargain militantly
making the best of today's certainties.
An eye on the whirring chopper overhead,
and wary of its machine-gun fire,
I take my year-old Lavannya
on her favourite evening bike ride.

20 October 1990

CHELIYAN
(1960–2018)

Cheliyan was the penname of S. Sivakumaran, who was born in Jaffna in the north of Sri Lanka. He wrote short stories, plays and five collections of poetry in Tamil. Joining the freedom struggle at an early age, he was a committee member of the Tamil militant group EPRLF. Becoming disillusioned with its direction, Cheliyan left Sri Lanka in 1986 for Canada, where he lived until his death. A prolific poet, he wrote about the grey areas of the struggle, often voicing critical views (especially of the internecine fighting between the various Tamil militant groups) others were too frightened to articulate publicly. Cheliyan's use of myth and allegory transformed poems that seemed simple on the surface into works saturated with cultural memory and meaning.

Those Who Enter the Pit

The exhausted wind sways
gently across the street

and announces its end
to a weeping sea.

The birds shake their wings, forming
a phalanx around the wind.

The trees shed their leaves and naked,
clasp their hands in supplication.

Insects climb mountain ridges
and stand yogi-like, on one leg.

Yet still, people speak only of the stars
that elude their hands and their eyes.

[tr. from Tamil by Shash Trevett]

Untitled

The rain enters a window
left open to the wind.

The cat takes no notice, and chasing
an elusive scent escapes from the room.

Unwitnessed, the rain murders
the poems quickening on my desk,

then walks out into the heat
and disappears from view.

It leaves behind no trace of moisture.

[tr. from Tamil by Shash Trevett]

Merciless Ones

the sun was floating in the temple tank

they tied up the sun head-down
hit it with sticks
rolled and pushed it
into the tank

in the cloudless expanse of the sky
rain was falling from the leaves
the tank was overflowing with tears
the utterly fearless little ones
had no mercy at all
they had climbed onto the dead sun
and were swimming and playing

the sky had caught fire
and was burning.

[tr. from Tamil by Rebecca Whittington]

On a Rainy Day

On a rainy day the kathirnaavaai yearned
to kiss the Sun. It told the leaves,
who, elated, whispered it to the branches.
The wind sped to broadcast the news.

The weaver-birds tore their wings
to aid the flight, leeches volunteered
to shoulder the burden that had turned
heavier in the heavy rain.

The bees collected nectar
from pumpkin blossoms; a sea-horse
dipped itself in the receding waters,
dived deep and came up with pearls.
Blushing butterflies penned
a beautiful poem with a fresh pattern.

Drenched in the pouring rain
water dripping down its cheek
the kathirnaavaai alighted
dragging the Sun along with it,
laid it flat and kissed it ecstatically.

[tr. from Tamil by S. Pathmanathan]

90

CHERAN

(*b.* 1960)

One of the best known and most influential of Tamil poets, Cheran was born in the village of Alaveddy, near Jaffna, in northern Sri Lanka. His father, T. Rudhramurthy (1927-71), known widely as 'Mahakavi', the Great Poet, was one of the leading literary figures in modern Tamil writing from Sri Lanka. Cheran grew up with a grounding in the Tamil classics, but from his early years he also became familiar with the works of the younger, left-leaning poets who frequented their house. He graduated from Jaffna University with a degree in Biological Sciences. As a poet and a political journalist, Cheran refused to align himself with any of the several Tamil militant groups that were active in Jaffna at the time. As a result he was harassed both by the Sri Lankan Army and, later, by the LTTE. He is now an Associate Professor in the Department of Sociology at the University of Windsor in Ontario, Canada.

Cheran's early poems were collected in *Nii Ippolludhu Irangum Aaru* (The River into Which You Now Descend, 2000). This was followed by *Miindum Kadalukku* (Once Again the Sea, 2004) and *Kaadaatru* (Forest-Healing, 2011). He co-edited a landmark anthology of Tamil political poetry, *Maranatthul Vaallvoom* (We Will Live Amidst Death, 1985). His recent academic publications include *The Sixth Genre: Memory, History and the Tamil Diaspora Imagination* (2001) and *History and the Imagination: Tamil Culture in the Global Context*, co-edited with Darshan Ambalavanar and Chelva Kanaganayakam (2007).

I Could Forget All This [1983]

I could forget all this
forget the flight
headlong through Galle Road
clutching an instant's spark of hope,
refusing to abandon this wretched
vulnerable life
even though the very earth shuddered
– and so too, my heart –

forget the sight
of a thigh-bone protruding
from an upturned, burnt-out car

a single eye fixed in it staring
somewhere between earth and sky

empty of its eye
a socket, caked in blood

91

on Dickman's Road, six men dead
heads split open
black hair turned red

a fragment of a sari
that escaped burning

bereft of its partner
a lone left hand
the wristwatch wrenched off

a Sinhala woman, pregnant,
bearing, unbearably,
a cradle from a burning house

I could forget all this
forget it all, forget everything.

But you, my girl,
snatched up and flung away
one late afternoon
as you waited in secret
while the handful of rice
– found after so many days –
cooked in its pot,
your children hidden beneath the tea bushes
low-lying clouds shielding them above –
how shall I forget the broken shards
and the scattered rice
lying parched upon the earth?

[tr. from Tamil by Lakshmi Holmstrom]

My Land [1981]

Nets spread like wings across the wide sea.
Above, the fierce breath of the wind.
From the sea, looking up,
fingers pressed against your flying hair,
you can see the shore,

palmyra palms, and tiled roofs here and there.
The waves, the sea-spray
as the engine roars!
How did such an hour and a half
come to an end?

Later, the wide expanse
with palmyras planted there,
each rising to a man's height
from the virgin sands.
As for the sand,
it is all golden specks,
seeded mirrors, inhabited by the sun.
Beneath the sand, the land extends
where, two thousand years ago,
my ancestors walked.
Our roots go deep:
one footstep, a thousand years.

Upon the jewels of bare-breasted women –
one, perhaps, standing sleepless by this shore,
watching and lamenting as stars scatter
and fall into the sea –
or another, waiting for a boat
to plunge through the horizon
and come safe ashore –
or upon footsteps buried deep in the sand
one late evening, perhaps, under cover of dusk,
here where the coconut-fronds sway –
my ancestors have left me a message.
I stand on a hundred thousand shoulders
and proclaim aloud: This is my land.
Across the seven seas,
overcoming the rising waves,
the wind shouts it everywhere:

My land
My land.

[tr. from Tamil by Lakshmi Holmstrom]

Nandikadal [2009]

When the platoons advanced
from all directions
inch by inch,
the land vanished,
the landscape blackened.

On the silent screen
the multitudes raise their lament:

Where can we go?

They had travelled, believing
the sea's lap and its kind shore
would be their harbour.
Before their very eyes
the sea shrank,
scattered,
vanished.

[tr. from Tamil by Lakshmi Holmstrom]

In May 2009, by the banks of Nanthikadal Lagoon, near Mullaitivu in Eastern Sri Lanka, the civil war came to a brutal end. The UN estimates that around 40,000–70,000 civilians were massacred by the banks of the lagoon over three days. Corralled onto a narrow strip of land they were shelled by the Sri Lankan Army on one side and prevented from leaving by the LTTE on the other.

Grave Song

Alone with the three
whose faces and hearts
were hidden in darkness

he dug his own grave.
His distress, the horrors he felt
were trapped within his unspoken words

which congealed in the air
above that grave.

The wind would not permit
the rain nor the sun
to approach them.

Those unspoken words sank
into the soil
entering the roots of trees.
The unceasing wind drew
them upwards in waves
radiating them along branches
from leaf to leaf
and beyond.

There are no ghosts
above that grave.
Nor gods.
There is no memorial stone.

Encased in the cruel grip of time,
a single patti flower
grows upon his grave,
burning bright like a lamp
on a darkened street.

In his final words
lives
the life of our land.

[tr. from Tamil by Shash Trevett]

RIENZI CRUSZ
(1925–2017)

The child of Colombo Burghers, Rienzi Crusz trained in library science in
England, and on returning to Sri Lanka in 1953 realised the new political
climate, and the breakdown of his first marriage, had scotched a possible
career as a librarian at the Central Bank. He moved to Canada in 1965 with

his three children, and much of his poetry narrates and mythologises the immigrant experience: instances of racism are depicted without adornment or disguise, and he establishes a thematic contrast between snowy Canada and sun-drenched Sri Lanka. Tropes and characterisations recur – the 'sun-man', elephants (he wrote an unpublished children's book about one) – in poems flitting restlessly between alternative points of view.

Song of the Immigrant

It's time
to break your elephant and wood-apple dream.
Honey and curd in your mouth,
the kingfisher ablaze by the Mahaveli's edge –
time to cast off
your batik sarong, wooden thongs,
the exotic shackles round your throat.

You only read
the language of signs,
a long silence in the snow,
a dark music   silent
and hammered in your blood.

No more shall the elders say:
Hold your tongue and wait,
this night will pass.
The civilised nerves
will first grow taut, then break;
then sleep beside your alien breath,
then love you with a tentative smile,
even bleed for your leftover pain.
Now you may talk loudly of crows
as stars in a dark night,
conjure peacocks from harvest cornfields,
look straight into the sun, the whipping snow
and not blink at all.
Be happy now.
Only death
can redeem
the original dream.

Leaving – Michael-style

These are the fractured journeys
of childhood
where the hairline crack
seems wider than a chasm;
where we learn
the true nylon toughness
of the umbilical cord,
how to love
what we think we hate
in the terror of the argument,
hate what we know
is not our mother,
only the genius
of a child's topsy-turvy room,
a set of rioting loafing toys.

So a hectoring voice
once again lays out the charges:
Michael, toys all over the damn place
and they're going
straight into the garbage!

Batman in the dumpster?
Tears drown out the thought.
He makes the traumatic decision.
He must leave…

Says so defiantly: I'm leaving!
And mum, cool as tea-country rain,
picks up the gauntlet:
Good. Let me pack your bags!

A sheet of paper
is left behind revealing
a superb map
of his 'leaving' itinerary,
his last stop, a legend
that seemed washed ashore
by the tides of the womb:
I WILL BE FOUND HERE!

The anchors hold.
Congenital love survives
the deep frost
as the fires of descent burn out
by the map's end.
This is a going, a kind of love
that always leaves a paper trail,
that never goes out at all.

The Elephant Who Would Be a Poet

High noon. The piranha sun
cuts to the bone.
Anula, the heaving elephant,
froths at the mouth.
The logging ends.

Without command,
he eases his huge body to the ground,
rolls over,
makes new architecture
from his thick legs,
four columns vertical
to the sun.

The confused mahout
refuses the poem
in this new equilibrium,
this crazy theatre of the mind,

this new way
of looking at the real world...

A.P. DAVID

(*b.* 1964)

A.P. David was born in Colombo and lives in Kandy: he is also a naturalised US citizen who has lived in England, Hawaii and Germany. He is a classical Hellenist who did his doctorate in the Committee on Social Thought at the University of Chicago. Besides *The Dance of the Muses: Choral Theory and Ancient Greek Poetics* (Oxford, 2006), he has published a number of scholarly articles and monographs and self-published several volumes of poetry (*Past Your Ear, Over the Moon, Bullroarer*). His current project is reciting and translating Homer, at homerist.substack.com. Formative encounters with poetry in English have involved Robert Fitzgerald's translations, Guy Amirthanayagam, Shakespeare, Chaucer, W.B. Yeats, T.S. Eliot, Ray Davies, Warren Zevon and Leonard Cohen.

Fishermen

Boxing Day 2004

Fault lines are cracks in a teacup
Earthquakes are an old lady's hiccough
And the prophetic tea leaves floating in the dregs
Fitfully tossed and finally side-stuck
Are so many dead fishermen.

Wives and sons and lonely daughters
Are laid on human biers,
Wail in strange agony with no lesson,
Clamber through the bric-à-brac
Become prey for the fishers of men.

How do we find the cause of this
Strange upswelling, this sea surge?
The farmer caste and the mountain dwellers,
Tea-leaf philosophers, would call them back
These fishermen, for questioning.

But they are gone, the way of graveyards,
Gone to flowers, an ocean bodily blooming;
And I stumble upon a vacant shark,
Remnant of the surge on a sea street
And question his dying, gasping, fish dignity.

'Sir Shark,' I said, 'why these wafting fishermen,
This surging sea calamity, ionospheric discharge
In a cracked teacup? Why the fish slaughter,
And the lonely daughter?' 'Fool,' he replied drily –
'Ask me at home. I am a fish out of water.'

MEGAN DHAKSHINI
(*b.* 1983)

Shortlisted for the Gratiaen Prize in 2021 – for *Softly We Fall*, her second
book of poems after *Poison Apple* (2018) – Megan Dhakshini is a Tamil
creative multidisciplinary who has worked in advertising, creative design,
voice acting, and singing. She counts as influences on her writing Sharanya
Manivannan, Ocean Vuong, Vivimarie Vanderpoorten, Nayirrah Waheed,
Charles Bukowski, Leonard Cohen and Anaïs Nin. She currently lives and
works at 'Navya Illam' in Colombo – her home and haven full of blue doors,
greenery, textured walls and spiders.

In Lockdown

I

There's nothing to it really.
It's only day 351 of being truly alone
day 1650 (or 1860?) of wearing masks
that are never really thrown away
and the bits of you under my nails
stay unwashed by anything.
Isolation is a laugh.

II

Time moves across this wall
in shadows, in a parade of ants
in stains shaped like dying animals
in 27 charcoal fingerprints
in peeling patches of age
creating maps of no place I've been.
Tomorrow we will observe ceilings.

21

(in memory of 21 April 2019, Colombo)

We trudge, heavily
through this daylight darkness,
nodding half-heartedly
at blackened people
dropping charred words
onto burned hearts,
watching greyly,
how the un-alive
bury their dead.

WIMAL DISSANAYAKE
(*b.* 1939)

Wimal Dissanayake is one of the leading scholars of Asian cinema and Asian communication theory and founding editor of the *East-West Film Journal*. He was the Director of the Cultural Studies Program jointly sponsored by the University of Hawai'i – where he works – and the East-West Center. He has published eight volumes of poetry in Sinhala and has won numerous awards. In 2012 he was given a lifetime award by the government of Sri Lanka, and he has received another from the Sri Lanka Foundation in Los Angeles. He has been the editorial advisor to many journals dealing with cinema, communication, and cultural theory, as well as the International Encyclopedia of Communication.

Anuradhapura

Monkeys in the pack
somersault freely
leaping from branch to branch nonchalantly.
Only I am imprisoned
in the past
in this old city
that's got angry with history.
I try indecisively
to suppress my emotions.

Sun's rays
filtering through the tall trees
fall on a moonstone
lighting the fingertips of the artist
trained for centuries.
The enraged wind
rouses the dust.
I walk under a tree
with a torn shadow.
At a distance is seen
the pinnacle
of the Ruwanweliseya,
war drums of the past
reverberate in the skies.

Suddenly
a bird dropping
falls on my head
and the bird flies away.
I stand
leaning on the wind
a withering bud seen
on a thorny bush.
A lizard, excited, quietened
blends
with that thorny bush.
A confused morning this is.
Monkeys, history, sunlight
and the dust.

[tr. from Sinhala by A.T. Dharmapriya]

Strange Flowering

On a night when the light of moon or star is forbidden
On some day in May, it is said, when the cuckoo calls
In the midst of a swamp lost in the jungle's thick gloom
When moaning water falls in dense groves hidden,
In a silent moment of midnight, a flower will bloom.

It is said that this flower, red as a clot of blood
Tells the world its tidings of grief in an undertone:
But the wild, without heart or mind, has not understood –
And before the coming of daylight the flower is gone.

[tr. from Sinhala by Lakshmi de Silva]

Homecoming

My grandmother, silver-haired and frail,
sitting on a mat, with the betel tray next to her,
used to spin endless tales
in those monsoon evenings, when
dark ropes of dusk coiled in the air.
My brother and I were turned into
silent statues of clay, kneaded in her narratives.
She told us stories of kings and demons,
beasts and flowers; one evening, I remember well,
a bird escaped from her story, rose to the sky,
flapped its wings, flew higher and higher, and
disappeared like a dot in the darkening sky.
Forty years later, the bird has come back,
wiser, if a little weaker, to roost in my mind.
It's a large bird with a long beak
and brown feathers. I'll show it to my kids
when they come back from school.

[tr. from Sinhala by the poet]

Anjali

It was the most welcome
thunderstorm that ever descended.
Under the dripping trees
without an umbrella
you and I were stranded.
That was our first meeting.

103

Caught in that incessant downpour
for over two hours
we couldn't help but talk.
I remember distinctly
the water was ankle-deep and rising.
Standing deftly on the sodden leaves
you asked me how long it would rain.
Perhaps I should have known the answer.
I said I'd no idea.
I laughed, and you laughed with your whole body.
That was how language began for us.
Our friendship lasted for three years.
We met regularly joked and laughed,
met at cinemas and cafés and fairs.
Gossip tied our fingers in marriage.
But our friendship withered away
unknown to us
like a tendril trapped in a severe drought.
Still, when a dark cloud descends
from our private sky
and trees start dripping
I think of you.

[tr. from Sinhala by the poet]

DUSHYANTHAN

(*b*. 1964)

Dushyanthan is the penname of Anton Jude, born in Jaffna, Northern Sri Lanka. His poems appeared in magazines during the 1980s and 1990s and he published a collection in Tamil in 1990. He left Jaffna to live in Germany and, though he wasn't prolific, his lyric 'They Do Not Know' became incredibly well known, for capturing the essence of Tamil experience in the 1980s.

They Do Not Know

Yesterday someone died.
It wasn't me, nor was it you.
Today someone died.

Not you, not I.
If someone dies tomorrow,
that may be you or I.
Definitely
one of us, my friend!

At dawn,
there will be more and more
military trucks,
and the roads in our village
will be blocked off with barbed wire.

Then,
you or I
will be abducted
or shot dead. Definitely.
They do not know
that you and I are human.

All they know is
that you and I
are not human.

[tr. from Tamil by Sascha Ebeling]

PATRICK FERNANDO
(1931–82)

Born to Roman Catholics, Joseph Patrick Fernando lived by the coast and
worked as a tax official until his sudden death. He wrote essays on theology
for Catholic journals. In his poems, which are formal but with room for a
spoken voice, measured evocations of particular locales alternate with remarks
on how the energies of animals and persons must either discover forms for
their expression, or face erasure. As well as speaking English and Sinhalese,
Fernando knew Latin and Greek and wrote translations as well as poems with
classical themes. He owned a coconut plantation at Mangala Eliya.

The Fire Dance

...and Simon Peter was standing and warming himself.

JOHN 18:25

The fire never repeats itself – always changing into
More impassioned movements: now swirling low and thick
Like the eddies I saw in water fishing in the starlight, now
Stretching into human form, yellow red-nailed fingers
Thin into vanishing.
Underneath her soft insistent feet, the logs degenerate
Into ever deepening ash:
Cruel ballerina dancing upon gathering pain.

But still, it's not only the high priest's vast aristocratic fire
That can execute such forms of dance as these;
Have I not gazed endlessly at fires we light on shore
– Burning centres of night-blossom petalled with crouching fishermen
And huddling shadows? Have I not seen the cold fear in fire,
When it stepped aside to avoid the predatory wind? And its joy,
Have I not felt it at my hearth at home, where it leaped
And laughed like a child?

But this is not the time for the mind to strive to understand what it cannot explain;
This is the time to be still, to conceal my face and escape detection and death.
So let me gaze deeper into the puzzle of the fire and cover my face with its glow,
While the heat unlocks the numbness in my bones and sets me free to go.

All round the shadows of Roman soldiery flit against the walls
Like insects in lighted rooms seeking for a place to rest.
Look how the fire's fingers interlock and hands clasp
As though in thanksgiving, or supplicating in some distress
Which only the suppliant knows and cannot yet divulge.

But now it assumes a quieter attitude and squats upon the ash: Dolopina,
The grey Thessalian witch next door, practising her craft!
And I can see the withered fingers now unweave before these startled eyes
The illusion I wove; and all my hopes of throne and power
Split in the backyard of my shame,
And I, an idle cat who dreamt in an empty afternoon.

Still I cannot call it all an imposture. I loved the man,
– A thing we hard sea-going folk never do
Unless there's reason for the trouble. Besides,
A hundred scenes begin to stir to life and I am tossed
Once more upon a sea of doubt:
Along the brook of the Cedron the water carriers walk with cautious grace
Talking wishfully of wine;
The man is now alive who was dead, spiced and embalmed,
I recall the waves whiten pale and run before the wind,
And hear the voice that calmed.

All these and many more to mesmerise a dull restless mind
– The endowment to the weak and poor.
But I shall know it all tomorrow. Tomorrow I shall come back
To join the crowd and cheer,
Or hide my face, ask pardon of my wife and take to the sea once more
With renewed loyalty;
Feel again its changeful pulse, listen to the wind chastise,
And light our little fires on shore.

Aeneas and Dido

Created in the image of God,
Though sprung from the womb of Eve,
He could impersonate the Lord
And win applause for Dido's grief.

Dark after-world is shot with light!
Torch-bearers keeping company;
Bringing to mind a certain night
Descending on Gethsemane.

He walks upon the fallen leaves
To where, nursing her new-born plight,
The lovely shade of Dido grieves
Now unconcerned with wrong and right.

'To leave you in that cold grey dawn,
My love, I swear was not my will;
Yet Heaven pushed me like a pawn
In strange furtherance of its will.'

Her anxious face, as some rare flower
Caught in a soft infecting wind
Dispetals, fell – she had no power
For speech and fled unanswering.

Returning over the trodden leaves,
Her conscience light and satisfied,
He joins admiring friends and grieves
Over her hard eternal pride.

Then sailing to a better land,
In obedience to God's decrees,
He takes a royal daughter's hand,
Enthroned throughout our centuries.

Ballad of a River

Dawn fires the surface into gold,
Gold-eyed the herons stilt and stalk.
At silver noon the waters hold
Wheelings of a mirrored hawk.

I've not seen water lie so still
As here. Perhaps an otter may
Disturb its peace, or white cranes till
The green edge wading tall-knee-deep.

In gusts of wind, a faint wood hum –
Plucked leaves and broken petals dance,
The wind departs, the wood is dumb,
And floating yellows gather brown.

To think up to a mile ago
This river bounded like a hound,
Convulsed and nearly wrecked our boat,
And lies here gentle as a pond!

A rich practical man I'm told
Demanded, why this idleness?
He got no answer and compelled
The river into harness.

Like frightened birds the minutes fled
Pursued by roaring steel and fire.
The river slaved and profits grew
To almost overtake desire.

Until, they say, one windy night,
In deepest vigils of the owl,
The river rose and foaming white
Descended like a murderer.

At dawn the waters shone restored.
The wreckage stood like blasted rocks
Round which the burnished mirror showed
Artistry of a wild brown hawk.

SANDRA FERNANDO

(———)

Sandra Fernando says that her poetry is 'influenced by the poetry of the hymnals we use in the various mainline churches'. She is a teacher and a member of the Wadiya Group. Her first book, *Candle and Other Poems*, won a State Literary Award in 2005, and in it she uses both tight and loose forms, combining careful description with satire. Fernando has read at the Galle Literary Festival and is also a playwright.

... and in the middle

and in the middle was a temple flower tree.
She would sit there in the evenings
sipping wine or sherry
watching the sun go down
letting the coconut trees whisper
away the fret of the day
talking to the orioles and kingfishers
counting the gardenias as they bowed
to their solitary audience
admiring the brush strokes on the crotons
nodding with the anthuriums.
She liked to come through the gate

into her kingdom.
It pleased her.
All was in order.
Until she arrived one evening to find
a rose bush
next to the temple flower tree.
A surprise.
Planted solidly.
Standing as tall as she
and half as wide again.
Holding out shards for thorns
and bud fists for flowers.
Wrenched and awkward
it ignored her.
The card in its branches said
…with love.
She pondered how
to weed it.

Setting the Table for Dinner

I want to ride my bike on the Galle Road.

He rolled up a newspaper.

Leslie says he'll show me how to ride his motorbike.

He stepped to the dining table.

The new auntie in the front house says she can lend me her nice,
    slinky black gown to go to the ball.

He swatted at the flies.

She says she'll be able to take me with her and pay for my ticket also.

He paused to let them return.

She'll have to pick up her boyfriend on the way, but he's handsome.

He watched the flies gather.

He works in a casino.

Her mother decanted food into chipped bowls.

He rides a trailbike.

Can I go for a ride on it with him one day?

She scraped the gravy carefully into the bowls.

Leslie smokes.

She wiped the splashes from the sides of the bowls.

Can I smoke too? Leslie's 16 and I'm almost 16.

He swiped the flies.

I don't want to go to school any more.

He swatted furiously at the board.

Rochelle's got lots of money. They say she sleeps with men after school.

He was sweating and gasping with effort.

She's having a lot of fun with her money.

He wiped the table with a cloth.

Why do I have to finish school?

Her mother laid plates on the table.

What good will three more years in school do me?

He put the knives on the right and the forks on the left.

Can I sleep late this Sunday and not go to church?

He laid out dessert spoons along the tops of the settings.

I had my first beer at Tania's place yesterday.

Her mother laid the bowls of food on the table.

It tasted really good.

He laid serving spoons beside each one.

As good as my first cigarette.

Come and have your dinner, he said.

You missed wiping away those flies on that corner, Daddy.

Shirt

I'll wear your shirt.
Can I choose my own style?
Does it come with those collars that stand up
Like an Indian tunic?
Do you have one with a neat collar
That buttons tidily like a Mao suit?
Or perhaps a pirate shirt with a long yoke
That ends half way to the elbow –
So the sleeves bell beautifully – with wrist frills?
No frills. They're too flippant.
No styles – a shirt like this must be dignified.
Do you mean workmanlike?
Can I at least choose the colour?
No, it must match your joy.
Does it have a pocket? Can I hang a pen there?
Or peg my shades through a button?
No adornments. Your shirt is your shirt.
You want it to swaddle and scour me.
Put shoulder pads in it, then.
When someone rests a head on my shoulder
It'll really scrape and chafe for the pads,
Like bizarre armpits of wire wool.
No shoulder pads. What about painkillers?
Or at least do this:
If I wear your shirt,
You wear mine.

RU FREEMAN
(*b*. 1967)

Ru Freeman (birth name Ruvani Pieris Seneviratne) is a Sri Lankan and American writer, poet, and activist whose work appears internationally in English and in translation. She was born in Colombo and currently lives in Philadelphia, USA where she teaches creative writing. She grew up reading the poetry of her father, Gamini Seneviratne and later her brother, Malinda. 'My phrasing comes from Sinhala and Sri Lankan oral patterns, but my concerns tend toward the global even in the most intimate sphere of personal relationships. The strength of Sri Lankan women, which arises out of our matriarchal/matrilineal tradition, is at the centre of what concerns me.'

Her poetry has been published in various magazines including *American Poetry Review* and *Poetry, Narrative and The Normal School*. She is editor of the poetry anthology, *Extraordinary Rendition: (American) Writers on Palestine* (OR Books, 2015/Interlink, 2016) and co-editor of the poetry anthology, *Indivisible: Global Leaders on Shared Security* (Interlink, 2019). She has also written two novels, *A Disobedient Girl* (2009) and *On Sal Mal Lane* (2013), which was a *New York Times* Editor's Choice Book – she has won two prizes for her fiction – and a short-story collection, *Sleeping Alone* (2022). She writes for the UK *Guardian*, *The New York Times* and *The Boston Globe*, and is the Director of the Artists Network at Narrative 4.

Erasure

A touch of cold   light frost
they cannot tolerate much
more than that   they seek
heat for life   & touch
they want that too the ideal
conditions given for what
you think they are: rooted
tubers pressed into service
from the altar of our bodies

& if they are   their mother
safe-guards against the mold
set of dark waters rising
the way it is told happened
in Ireland's occupied soil
story of hegemony & peril
not unlike this: dark crown
forced upon the virescent
girl still becoming woman

You would like to imagine
my children thus To dig
& rinse & peel their skin
memory of country shed
You   would prefer them
placed upon your table
no longer brown but *clean*
a touch of   *something* come
from nowhere & no one

My loves bloom otherwise
              hypethral
held fast by the subterranean
Networks beneath their
life above-ground & free
Nourished by the unseen
mycorrhizal secrets whispered
like another foreign word
corazón corazón corazón

Loose Change

It's the change of the dollar that makes
all that noise I heard her say   She comes
from an island and like mine hers made her
root & dance so the hard waves licked
incessant on us Mandrake women who
like the devil trees accrued dark courage
learned the currency that exes exchanged
leaving less worn tokens in our hands
skipping turnstiles to move bodies less
warm with each revolution of steel
Selfie-stick wielding activists what do they know
of bargains struck dumb we are pitched
black and wear gold scream colours
from head to toe Say keep it keep
the change keep the change keep
all the noise-making metal   Give us the rest
whatever that is   in this every man an island
country of deceit   We are far from home

In Your Hour of Need, God

But Lot's wife looked back, and she became a pillar of salt
GENESIS 19.26

People say I turned out of weakness
I loved the things of the world.
Lust of the flesh

Lust of the eyes
pride of life: daughters,
more, grand-daughters.
I refused to believe.
I refused God.
           And yet –

When women leave men for other men
When child scream and child laugh
wrestle our hearts to the fecund earth
When the blues bands wail our sorrow
and we are still from what ails us now
When no taste remains but mine
bless me for my choice
               O sisters, O brothers;
                    falling
               these fingers at the end of this hand
               these arms which hold and
                   release
                   this body which pleases. Look
up at that famous ceiling
see what was hidden from us:
it is the old man who yearns
it is the young man that gifts
his nakedness content
If life was exchanged who is to say
it flowed one way and not the other?
Look up at that famous ceiling, wonder.

When lips touch lips and the taste of her
remains in the afterlife left
when the olive mango avocado grows and falls
              as naked into your hands,
              as dressed into your mouth
                   consider the divine:
What I mourned you possess.
That smear upon your tongue, that spice,
               that is I –

On Jebel Usdum on the western shore
of not-lake-not-sea, I stand.

God, I forgive you

BUDDHADASA GALAPPATHY

(*b.* 1947)

Buddhadasa Galappathy published a collection of poems in 1971 with two colleagues, Sunil Ariyaratna and Jayalath Manoratna; since then he has published ten books of poetry in Sinhala, five collections of short stories, and has won the Poet of the Year Award at the State Literary Festival in 1999, for his collection *Thuruliya Akuru Wiya*. He is considered one of the leading poets of the 70s, alongside Parakrama Kodituwakku and Monica Ruwanpathirana; his influences include Ediriweera Sarachchandra, Gunadasa Amarasekara, Siri Gunasinghe, Mahagama Sekera, and Wimal Dissanayake. Galappathy has also won the Best Column Writer award twice, and a Lifetime Award for Cinema Writing.

I Am Not Sita

The cold wind creeps, a thief
between the window panes
the dim moon shining over the desolate earth
lets a thin sliver fall.

Breaking the desolation of midnight
the waves fall, wailing, solitary,
the boat that you rowed out to sea
is now a speck on the distant ocean.

The wind already is softly whispering
that he is come and waiting
outside the window of my hut.

Be not angry my husband
think not too ill of me, my husband
I cannot be
another Sita.

[tr. from Sinhala by Ranjini Obeyesekere]

Alms for King Vessantara

When King Vessantara gave away
His children, his wife
His retinue and his servants

Brahmins queued up in the streets
Waiting to receive those alms.

But a mother with her child on her shoulder
Looking on from the corner of the street
Waiting

To give away her little son
To King Vessantara

She did not have
Strength in her arms to carry her child
Or milk in her breasts to feed him.

[tr. from Sinhala by Malini Govinnage]

KAPILA M. GAMAGE
(———)

Born of Tamil and Sinhala parentage, Gamage is a veteran journalist of Sinhala radio and television who has fought for the wellbeing of agricultural communities through his broadcasts on Mahaweli Community Radio since it was founded in the early 80s. He has also worked for the Sri Lanka Broadcasting Corporation and the Sri Lanka Rupavahini Corporation, and lectured at educational institutes and universities. He is at present a scriptwriter. 'Prose, poetry, painting, sculpture, cinema, drama or photography… develops a strong platform for a realistic debate or discussion between nations and ethnicities enabling to understand their cultural life. Art is also a gateway towards intercultural education.'

Teriyum Kokila

There are no dreams now
that I cannot not let go of
only the day you came by
is my world's vasantam

Not the hare in the moon
nor the daughter to God
the dust-smeared jasmine
still remains untouched

'Aney, annei inga vāngo
it's too arid here'
but the pottu on your forehead
still looks fresh

True, Kokila, you are dark
but your smile is ever so white
the dream you dreamt every night
seems too heavy for you

A house, an American roof
and a long Austin car
the books you read over sleepless nights
have made a stethoscope-necklace for you

Whacking the polished floor
with a slender high heel
wearing a jasmine behind the ear
and the pallu hugging a shoulder

At the Jaffna hospital
caring for her sick folks
she keeps their smiles close to her heart
the smiles that say 'seeing her is bliss'

This was your old dream
the one you said wasn't too heavy
I saw you at Nallur kovil
like an unfamiliar dream

On the head adorned with jasmines
were scattered white strands
the pottu on your forehead
was your heavy old dream

Leaning on a crutch
a hand's fingers stretched
Kokila, your white smile
is even whiter now

My mother speaks Tamil
like flowing water
to me Tamil is konjum teriyum
how embarrassing is it, Kokila?

My child hates Tamil
how it angers me
and I can't forget how you lost
your foot once graced with marathondi

[tr. from Sinhala by Chamini Kulathunga]

Prayers to Konesvaran

Tiruvaran
you wake up
to welcome the brothers
piled up along the lagoon's shore
once more you must wake up

To the fine season
where the grand tides
that buried secrets
beneath the singing waters
of the lagoon
crash and mourn
against the Kallady bridge
Tiruvaran
you wake up

Can the fragile lantern light
that took us to life's depth
sight a coast
or a lighthouse?

Like his name
Nimalachandran
was not a moon
but a hand full of pure water
a heart full of warmth
like a hot spring in Kanniya

On a night
the breeze murmurs
the melodies Isaipriya sang
the fish in the lagoon waters
listen in silence

Tiruvaran you wake up
aborting the past
making a shrine
out of the new womb
now you must wake up
holding in your hands
the things you've got to say
to go to Konesvaram
Tiruvaran you wake up

[tr. from Sinhala by Chamini Kulathunga]

V.V. GANESHANANTHAN

(*b.* 1980)

V.V. Ganeshananthan is the author of the novel *Brotherless Night* (2023). Her previous novel, *Love Marriage*, was longlisted for the Women's Prize and named one of the best books of the year by *The Washington Post*. Her work has appeared in *Granta*, *The New York Times* and *Ploughshares*. A former vice president of the South Asian Journalists Association, she has also served on the board of the Asian American Writers' Workshop. She is on the board of directors of the American Institute for Sri Lankan Studies and the Minnesota Prison Writing Workshop. A co-host of the Fiction/Non/Fiction podcast on Literary Hub, she teaches in the MFA program at the University of Minnesota.

the faithful scholar dreams of being exact

the faithful scholar dreams of being exact,
invites unsorrowing reason in, builds
a church of math: illuminates this volume of
violence with formulae, brackets the absence
with love for the civilian dead approaching infinite –
he divines the loss, the imaginary number,
exacts the hour: the distance travelled over time,
the task, the force plus mass, this hour weighted
enough for him to step tender again into the garden
still watered with falls. into each blank, a variable –
son minus father; corrected for orphans, widows
over children, vanished over zero. a line beyond
which unrelenting fact reveals that of every eight slain,
two crossed the bar entwined. the calculus celestial:
the impossible sum in which one must already
believe to pursue proof, though in all this
reddened heaven and earth, desire reduces
to reversal: the apple lifted from the air,
shot above no one's head, uneaten, unbruised,
returned to the heart of the tree still blazing green –

from The Five-year Tongue Twisters
[*five times five things to try to say quickly*]

1

The misters assisted in shelling these shells on the seashore war,
The shells they shelled were not sea-shells, I'm sure.
Some of the people they shelled aren't there any more.
And if they shelled the seashore during the war
Then I'm sure that whoever sells them the shells has more.

Hard to say. Hard to ring any bells. What are tongue-twisters for?

The terrorists failed to resist state terror and in fact assisted
In placing the targets that were shelled in the seashore war,
When people tried to flee to the sea they decreed
Give us one child, another, more –

And as the misters shelled the seashore during the war
The terrorists held the people as shell-shields before –

Hard to say. Hard to ring any bells. What are tongue-twisters for?

2

The mighty military mounted a magnificent Mullivaikkal monument to most magnanimous majesty Mahinda. Mahinda manages most magnificently militarily!

5

Tourism (terrorism) terrorism (tourism) tourism (terrorism) terrorism (tourism)!

10

The torturers took Thambi's thumbs.

12

Our ūr, your ūr. Your ūr, our ūr.

13

The widowed women wandered, wondering whether they were widowed.

YASMINE GOONERATNE
(*b.* 1935)

This novelist, academic, biographer and poet wrote studies of Jane Austen and Alexander Pope, and her own poetry is ironic, satirical, guiding its usually tight forms towards moments of withering commentary – her rhymes in particular can be polysyllabically ingenious. Born in Colombo, she studied at the University of Ceylon at Peradeniya before going on to Cambridge and then teaching at Macquarie University in Australia, where she was the founding director of its Post-Colonial Literatures and Language Research Centre. Her collections of poetry are *Word Bird Motif* (1971), *The Lizard's Cry and Other Poems* (1972), *Six Thousand Foot Death Dive* (1981), and *Celebrations and Departures* (1991), which includes poems written over four decades, some outside Sri Lanka. She has also published four novels: *A Change of Skies* (1992), *The Pleasures of Conquest* (1995), *The Sweet and Simple Kind* (2006) and *Rannygazoo* (2015).

In 1990, Gooneratne was awarded Australia's highest national honour, the Order of Australia, for her services to education and literature. She has been Patron of the Jane Austen Society of Australia since its inception in 1990. She won the Raja Rao Award in 2001 and Sri Lanka's Sahithyarathna Award for a lifetime's achievement in literature in 2008. She has been a patron of the Galle Literary Festival from its inception.

Horoscope

The Stars Foretell Your Future is a solemn
journalist's joke that fills a daily column
enchanting Britain's secretaries and slaveys
who like to think that in a weekend's series
of amorous encounters they discern
the great Goat's hoof-beat, downy pelt of Aries.

Its counterpart with us tries no such jest,
stricter than moral law and rather less
kind than divine, slips from its secret sheath
with boy's first breath,
preoccupies his thoughts and, pitiless,
measures his minutes, hours and days till death.

At three the Planets wrest him from his mother
asserting that they cannot thrive together;
predicting a divorce at forty-five
the Constellations freeze his heart. He strives
to show some disbelief, and when another
star augurs fortune, seeks it in a wife.

Rise for the bride, in whom all virtues blend,
nurtured these eighteen years towards this end
by watchful womenfolk, the same that hover
about her now; their duty to discover
budding self-will, to root it up, and tend
the shame-fast fear that gratifies a lover.
She draws upon her our admiring eyes,
her own correctly lowered now. A prize
duly annexed together with the dower
her father yields, and trusting in its power,
she dreams of happy hours, nor knows what lies
ticking relentlessly among her flowers.

Peradeniya Landscape

(to Chitra)

Examination time is here. Again
The April jacaranda in the park
Sprinkles the burning grass with purple rain.
Threading the April heat the students mark
Its lovely canopy as we did, take
The long way round beside the little lake
As we did once, to walk beneath its shade.
Behind our splendid hills each cooing pair
Still make the most of Spring before it fades,
The Library's still crowded, not a chair
To spare behind the wooden barricades.
To see it now, you'd never think a thing
Changed, though one knows quite well the future dawns
Less brightly for them, and a muttering
Protest hushes birdsong on these well-kept lawns.

The Brave Man Who Keeps Snakes as His Pets

The brave man who keeps snakes as his pets
In his laboratory
Showed me the other day a cobra
In a glass tank
That spat and struck
And then caressed the stick held out to it.
On the lowest shelf of a cupboard
Coiled neatly among books and papers
A python lay, deeply asleep,
Shifting only a very little at the nudge of its master's boot.
In a metal cage, a Russell's Viper
Shrank and hissed at our approach
With a sound like a singing kettle.
All very domestic!
He takes them for a run in the evenings, it appears,
As some people take their dachshunds and pekes.
One hopes they all get safely tucked up again at night,
Each in its little tank and cage and cupboard.

And much luckier they are, after all,
Than their cousins that I used to see
High on a shelf, above the clicking typewriters
In my father's provincial office,
Green and yellow diamond-backed, and slimy white-bellied,
Coiled in shimmering rings and figures-of-eight,
Floating in a transparency I now know to have been formalin,
Bottled in formalin, safely stoppered.

Since snakes exist
With us and in us,
And are beautiful as well as fierce
And unpredictable,
Should we bottle them up, or keep them as pets?
I am not sure that loving-kindness enters into it
Since a snake, if startled
Or provoked, may strike
And can presumably
Kill.
I think it is wisest, when you have to live with snakes
That are not safely pickled and stoppered,
To let them doze companionably in cupboards
Well fed, content,
To let them lash harmlessly in a transparency of words
Where you can observe their curious markings
And admire
Their vicious grace,
And exercise them, when they need a run,
In the airy enclosure of a poem.

SUNIL GOVINNAGE

(*b.* 1950)

Sunil Govinnage has written poetry in Sinhala since 1965, and poetry in
English – he taught himself the language when he was 17 – since 1989. His
poems have been published in Sri Lanka, Australia and the US, and broadcast
on radio. Formerly employed by Sri Lanka's Health Department, he worked
as a full-time civil servant in Western Australia from 1988 to 2014, and as a
visiting lecturer teaching sociology and social justice from 2005 to 2008 at
Notre Dame University, Perth. He has published seven books of poetry; his
Sinhala collection, *Mathaka Mawatha*, won a prize in 2010, and his English

collection, *Perth: My Village Down Under*, received a publisher's award in Sri Lanka in 2012. Govinnage's other work includes the short story collection *Black Swans and Other Stories* (2002) and a novel, *The Black Australian* (2012). He was a finalist in Sri Lanka's State Literary Awards in 2013, and was an Elder-in-Residence (2022 program) at the Centre for Stories, in Perth.

The City of Light

Perth: the city of light
Home away from home;
Floating at the edge of the Swan River
Like a picture postcard,
Where people ask me
Every day
Where I come from.

My English Verse

I battle with syntax and grammar,
Subjects, nouns, verbs and adjectives.

Meanings reach base simplicity,
And metaphors scurry
To hide in corners.

My Sinhala poems sleep in a back room
Lamenting their exile
Like children forbidden from play.

They will never be read
By Dennis, Bruce, Adrian or Andrew;
Not at all by Murray;
And will never appear in an anthology
Of new Australian Verse by Peter Porter.

On Becoming an Intellectual

'You have lost your Third World touch'
He said when I talked of Derrida and Foucault.

He thought they were Tamil Terrorists;
Then I explained.
He said:

'Be pragmatic,
Look for simplicity;
Philosophy is dead and nutty.
Literature doesn't make you rich!
Try to improve on your accent and
Consider doing an MBA.'

He showed me the key
To his brand new car.
I walked to the station.

AMALI GUNASEKERA
(*b.* 1971)

Amali Gunasekera grew up in Kandy. After living in Mozambique, Kenya and India, she is now based in Cumbria. Her first collection, *Lotus Gatherers*, was published by Bloodaxe in 2016 (under her former name of Rodrigo). This book included a short sequence based on a translation of medieval graffiti poems etched on the mirror wall in Sigiriya, Sri Lanka. She was selected for Arts Council England's project *Breaking Ground: Celebrating the Best British Writers of Colour* in 2017. Her second collection, *The Golden Thread*, was published by Bloodaxe in 2022. She describes herself as 'deeply preoccupied with exploring liminal spaces or the in-between of "thing" and "no-thingness"', and as seeing the poem 'as a primordial, timeless life force that through the green fuse dives the flower (Dylan Thomas) into expression, into utterance'. Gunesekera received a PhD and the Chancellor's Medal from Lancaster University and currently works in the field of Archetypal Psychology. She has won prizes in several poetry competitions and is a member of the Rathbones Folio Academy.

How to Watch a Solar Eclipse in a Bowl of Water

(Kandy, Sri Lanka, Insurgency 1987-1989)

The unbearable lightness of being no one
SLAVOJ ŽIŽEK

By day, stay close to home
  speak in modulated tones.
If the paper seller's son is gone
  don't ask after him.
Smile at the vegetable man's daughter
  even if you wonder – was it she
who slips *hartal* notices
  beneath coconuts, carrots?

Night after night
  let the house disappear,
the town
  with it the island.
Beyond the sea
  you may sense a lit planet
but know this darkness,
  how demarcations
are undecided.
  Lose your bodies
and live in voices.

Experiment with dumbness
  of hands, faces.
Scale dark hours with words
  learn the patois of silence,
its hesitations, swift leaps.
  Marvel
you are seventy per cent water, yet
  how easily you combust or float.

Like hunters beside night-fires,
  predators at bay
hush-hush
  tell tales, if only
of what you've heard –

how everyone stays away
        from the river,
after a raised arm
        in the murmur
drew eyes to those rocking
        downriver
like felled trees.

Outside, frangipani, verbena
        are at their most potent.
Breathe in these nights.
        Hope
to find no proof of anyone
        hula-hooped
in tyres and set alight.

It is your metronome of breath
        and winged gaze
like Minerva's owl
        that makes you real
without
        your animal body.

It is the world – trapped –
        that shatters again
and again
        in the skin of water.

from Beloved

Mother believes I will roam from sorrow to sorrow in the endless
tracts of samsara because I refuse to renounce the exquisiteness of
this perishable world. *Colours are the most essential qualities of a thing
not lines* writes Miłosz. He's thinking of Cézanne. Having puzzled
over the demarcations of colour, I see lines are fences that keep
each one safe yet imprisoned within. Does *I*, being the first person
suffer the same fate, hemmed in by a narrative from life's unspooling
mystery? Isn't the greatest terror of the heart like the golden tiger
that's caged by the freedom it senses in the spaces between bars?

Yes, there have been comings and goings; the burning tunic of the body, distant music. But none have moved your heart just so, to this exact pitch. *I am* not *my beloved's my beloved is* not *mine*. One day when all the divisions of your heart have given themselves up, you sit suffused in jewel-filtered light beneath a rose window and finally know love, love that comes too late perhaps for this dwelt world, when love with all its tenses has wandered in circles, when all the impostors are gone. Perhaps the most austere practice is not the relinquishment of the *sins* of the senses but a necessary forfeiture to know the true essence of the Beloved.

Then *You* is like earthrise, distant enough to see clearly and staggeringly beautiful. Not a state of enchantment but recognition. Like the moment I catch myself in the mirror and, for the first time do not flinch. *Catch us the foxes, the little foxes that spoil the vines, for our vines have tender grapes*. When we say *you are loved*, how often do we mean I see you? Jacob, waking, believed god was in the place the dream was dreamt and erected a visible monument. My palm shall never graze the temple of your body Beloved, but I feel the rough stubble of hair in new cut grass. As the ocean accepts rivers or rain, each of us accepts love differently, and sometimes we are unable to receive being too full of terror of the thing asking to enter us.

Peace

(Sri Lanka, 2011)

Within weeks of war's end, women everywhere began to find teeth marks on their breasts and bellies, often on the tenderest parts of their upper arms. Some woke to it after a restful sleep. Some were roused past midnight, finding no cause, turned over a new leaf of sleep. Days passed. Each found an echo of a narrative but no memory. Each found, how this confluence grew into a naked man, slathered in black grease, all of him faintly glistening as he moved like a night-river. They named it the *Grease Devil*.

In naming, this singular pain grew worse, so did the devil's ardour and night after night blood tie-died their sheets. Village men banded for vigilante night watch. Clutching at shadows, all they ever came away with were blackened, slick palms. Often there wasn't even that. If sometimes, a woman found flecks of skin beneath her own fingernails, she thought nothing of it.

One night, when they were all out to lasso this night-river, memories found them staring downstream with arms upraised as if in praise or supplication or surrender. When they came to, no one could tell which. But they sensed peace.

I could say peace was a river with time on its hands or a white elephant escaped from memory. I could say peace was stubborn as a water buffalo or shy as a sun-basking snake noosed in grass. But it wasn't like that. Peace waited all night to take in the faithless lover. Peace cursed like a fishwife brimful of toddy with her man so much at sea. Peace was less a woman with bitten breasts, though even now, some claim otherwise.

DAYASENA GUNASINGHE
(1936–96)

Dayasena Gunasinghe was born in the village of Ingiriya in the Karatara District. Initially a teacher, he later entered journalism and became Editor-in-Chief of several national newspapers. His debut collection in Sinhala, *Ranthetiyaka Kandulu*, was published in 1974 followed by *Novadhim Sidhuhath* in 1983 and *Doramadalawa* in 1991. His collection of short stories, *Canal Road Nigacharayo*, was released in 1985. He was also a well-known newspaper columnist and published a collection of his columns, *Raigam Rada*, in 1989. He won several state awards for his short stories and poems.

Denagama Siriwardhane, who published a biography of Dayasena, *Podu Janayage Pattarakaraya*, in 2020, refers to him as the people's journalist: 'From the outset, he was with the people and never went after politicians. He had a dream of creating a people's newspaper which discussed people's problems and their rights. I never met a journalist like him, as I frequently saw journalists who worked for politicians or the owners of the newspaper company or for money.'

The Blue of My Eyes

Listening to the pot of rice
bubbling merrily for you,
blowing embers into flames
to make it taste like heavenly food,

the blue of my eyes burnt out
disappeared in smoke.

When the sun set sail to the west
not saying when he'd be back
I sat with my face to the night
alone with the weeping world
many life-times of years,
and the blue of my eyes, unnoticed,
dissolved with the dark.

When after a hard day's labour
to eke out a mouthful for two,
you sprawled on your sleeping mat
for a moment's ease;
the sound of your sighs and groans
squeezed my heart out in tears
that washed out the blue of my eyes
unawares, as they flowed.

The blue of the deep blue lotus
the blue of the distant sea
were nothing in comparison
to the blue eyes of my youth;
so you once said, my husband.

Gaze not into my eyes
with thoughts of what is past,
look rather at your daughter
whose eyes look on the future.

[tr. from Sinhala by Ranjini Obeyesekere]

SIRI GUNASINGHE
(1925–2017)

Siri Gunasinghe was an academic, poet, Sanskritist, art historian, author and filmmaker. He was born in Ruwanwella in the Kegalle District, and educated in Galle, at the University of Ceylon, and then at the Sorbonne. A pioneer of Sinhala free verse, Gunasinghe advocated the use of spoken not received literary language. *Mas Lea Nati Ata,* published in 1956, was a transformational work that led to Sinhala poets considering free verse as a viable and liberating form of poetry: 'I found the traditional four-line stanza very limiting [...] It typically led to soppy language. In fact it crippled the language. I realised that there was a lot of natural rhythm in the Sinhala language which could be creatively exploited in free verse.'

Gunasinghe's novel, *Hewenella*, published in 1960, is also considered ground-breaking in its style. His other poetry collections include *Abi Nikmana* (1958), *Rathu Kekula* (1962) and *Alakamandawa* (1998). He taught at the University of Peradeniya and the University of Victoria, in British Columbia, as a Professor in the Department of History of Art. He then travelled to Paris where he continued his studies and wrote *La technique de la peinture indienne d'après les textes du Silpa*. Gunasinghe lived in Canada from 1970 until the end of his life.

A Memorial

Forsaking me
leaving my limbs death-stiff
she left – disappeared –
went away;
and I became a prey
to a flock of wild-beast memories
a bloody prey.

The thick dark of time shrouds
but in the flickering light from my heart
her body glows
gleams before my eyes.

Like a cool streak of water
between rough rocks
she flows
soaking my heart.

The colour of clear skies is her.
The texture of flowers and trees is she.
All the colours of the world are her.

I struggle hard to shut her out
but she lurks in the very lashes of my eyes.
The tough dry skin of forgetfulness
splits apart
and your eyes peer at me, beloved
I still see the trembling of your lips
as you embrace me.

The only happiness life has
the one lovely object the world holds
is she – companion of my loneliness –
vanished now;
the only woman who shared my loneliness.

[tr. from Sinhala by Ranjini Obeyesekere]

The Water Buffalo

My beard on fire
in haste, I was running, running down in the dawn,
bearing the burdens of life
all on my back;
at the edge of the road, in a large clump of grass,
like a fat merchant sprawled on his easy-chair
I saw you lie.

Both eyes closed;
and at the earth-shattering
battering of my feet
you did not even start.
Ears turn down;
my sky-thundering
lightning-like haste
did not surprise you.

Teeth uncleaned
face unwashed,
in the mountain's moist lap
of lush marsh grass
mud splashed:
What if, like you,
I too
could laze?

Tell me my buffalo,
you who can't even stand
yes you, Reverend Sir!
Are you observing rites,

134

contemplating the impermanence of life,
belching with both eyes closed?

Or do you count beads
with each slow puff
of dilated nostril?

Like eye-flies slowly crawling
from a partly opened flower
are the thoughts that seem to teem
from those faintly twitching eyes;
what secrets do they hold?

Head half-lifted up
spit drooling, lips that chap
like a toothless mouth chewing betel
all alone;
a lazy past was yours.

The full weight of earth and sky
bundled in one load
like the wisp of a cotton flake
you bear
on those handsome, upturned horns.
How do you do it
oh buffalo?

You do not know of yesterday
nor have yet come to know today.
Tomorrow you know nothing of.
Undying time alone is yours.
You are my only idol
all in stone.

[tr. from Sinhala by Ranjini Obeyesekere]

Renunciation

It is a long journey,
a grief-filled journey.
A journey progressing
from darkness to darkness.

Battling that darkness
stifling the weariness
sweat dripping from quivering flesh –

I came,
across vast deserts of madness
to ford the river
Neranjara:
On the further shore –
a vision – white, filled with laughter.
Sometimes, someone
standing on a mountain
throws out a light, with a flare,
fire-fly-like;
The black sky of ignorance
swallows it instantly.

I, seeking light,
was led by blind-darkness
to this river's edge.

I must cross this river
Neranjara.
Will I be able to – can I ever –
cross this river
Neranjara?
I have struggled so long just for that.

Life,
snoring,
spit drooling, naked,
beside the bed
curled like a maggot clump, lies.
The day the singing and dancing ends
death splits them apart –

I left the harem,
left my wife, my son,
came here at midnight
but that too is my life.

That white hot radiance
on the further shore

was light
so they said.
I came, leaving everything,
all life's pleasures, which are also grief.

In a myriad shapes
in a thousand dances
in the sound of sweet music
life clung to me
wailing.

I brushed her aside
and at dead midnight
made the final act of renunciation.

I snapped
life's chain that bound my feet
and on a borrowed steed
came speeding.

With the waters of intellect
I marked a line round my neck,
severed my head
offered it in alms;
that I might reach the light on the further shore,
my heart's crystal eyes,
I plucked out and gave away.

All the joys of life
all its sweetness to the
Jujaka of intellect
I offered, as wife.

Like early morning spittle
I spat it out.
Elated, I came
seeking undying life
to cross the river Neranjara.

[tr. from Sinhala by Ranjini Obeyesekere]

YVONNE GUNAWARDENA

(1926–2022)

Yvonne Gunawardena was born in Kurunegala. She was a musician, as well as a poet. In 1950, she won a government scholarship to study at London's Trinity College of Music. In 1973, she moved back to London for a substantial period of time. She won the Sri Lanka Arts Council Prize in 1988 for her first book, *A Divisive Inheritance*, described by Gamini Seneviratne as portraying 'the predicament of the expatriate with a pithiness born of honesty'. *Arrivals and Departures: Thirty Poems* was published in 1996, *Collected Poems* in 2005, and *Harbour Lights* in 2011. Yasmine Gooneratne describes Gunawardena's poems as 'quiet and thoughtful, recording brief and witty, carefully crafted impressions of life', though in the later works the wit takes a backseat, given 'the inescapable challenges posed by expatriation, sickness and death'.

Homecoming

'Ten years have passed,' the young man said.
Worn down by the sea's incessant churning
The firm line of the horizon had shrunk to a tenuous thread.
The old house had groaned at each leave-taking,
And immigrant sparrows bickered in the eaves
Querying their rights and the gifts of the dead.
Such a waste of so many golden sheaves!
'There's iron in my soul,' the young man said.

Colombo, 1981

Ancestral Voices

She sang quietly under her breath
an old song about fallen heroes
and a rough sea passage.
This was the burden of her journey.
A cleaner at London's airport, she paused,
sighing for the golden mustard fields she'd left.

On these drab North London streets
more shadows pass me.

I make a mental note of their names
and of this particular mannerism or that.
See in a pair of light eyes a Burgher from
the Dutch East India Company; or I search
the old maps and prints to be rewarded
with a single-minded conquistador
sitting po-faced at his interminable ledgers.
Perhaps he is an ancestor of the Krauses, Kochs,
or de Witts, or of Clasz the music lover and
the gifted organist we knew named Herft.
These had crossed frontiers too, spurred on
by fear or greed; they rode their slim caravels
through unfamiliar seas to exotic spice islands.
Some returned. Some stayed and mingled their blood
with those they called the 'lesser breeds'.

Today, I would like to tell the singer
that the burden of her song is mine too.
We share a common enemy; a faceless
establishment moves the pawns. We must
cling like barnacles to the rock's scabrous surface.

London, 1982

Thoughts on a Train Journey

The grim squares and dwelling places recede
and out of a maze of steel configurations one
track emerges in a solo line.
We are moving away from the monotony of corrugated iron
and the weekly washing of polyester and cotton sheets.

An alien landscape: yet nothing here is unfamiliar
for are we not the rump, the sacrificial lambs left over
from the great cataclysm of old?
The last of the middle-class diaspora, the ones reared
on 'a host of golden daffodils' and 'babbling brooks'?

The young think we were mostly cardboard cutouts:
shadow puppets from another time, nostalgia pedlars!

I cannot bear to tell them how deep our schisms run
or why they came to exist; instead...

I take my chances as they come,
allowing my eye to feast on the fleeting
silver birches, and I follow the starlings
in flight from their chill Siberian homelands
(this being an act of faith).
Perhaps a kinder winter awaits them on
these fen marshes; these are birds of passage.

Cambridge, 1986

Letter to England

Spring was the only time I woke
to a feeling of weightlessness,
a kind of silent exhilaration, the ebb
and flow of it relatively painfree.
I should have thanked you. Pardon me.

The pastel shading of your landscape,
fields layered with greening cress;
your hoary lichen-splattered oaks; your
village greens, where a plethora of
tulips jostled for space, streaking
through the long-stemmed grasses.

It matters little now that you scarcely
knew me (except as a species
of ephemeral exotica), a seed blown over
from the distant tropics, germinating
here through some quirk of time.

The anonymous silence you so value
kept me silent too. This way, I felt
your insistent rhythms better, knew how
your pulse fluctuated between indifference
and boredom at my intrusion. For my

part I tested you at your chillest depths,
yet softened when the next spring came round.
Your chorus of fertility, the gentle merging
of one sequence with the next, the virility of
each ubiquitous weed, your fine-veined
pampered roses: all these claimed me.

London, 1987

ROMESH GUNESEKERA
(*b*. 1954)

Romesh Gunesekera is internationally acclaimed for his poems, novels and short stories including *Reef*, shortlisted for the 1994 Booker Prize, *The Sandglass,* winner of the inaugural BBC Asia Award, and *The Match*, a groundbreaking cricket novel. His debut collection of stories, *Monkfish Moon*, like his dystopian novel *Heaven's Edge*, was a *New York Times* Notable Book of the Year. *Noontide Toll*, a cycle of linked stories published in 2014, captured a vital moment in post-war Sri Lanka and was featured in *The New Yorker*. His 2019 novel, *Suncatcher*, shortlisted for the Jhalak Prize, returns to an earlier era and a story of divided loyalties and endangered friendship in the turbulent 1960s.

Gunesekera's poems have appeared in the *London Review of Books*, *Guardian, Poetry Durham, Sunday Times* (Sri Lanka) and in anthologies published by Norton (USA), Bloodaxe (UK) and others. He is a Fellow of the Royal Society of Literature and has received a National Honour in Sri Lanka.

The Big Wave

The boat is made of coconut palms:
a wooden whale hollowed out
with two ribs stuck in a second hull.
A fisherman's rough catamaran.

Kapu perched on the outrigger
would sail into the night, but not too far.
His lamp, he knows from his father's short life,
must always be seen from the shore,

'Malu, malu, malu,
dhang genapu malu,

141

Suranganita malu genavaa…'
Fish, fish, fish, he sings,
just brought in,
for Surangani I have brought fresh fish.
A simple song that rises from the dark
lisping coastline,
a hungry heart,
an offering of netted moonlight.

This morning when he rides back
on the slow deep swell,
he comes with no slivers from the moon.
Not a single one.
He pulls the boat up the beach,
his brother and his son,
their shoulders to the two ribs,
nudge it out of the water's reach.
'Koheda malu?' his Surangani asks,
tightening the green cloth
around her waist.
Where is the fish?
Kapu brings out his empty net.
'Puduma vade, malu na.'
Strange business, no fish.
It is a mystery to him.

His son curls his toes in the white sand.
What could have happened to the moon?
Where would the fish go?
The blue line of the sea
marks the end of the world.

Circled by Circe

After twenty years muzzled in North London
you tell me over a cup
of treasured Tangana tea, you have decided
you must now go back.
Back home to that repository of such
complicated images to find

a less constricting mask
and unthrottle
an old lion in your throat.
You kneel before a temporarily placed
music-centre; as the record spins
I listen and try to understand
how you imagine your future
will unravel from such a private past.

You have been heading for this announcement
over many years. Each time we met
your conversation grew more spiced
with images of gold sand, tamarind trees,
the cacophony of traffic – lorries, cars,
bullock carts, bicycles –
rising out of the deep roar of the sea
soothing life in a Wellawatte boarding house.
Have you found in old Galle Road
a histogram for the politics of development,
a place for the dry knowledge you extracted
from that heap of economics textbooks?
How quickly they invaded those bookshelves
that once encased
arm-loads of dog-eared poetry
and far-flung magic histories.

For twenty years you dug your heels
and watched the catkins' obstinate return.
You inscribed Keats, Marx, Paranavitana
on every inch of your eclectic skin
to come finally to such disillusion:
now you say you must measure your roots
and distance yourself
from an increasingly hostile climate.
It seems you must exchange
one mirror image for its reverse,
confound exile and pin your hopes
on a fragile memory
of things as they might have been.

ROHITHA GUNETILLEKE

(*b.* 1954)

Rohitha Gunetilleke was born in Gampola and now lives in Los Angeles. He
left Sri Lanka during the rioting of 1983, and has watched from abroad 'my
country being torn apart, lives destroyed in the name of a religion, and for
the sake of a language. In my self-exile, I yearn to tell the stories that I had
carried in my palm.' Carolyn Forché's anthology, *Against Forgetting*, inspired
him to write the poems which have appeared in, among other places, *Indivisible:
An Anthology of Contemporary South Asian American Poetry*, *Malpais Review*,
Chicago Quarterly Review, *Catamaran*, *Muse India* and *Poetic Diversity*.

Eventually,

You no longer notice the tarred-out road signs
you get to where you got to go.
The sea lulls you
to see only what you need to see.

You stop gathering the garlands
those placards and slogans
now pulped and paper-mâchéd.
Your three-brick stove
wouldn't know what you ate,
petrified kindling carries no taste.

You forget the Morse code,
the alphabet soup of UN, NGO.
Refrains fade and the jeeps go home.
You stop
counting the dead.

You don't hear the waves
crash at your feet,
or feel the sand under your sole.
You don't wait for the unarrived bus
you walk and you walk,
you ignore the burden on your back.

Cowboys

His dark skin glistened like a bottle bottom –
button eyes cindered knee-high – beside
my white horse. We galloped away
chasing the renegades, shooting from our hips.

Elastic waist pants slipped down
our kindergartner behinds –
we were all shades of brown then.

We prayed to the Hindu Gods
in the Bellanvila Buddhist temple.
Tonto carried the offering –
fruits and incense flowered
over his head in a rattan basket.
We smashed coconuts, dotted
our temples with kumkum –
sat all-night on paduru mats
enfolded in the pirith chant
tethered to a holy string.

We didn't know then –
one day they would come
carrying voting lists, sticks and stones
fire bottled in their fists –
looking for the others among us.

In the distance, the roofs burned
like camphor
but with no scent.

I lost track of what happened
to my dark mask, white cape
those ivory handled pistols.
I thought I'd saved the world.

APARNA HALPÉ

(———)

Aparna Halpé is a poet, musician and scholar from Kandy who lives and works in T'karonto, where she is a Professor of English at Centennial College, researching the function of myth in contemporary postcolonial fiction. She is the author of a collection of poems, *Precarious* (2013), and her creative writing has appeared in many journals including *Postcolonial Text* and *Indialogs*. Her interview with the Tamil poet and activist Cheran appears in *Creative Lives: Interview with Contemporary South Asian Diaspora Writers* (2021). She is co-editor, with Michael Ondaatje, of *Lakdhas Wikkramasinha: Selected Poems* (2023).

Poson

My dreams are full
of strange copulations;
locusts swarm
and scarab-women
flee.

Highways dissect the land
like gleaming swords,
and ants
scramble ever northward
to their mud-hives
and
mines.

Elephants ramble
the lost ways
and ghosts
death-dance
in their battering
limbs.

Morning,
and the cadjan
ground
to dust.

The boy asleep
in his own
blood.

5.45 at St George

So last Wednesday
I was in the subway
you know
sitting across
from this old guy
and he's obviously
a little,
you know, touched
in the head
but so
so innocent.

And like,
he pulls out
this page
of the NOW
starts like
cutting
cutting paper angels
out of it.

And you know,
people start
to get edgy
don't know
what to make
of another crazy person
and stuff.

And he cuts
his paper angels
out
and turns to this chick,
this honey blonde strawberry soft
pamplemousse
chick
and says 'LOOK'
'Look at my ANGELS!'
and he tries and tries
to give them
to her.

And she
looks
and blinks and gets up
and leaves.

And
he sits there
just
looking through
me
and there's
so much sadness
in his sad blue eyes,
in his
big baby blue
blue eyes.

And I mean, like
when your heart
breaks
it is so totally
random.

ASHLEY HALPÉ
(1933–2016)

Ashley Halpé studied at both the University of Ceylon and the University of Bristol in the UK. Known too as a visual artist, he also worked in theatre as a director, designer and actor. Publishing prolifically, he translated from Sinhala both modern and classical verse, as well as the novels of Martin Wickramasinghe.

Halpé's poems are appealingly abrupt; the time-signatures of his lines vary jaggedly, keeping his reader on their toes. Though his lines can be melodious, he prospers more often through cunning juxtapositions of cudgeling detail. It is perhaps unsurprising that, working in art and theatre, he became the poet-as-arranger, walking the line between being shocking and being wise.

the tale of Divnuhamy

Millawitanachchi Divnuhamy
was ninety.
Her son Mendis
sixty.
Millawitanachchi Divnuhamy
died an hour before dawn
on a muggy night in May.
Her son cut her throat.

The witness said
that Mendis
was up in a tree
when he first saw him that morning.

Mendis told him
that he had given his mother a good dinner
arranged her comfortably on a bed in the veranda,
read her to sleep.
At four in the morning
he had got out the chopper.
He bowed to his sleeping mother,
his hands joined before him.
He did likewise to the chopper.
Then he cut her throat. After which
he had climbed the tree
to hang himself.

Mendis, M.W.,
why did you come down
to pick up the chopper again
and cut her head off?
What did you want to be sure of
before you hanged yourself?

You went to your tree.
We have no right to ask you
what deliberations disturbed your intent
on your road upward, whether
the chill light of dawn dissolved
certainties which we may guess at
but should not utter.

You went up your tree
and there you were as rural morning
gathered to savour
the piquant juice of your privacy.

It was surely embarrassment
that made you ask your cousin
for a chew of betel
the smooth old rope dangling behind you
the bloodstain vanishing into the well-stamped earth.

Mendis, M.W.
your confused old eyes
are quiet mirrors.

all our Aprils

The smell of all our Aprils hangs upon
cool jacaranda and lucent flamboyant,
each annual recession hurries on
day of the hawk and hour of the ant

if I were rock
if I were island

Jacaranda and lucent flamboyant
forever bear the stain of wasted blood,
bones whitened by the cold relentless ant
smell still of slaughter, fire and mud

to be rock
or island

Day of the hawk comes closer with each year
shall brute power cancel every covenant?
Must these lost youths be hostage to our fear
refuting jacaranda and flamboyant?

If I were sharp rock or tender island,
bland stone or soothed solitary reef,

150

whole, all limits precisely defined –
but I am dented, blurred and blind:
no rock, no island.

The Second Reading

(FROM *Writers Reading*)

In first grade he had a toilet with zinc urinals
And no doors
As in the men's room at the Syracuse Community Centre –
So we have a humourist tonight, an observer of manners
And collector of mannerisms.
He affects wise eyes and a modest vocal style.

Two grades later he gets off with Mrs Sullivan
'who wasn't Mrs Babke who wasn't Mrs Lapke'
With *Les Misérables* as soft corn
Popped at the toptable, when he wasn't
Going to the dime movies – *Samson and Delilah*
'Having one's cake
          – sin –
And eating it too
          – piety –

And *Babylon* – 'America wrapping itself in the mantles
Of previous Chosen Peoples', the leading lady
Lamarr – or Lamour –
Bruised by holding together her glamour
For ten more years

The audience is in gurgles and burbles
The reading pedals on madly
He still looks like the man who taught
fifth grade PS 75 (Upper West Side)

He's going about 70 an hour now
And beginning to swallow syllables

Then he read a poem
About nothing touching him,

About learning to honour
His emptiness. His father
Called him a cold fish
When he was nine. He has since
Spent so much life going around
Proving warmth, aware
That there were continents of numbness
To discover

The numbness
Communicated, the emptiness
Opened with a thin sweet smell
Like overripe guavas

TASHYANA HANDY
(*b.* 1998)

Tashyana Handy is a performance poet based in Colombo, Sri Lanka. As a performer, her work has been featured at many festivals including KACHA KACHA and the Galle Literary Festival. Her poetry has also been featured on local platforms such as the Kopi Collective and Groundviews. She is part of the artist collective 'The Packet'. Inspired by Hanif Willis-Abdurraqib, Ilya Kaminsky, Pádraig Ó Tuama and Ramya Jirasinghe, her first collection, *A History of Want* (an ode to the teen-girl diary), explores intimidate histories of migration, grief and violence. Her poetry has often left her preoccupied with the failure of speech, and the many shapes that language may take in its absence.

C189

The Shop and Office Employees (Regulation of Employment and Remuneration) Act No.19 of 1954 (as amended) and the Wages Boards Ordinance No. 43 of 1941 (as amended) stipulate the basic conditions of work.

Do not make their house your home,
It is not.
Memorise every crevice every corner every crack
And plant your body there.
It simple, just another chain in the industry.

Balance the break-evens
on your back
As if your life depends on it
And your life does depend on it.
Do not let them see you sleeping.
Work till your hands bleed.
Work till your bloodline drips down to your feet
Work till it's clean.
Know
That no one will know of your existence.
Don't you know they are dealing with a history of slavery and subjugation?
A history of want and women.
We are sorry, but
Your struggle is not struggle enough.
Come back tomorrow.
You are not an exception.
You are the backbone of this economy so act like it.
You cannot afford to break.
You cannot afford to bear the pain of everyone who came before you
And who will come out of you.
Remember they are not of you.
They are not your children.
You left your children
In the arms of someone else,
Cradled by their mother land in the absence of their mother.
Consider this atonement for your sins.
If you are tired or growing old,
You do not age.
Your body does not wither like everyone else.
If by chance it does,

Sweep the dust away from your bones and bury it in the floor.
Pour concrete into every opening.
Hammer together the joints that no longer work.
Build a firm foundation.
You are the house we stand upon.

LAL HEGODA

(*b*. 1947)

Born in Colombo, Lal Hegoda is a veteran both of poetry and photography. His debut, *Ma minisek oba gangak nisa* was published in 1994 and won a State Literary Award – he won a second in 2000. He has written seven further collections in Sinhala including *Pasaloswaka Sanda Mageya* (1996), *Sandun Aratuwa Dalluye Obai* (2001), *Ganga wak wee Galana Thena* (2003), and his most recent *Komalani* (2021), which was published by Vidarshana Publishers. His poetry is distinguished by its novel approach to both content and form; he believes in the value of lyric concision, yet also writes prose poems that resemble short stories.

I'm a Man Because You Are a River

On this river bank
in a most pleasant seat
under a cool canopy
of Kumbuk trees
I will rest awhile
for a brief respite in life

    Here and there in the high canopy
    caressed by long fingers
    red leaves rustle in the breeze
    they move and show
    the blue sky in a floral pattern.
    its shadow falling on the water
    breaking into a thousand little fragments.

When the sun's brassy rays
flow along with the river
the jewelled lights
float in the soft darkness beneath the canopy
the grandeur is beyond words
and only a poet can sing of it.
Free from other 'samsaric bonds'
my mind falls in love

    As with a language so familiar
    I understand what you say so coyly
    smiling like the foam

as you go winding along
amidst the rocks
breaking into a symphony

I will throw away the watch in my hand
I will throw away the shoes on my feet.
Leaving you where else can I go?
As I shed my clothes
one now and then another
I see my own body's image
like a dark shadow

Because I am a man
and you are a river
let's melt softly
in a loving embrace.

Is there another way?

[tr. from Sinhala by A.T. Dharmapriya]

Bhikku at the Ferry

So, what is in that pouch
You carry?
Is your helper not too exhausted?
Are your eyes not throbbing, as you search
For the ferryman
This misty morning

He too crossed over from here
With no pouch, no helper

The bhikku waited, with his helper
And their heavy pouch
But the ferryman did not return

[tr. from Sinhala by Manoj Ariyaratne]

AJITH C. HERATH

(*b*. 1967)

Ajith C. Herath became involved in student politics during the JVP uprising in the 1980s in the south of Sri Lanka. He was arrested by the military in 1989 and tortured, witnessing terrible brutality and experiencing the deaths of many close friends. While imprisoned, he wrote – says Frances Harrison – 'passionately and prolifically', expressing his loss through poetry as a way of overcoming his own pain. These poems were published frequently by the alternative Sinhala media in the 1990s. He is also a painter, political cartoonist and political analyst who worked as a journalist until he was forced into exile in 2008, when the civil war was reaching its dénouement. Ajith received a scholarship and stayed at Böll House in Germany in 2009-11.

Last Station

(A watch worn by a passenger who perished in the train wrecked by
the Tsunami at Peraliya had stopped at 9.25am)

'The train shall now recommence its journey.
Passengers are requested to return to their seats... Calling at all stations!'

Does someone
turn back time from 9.25 am
bidding the enraged
dark waves to return to
some unseen abyss,
long away from the shore,
as a telephone rings ceaselessly,
unanswered at the last station
before death?

Time has stopped with a train,
between the waves and
a graveyard,
an indelible print of eternal regret.

Laughter and banter
still seem to echo
with the dying notes
of a blind beggar's fiddle,

as a child is looking steadily
towards the far horizon.

After that moment no further chatter,
only the interminable search,

mine, for my dead...
yours, for your dead...

You must be careful, where you step,
as bodies are laid out.
One false move, even a diary
beneath your feet may weep in pain.

The mechanical arm of a JCB
digs deep through
the hearts of the undead
searching for their departed souls
with each breath.
Time starts moving once again
in some parallel universe
and a whistle is blown
for the journey to resume.

'The train shall now recommence its journey.
Passengers are requested to return to their seats... Calling at all stations.'

Passengers, arise from your sodden graves,
take each other's swollen hands
and board the train.
Your loved ones await you
at the last station.

[tr. from Sinhala by Prathap de Silva]

from Seven Dreams

First Dream – u never noticed

I was falling
From unimaginable points of infinity.
Mucky water surged
Through the streets of the city.

157

Moments before I fell
On to the water,
I woke up an infant
In a cradle floating among debris.
I passed men and women
Smiling and waving at me,
Wading through muddy water,
Gathering up their clothes.

When the cradle toppled
Into a sewer,
I leaned out,
Shivering and unbearably cold
I crawled out of the cradle
Eagerly following you,
But you never noticed!
Suddenly, someone grabbed me
And threw me back into the surge.
Once again I was falling and falling.
Just before hitting the ground,
I felt I was waking up.

Fifth Dream – Blue tarpaulin pyre

When the cradle was burning
Along with the camp hut of blue tarpaulin,
You came out crawling
Your tiny hands and legs burnt,
As I was helplessly watching
Your fearful struggle.
Once, for an instant, our eyes met.
I will never know, if you noticed.
Crawling
You passed fossilised me,
Fell into a ditch
And disappeared amongst
Dead bodies and smoke…
The ditch that protected you
Was leveled into a tomb by bulldozers.
As they faded into the distance
All I could see was that tiny hand
Above the sands.

Once the search operation had been completed,
The soldiers left.
And in the demolished room I found
Our group's last portrait
Torn into shreds.
Lingering on those time-faded scattered pieces
Was our smile
Of the last moments we spent together
Just before going our ways
Towards unknown destinies.
I placed the pieces on the window sill
Wanting to mend them.
A sudden mysterious wind
Stirred them up.
Piece by piece they scattered
With the last autumn leaves
Moving to sites far away.
We had become tiny pieces of paper
Tumbling away in the wind.

[tr. from Sinhala by the poet, Dawson Preethi and Karin Clark]

VIPULI HETTIARACHCHI
(*b.* 1968)

Vipuli Hettiarachchi is a poet, children's fiction writer and critic who writes in Sinhala. She was born in Colombo and currently lives in Makola. She began writing from a very young age and was frequently published in newspapers and magazines while still at school. She has published four collections of poetry for adults: *Nikmanaka Nimiththak* (1993), *Sakuntawagen Chula Kawyak* (2000), *Sandaga* (2008), *Roo – Kavya Roopaavaliya* (2015), as well as three collections of poetry for children: *Samanala thatuwaka Nagala* (2004), *Seethala Punchage dange* (2012), *Sathutu Ko-chchiya* (2013). Her children's fiction books include *Dingaata Paadamak* (2006), *Ran Kumbala* (2006) and *Seeya harima aadarelu* (2007). She works as a teacher in Colombo and is an advisor on the government's education panel. Her poetry has been translated into English and has been widely anthologised. She won the State Literary Award for Best Children's Book in 2005.

We Are Women...

'Anyone home…?'

Housecoat buttoned quickly up
over the night dress
the voice hardly able to reply

'Is there anybody here…?'

They have come on a task assigned

Still half asleep
Mother struggles to find words and
to prevent her face and body freezing
I switch on lights from room to room

To ensure safety in the town
they search a house that has
no visitors or lodgers, not even a dog

'Where are the men of the house?'

Sniffing even at our minds
that have harmed not even an ant
they look around with suspicion

'Only both of you?'

On other days my mother would lie
that her husband would return soon
and her son was at work
but her wits that always found the right word
for the right time and place
were not working today.

In front of a crowd of men
wearing uniforms and stars
with guns in their hands
I scream

'Yes. Who else?

We are the men
who have survived in this home.'

[tr. from Sinhala by Liyanage Amarakeerthi]

Balachandran

Shots fired
shattering dreams
like stars displaced,
scattered.
Combing the north sky, is it
the rabbit in the moon you seek?

[tr. from Sinhala by Shirani Rajapakse]

Balachandran was the 12-year-old son of LTTE leader Prabhakaran. He was handed a snack and then executed by the Sri Lankan Army in 2009.

'Iron Lady'

It isn't number
10 Downing Street London,
but Londonwatte,
residence of
Margaret. A tiny hut
made of corrugated iron sheets
and wood is what she calls home.
No metal wheels
no Maruti to call her own
Margaret
moves from house to house
collecting old newspapers
pieces of scrap metal
she sells by weight.

161

The businessman comes on strong. His grip is
as hard as iron. She breaks free from his
embrace, grabs an iron rod
and strikes like a furious Leopard.
He falls at her feet.

Iron lady
her steely arm speaks
her iron body hefts
her iron heart
melts
frequently.

A determined woman
she bears grief.
She's an iron that smelts
yet doesn't bend. She's like a flame.

'Margaret' is her name
she is 'sister'
'aunt'
'mother'
in her realm.

She hurts
She shines
She warms
She burns
She's firm
She is
'the iron lady'.

[tr. from Sinhala by Shirani Rajapakse]

ERIC ILLAYAPPARACHCHI

(*b.* 1954)

Eric Illayapparachchi works across genres, and has published novels, short stories, poems, translations and academic books in Sinhala, including *Madiyame Geethaya, Aalindaya, Mage Kolambata Handa Paayai, Kisiwek Kaviyan Nomarathi, Piththala Handiya, Kaputa Saha Sitaano* and *Dasa Bimbara*. His translator, Gaya Nagahawatta, describes him as exploring 'a range of perspectives, from the mundane everyday to the exotic – as well as perspectives of those who do not have a voice. The most colourful of Eric's poems are so immersed in Sinhala culture and idiom that I would categorise them as untranslatable. The two poems translated here describe the war in Sri Lanka and the urban chaos it caused. In his devastated urban world, it seems that only nature and wild creatures enjoy any measure of happiness.'

The Bomb at the Rooftop Restaurant

Free of routine worries
sky-high on feathery softness
snugly seated in cushioned comfort
I sipped good liquor
when the Tigers surrounded,
shot and grounded my dream

As my dream sprinted, naked
as a girl child on the Vietnam roadway,
many photos sourced from BBC News
appeared in local newspapers

Later, after the battle fire died,
my ghostly dream, wrapped from feet upward
with rust-gathered injection needles protruding,
was centrally installed at the National Art Gallery
called a modern art sculpture

My healed dream muses upon the lost legs
and lies wheelchair bound.
On days when the sky is not dark,
it gazes up at the nurse moon white among the clouds.

[tr. from Sinhala by Gaya Nagahawatta]

Against Colombo

The angered devil, the sun, approaches,
splits shutters and unlatches windows;
sharp fingernails pry open sleepy eyes
forcing me to observe
the still sleeping, rag-covered city in disarray

A baby cries on a pavement cradle.
The company cow selling milk powder
shoves the rubber teat into the street-child's mouth

The fanning ocean cools the noon heat,
making doves fly gladly,
their wings flapping in delight

Engaged in a hundred-day hunger strike
at the base of the Olcott statue,
labourers' eyes register
the fate of strike action gone wrong

A poet roaming in the city of Fort,
wearing a drab national dress and Nehru headdress,
sells poetry leaflets

The thugs of Fort are apprehended,
grabbed by their throats.
I accompany them to file a case against Colombo.

[tr. from Sinhala by Gaya Nagahawatta]

FAHEEMA JAHAN

(*b.* 1973)

Faheema Jahan was born in Melsiripura, Kurunegala District, Sri Lanka and is a poet and a teacher of mathematics. She has published three collections of poetry in Sinhala: *Oru kadal neerootri* (2007), *Aparaathi* (2009) and *Aathith thuyar* (2010).

The Sea's Waters

The sky spread above us, burgeoning with stars.
Behind us
a shimmering moon followed.
A white mist covered the faraway fields.
The sound of waves falling against the bay
clashed against coconut palms, pierced through hutments
and entered our ears
as you and I walked up to my lodgings.

Just so
during so many nights
for so many hours we argued.
At the end, we always parted
with no hope for the future.

Later, at a tense and fearful moment,
you shook off all that stood in the way
of your passion for freedom
and entered into the forest.

Parani...
At a time when memories of you were fading,
one rainy season, at dusk,
you returned,
water dripping from your wet uniform.

You had to complete a particular task
by the spreading sea and its lapping waves.
And so you left me.
I had no words to wish you well,
and you had no desire to embrace me.

Outside, as the downpour
streamed down my own cheeks
you disappeared into the rain's complaint.
You became our treasure that travelled the sea.
Over the entire ocean, the fire of the apocalypse
rose up, and then died.
You never returned.

Today, the deep silence of our sorrowful times
envelops the graveyards where our soldiers lie.
But you who chose the very ocean for your mausoleum,
should the sea fill, with its waters,
your empty grave?

[tr. from Tamil by Lakshmi Holmström]

After Catastrophe

a bird perched
on the stump
of a felled tree.

today it has
no flight
and no song.
before its eyes
a vast expanse
is stretched out, blazing in the sun.

is it cursing those men
or longing for its own nest?

[tr. from Tamil by Rebecca Whittington]

V.I.S. JAYAPALAN
(*b.* 1944)

Born in Delft in Jaffna Province, Northern Sri Lanka, Shanmugampillai Jayapalan is a prolific Tamil poet and short story writer whose work is part of the syllabus at universities in India. He began writing poetry in the 1970s and has published over twelve books of poetry and short fiction. During the civil war, he fled to Oslo, and now divides his time between Norway and Tamil Nadu. A lyrical poet, Jayapalan has championed the oppressed and was uncompromising in his condemnation of the LTTE for their brutality towards Muslim Tamils during the 1990s. He writes with longing of the landscapes of exile. In 1995, the Norwegian Writers' Association designated him the nation's best immigrant writer, and his poetry has been translated into Norwegian as well as English and Sinhala. In his later years he has enjoyed life as an actor and received a special jury award at India's National Film Awards in 2011.

One Night in Frankfurt

Packed like litter in the belly
of a pregnant sow, a group of men
from Jaffna lie seemingly lifeless
in a room in the heart of Frankfurt –
their bodies curled in blankets
wrapped tight like Egyptian mummies.

Work uniforms soak in the bath.
Saucepans litter the floor as time
meanders aimlessly. They are rootless
like stray dogs, limbs lying askew
like clubbed snakes. The darkness
of the night invades their days.

The mercury dips below zero.
On this night one of them sobs, thinking
of lands back home lying mortgaged
in the strong box of the village Big Man.
His sisters wait, anticipating a hopeful future.
He is like an orphan in his own country
a refugee in this foreign land.

On this night, like storm ravaged Batticaloa
his oppressed young life unravels.
A thorn pierces his wounded heart
as he crumples a letter bearing news
of a beloved's betrothal.

There will be no auspicious day for the man
who abandoned his home to the mosquitoes.
On a snowy night in Frankfurt
he cries in bewilderment
feeling the bite of the cold.

[tr. from Tamil by Shash Trevett]

Hope

like the sorrow
of a koel bereft of its lover
gently gently
the river seeps.
the varaal fish jump
gasping for breath
among the reeds set dancing in the wind.
a summer evening.
next to me on the warm white sand
I see
lying drying
rinds of banyan fruit
and five or six little seeds,
even though
somewhere far off in the distance
in a sweet voice
a Vanni boy
is singing of rain.

[tr. from Tamil by Rebecca Whittington]

Blue

My love,
do you remember the days
we strolled on the shore
searching for shells,
the waves foaming at our feet
erasing our tracks?
Something blossoms within us, I said,
an expanding blue, like the blue
of the sea and the sky.
You stood still and upright as a stork
about to spear a fish. The only movement
my image reflected in your eyes.

You said: you are old in years
yet your mind shows no trace
of grey. My love, I said,
To be young is to desire life.
To be young is to desire learning.
To be young is to search endlessly.
To be young is to have an inexhaustible appetite.
To be young is to dance and sing tirelessly.
To be young is to be eternally in love.

How *old* are you, she said.
My love, I am he who will live
fully until death.

[tr. from Tamil by Shash Trevett]

from Song of the Defeated

1

The song of the victors
rises from every direction.
The song, reaching its crescendo,
lands like spit on our faces.
And yet, they are afraid.
Why? Because they lack
the armour of justice.

169

Like the shoots of grass
growing from the ashes
of burnt pastures, we too
have our songs.
Our songs, which are like
warriors in camouflage:
the victors call them dirges.
Many epic vows begin
from laments. As they say,
tears caused by a tyrant's rule
will wash away his royal wealth.
There are songs like this
in the epics, that begin
with the defeat of justice.
All through time, new histories
have been born out of defeated justice.
Today, we are the defeated.

The victors are celebrating these days
by liberally throwing bits of bone.
Their drunkenness and ecstasy
make us afraid.

At night they will drag away
Tamil women from the camps, for interrogation.
Or, for the sake of spectacle
they will shoot Indian Tamils at sea.

We choose restraint.
The nine-headed is not Ravanan.
The five-faced is not Murugan.
The three-headed is never Brahma.
We are many-faced ardhanarishwaras,
halfwoman halfman,
with faces in both the North and the East.
If any face is missing, it is not us.
Even if chosen, it could end up a mistake.

Freed, our people
And our Muslim brothers chased to Puthalam
Have to return home
To give birth to a new era.

4

Motherland, do not mourn.

You are torn into the North and the East
and our women who die protecting you
are ghost-fucked by Sinhala soldiers
who sing and dance. Even on a day as cruel as this
don't be shattered,
but sing the war-song of tomorrow's life.
Sing the song that brings sap to burnt roots.

No fire will last on the bones
of our honoured ancestors.
So, for this day of black ash,
sing a song of butterflies
serenading buds that burst
into a rainbow.
As the howls of our kin die down
play the vital music heard
from the drums of comrades.

Mother!
on a pleasure-filled day
my father and you sculpted me with love,
with the soil and water of Eelam.
Now, with my five elements
I will sculpt you a fortress.
If it cannot curse the legs that kick you,
what is the use of this song?

11

Mother, do you remember
What I sang when Vietnam burned?
'Any number of forest fires will be extinguished
And green pastures will blossom.'
O heart, sing that song even today
Standing in the midst of fire
In my motherland.

[tr. from Tamil by Meena Kandasamy]

171

RAMYA JEGATHEESAN

(*b.* 1993)

Ramya Jegatheesan works across many forms, including poetry, short story, and longer narrative fiction. Her short stories can be found in the UCL Publishers' Prize anthology, *REWRITE READS* and *Lucy Writers*. In 2020, her novel in progress was shortlisted for Agora Books' Lost the Plot Work in Progress Prize and longlisted for Penguin WriteNow. In 2021, she was also a Hachette THRIVE Grow Your Story writer. Through her visual arts and creative writing project, Spinning Straws, she brought together photographers, fine artists and writers for short, hybrid pieces. Ramya feels privileged to have inherited two literary canons: the Western canon through her British identity – she was born in London – and Tamil literary precedents through her Ilankai Tamil ancestry. But she is also mindful of A.K. Ramanujan's words, 'Even one's own tradition is not one's birthright; it has to be earned, repossessed.'

from The Ariel Collection
Or
Colonise my tongue and laugh at the irony

I   my library
          Was dukedom large enough
                    WILLIAM SHAKESPEARE, *The Tempest*, 1.2

          Four foot high is the right height
          To be in a library.
          That Holy Grail quest to reach up and
          Achieve that cup, that book, my book.
          The word is my family
          The paper my city
          That book my country
          And that library my world.
          When my library burned
          You killed us all.

II   Good wombs have borne bad sons.
                    WILLIAM SHAKESPEARE, *The Tempest*, 1.2

          When you were born, I held you
          Clothed in the blood of me.
          I saw your sleeping face and vowed
          You would want for nothing,
          Not in this world, even if I had

To tear open my pelican heart.
You grew up, grew taller
Grew stronger, grew wiser
And my mother's heart
Saw you never cried, not even in dream.
But now you come to me,
Cloaked in blood
That might as well have been my own.

III   'This is the third man I e'er saw, the first that e'er I sighed for.'
       WILLIAM SHAKESPEARE, *The Tempest*, 1.2

In the town where I lived
There were only three men.
I think the rest had got lost long ago.
When in the night, I crashed into bad dreams
I asked my mother for advice.
She took a sip from her whiskey-and-coke
And said
'Ask the men, they're supposed to banish the dark.'
I turned around and heard her say
'Aye and bring it with them sometimes.'
I went to see the butcher.
'Something for the dark?' said I.
He gave me a slab of meat.
'It's meant to be good for your eyes' said he.
I left the meat for the pies.
And went to see the baker.
Something for the dark?' said I.
He gave me a loaf of wholewheat.
'It's meant to be good for your thighs' said he.
I left the bread for lecherous sandwich
And went to see the candlestick maker.
(He was young and tall)
'Something for the dark?' said I.
He leaned closer
(He smelt like mint and rosemary)
'Something for the dark or
something to help you see?' asked he.
I had no idea what I had come for.
Months later
With the candlestick maker in my bed
I turned and sighed, and put out the candlelight.

A. JESURASA

(b. 1946)

A. Jesurasa was born in Jaffna in the north of Sri Lanka and is one of the country's most influential Tamil poets. He also writes short stories, is a translator and editor, and is passionate about film. He has published ten collections and was awarded the Sri Lanka Sahithya Mandalam in 1974 for his short story collection *Tholaivum Iruppum Enaiya Kathikalum.* In 2015 he was presented with a Lifetime Achievement Award at the Jaffna International Cinema Festival.

As an editor, Jesurasa provided a platform for Tamil poets writing during the war years. He co-edited the seminal anthology of Tamil resistance poetry, *Maranaththul Vaalvom* (1985), and co-founded and edited two important literary journals, *Alai* (1975–90) and *Kavithai* (1994-95). Some of Cheran's earliest poems were first published in *Alai* by Jesurasa. Jesurasa's poetry engages the struggle against inequality, whether economic or caste based, and enriches modern Tamil poetry through its Christian perspective.

Under New Shoes

(1979)

I walk along
the darkened tar road
running straight ahead of me.

In front of me
the looming black mass
of the Dutch Fort
stands solid and huge.
At its corner,
clearly visible, the gallows
which threatened our ancestors.

On the wide, grassy lawn, outside,
soldiers in khaki,
bearing arms:
the government's machines,
their instruments of security.
They march in formation
ever ready to spring to their duty.
Fear spreads
even in the surrounding breeze.

174

Three hundred years have passed,
but the colour alone has changed,
the language alone has altered.
Today, too, we are under
the same rule of oppression.

[tr. from Tamil by Lakshmi Holmström)

In Memory of the Nameless
(1973)

It is All Souls' Day, the day of the dead.
All day crowds stream through
the wide-open gates of the cemetery.

On gravestones the skilled work of masons
detail lives lived in comfort. Names and dates
flower alongside crosses, angels, the Virgin Mary.

In the south-east corner lie
the orderly graves of the clergy,
their memory etched in marble.

By the well, under coconut trees,
patti flowers bloom among sea-shell crosses
marking the nameless dead. Here lie buried
those who have passed out of memory.

Yet, it is still possible to decipher
their stories, to feel a connection,
a kinship to them.

'Here lie those who stood on the shore
hauling a catch for others to grow fat on.
Here they are, desiccated like dried fish.'

'Here lie porters who bore great burdens.'
'Here, firewood sellers who dragged
their wares daily, in handcarts.'

'Here lie those who at dawn
carted away the effluence
from houses criss-crossing the city.'

Here lie buried those who laboured
on the soil. Yet even here,
boundaries enforce the rigidity of class.
Even in death, even in death.

[tr. from Tamil by Shash Trevett]

Afterwards
(1975)

It is all over, what is left to follow?
　　'Eloi, Eloi, Lama Sabachthani'

The memory of the voice from the cross
fades before her, before him, today.

In the vastness of the heat outside
are you wandering, searching
for green pasture?
On an island set apart
for whose boat are you waiting?

'It is finished.'

[tr. from Tamil by Shash Trevett]

Yet, time remains
(2010)

My son
this is how life
chews and spits out dreams.

Mountains obstruct your path
a vortex of sorrow discards you
into a valley of disappointment.

Your mind is shuttered
like a night sky
heavy with darkness.

However, my son
you are not like those

who 'fall like detritus from grace
as hair falls from the head'.*

Your time still remains.

Rise, get moving.
Live true to yourself.
You alone must provide meaning
for your life.

[tr. from Tamil by Shash Trevett]

* This is a quotation from the *Thirukural*.

RAMYA CHAMALIE JIRASINGHE
(*b*. 1971)

Ramya Chamalie Jirasinghe lives in Colombo, where she has spent most of her life. She won the Sri Lanka State Literary Joint-Award in 2011, for her book of poems, *There's an Island in the Bone*. Her poetry, short fiction, and journalism have appeared internationally, in *The Tipton Poetry Journal*, *The New Republic*, and the *Penguin Anthology of Sri Lankan Literature*, ed. Shyam Selvadurai (2014). Within Sri Lanka, her work has appeared in the *Sunday Times*, *Sunday Island*, *Island* and *Daily Mirror*. Her second collection, *Love Poems from a Frangipani Garden* (2018), was published in UK by Mica Press. Jirasinghe was longlisted for the Fish Poetry Prize, Ireland in 2011, and was joint runner-up in the Guardian UK's Orange First Words Prize of 2009. She holds a MA from SOAS, University of London, a PhD from the University of Colombo, and is also the author of several books of non-fiction: *Rhythm of the Sea* (on the Asian Tsunami), *Trinity* (on a missionary school in Ceylon) and *When Life Touches Life* (a biography). She acknowledges Anne Ranasinghe as a notable influence.

Food for My Daughter

Before your friends and even I
teach you the comfort of home delivered pizzas
and machine-crumbed chicken nuggets,
I will begin my mission.

I will puree the belli fruit into an ochre gel
the ash plantain into a grey heap
and surprise you with the purpleness
of purple yams.

You will learn to wonder at
the farmer's blood in the ripe tomato
the warm hands in the home baked bread
the myriad flavours you need to search for
over a slow dinner
in your great-grandmother's fish pie
your grandmother's black jak seed curry
the tartness of narang from the garden
the char of roasting coriander
the silk of the real white roux.
Let these fill your heart, even before
you know what they mean.

This crash course in food tasting
your mother's over-moral guide
to good cooking and real ingredients
will end before you are five,
when flavours that do not need tasting,
when pain and death, the only filling in sausages
become your breakfast, lunch and dinner
and everything in between.

Yet like the immigrant in the big city
whose search for their mother's food
becomes a lifelong obsession (the salt fish
the paprika goulash, the coconut roti)
let your memories of sunshine, sourness and love
bring you back to a scratched wooden table
and the hearth of an old grey kitchen
once you've had your fill from styrofoam packages
and plastic ketchup cans.

On Waiting with a Friend Getting His Heart Tested

A calm has engulfed us, flat lines are
The vagabond's pathways to
Abstractions: light and tomorrow.

The doctor and nurse watch the monitors.
I try to imagine what you must be dreaming.

You are so perfect, a body in repose

The morning city is waking up around us
Construction workers from the villages begin
Crawling up scaffolding of apartments shooting skywards
Coughing concrete dust they will take home
To their grandchildren.
The crows will be forever searching
For lost nests in the felled trees.

Never will there be such stillness
In your heart once it returns from
This sleep.

MADRI KALUGALA
(*b*. 1990)

Madri Kalugala was born in Colombo and grew up in Brunei, prior to her
family's return to Sri Lanka in 2001. The first fifteen years of her life were
therefore shaped by one island nation torn apart by war, and the tensions of
another dubbed the 'Abode of Peace'. Her family experienced financial loss,
poverty and sickness, followed by the death of her differently-abled brother.
All of these experiences were formative.

Madri has been writing poetry, accompanied by art, since childhood, and
has been featured in newspapers for her children's poetry, which won an
Edward Lear Prize in 2017. Her first collection for adults, *An Almond Moon
and the White Owl* (2016), was described by Vihanga Perera as the work of a
writer who had 'delicately studied and taken under her wing, poetry as a craft
and expression' and who had 'internalised a range of forms and styles'; he
praised her second, *Exulansis* (2021), as 'true poetry'. Madri has also published
short stories and is experimenting with longer prose forms and non-fiction.

Last night I dreamed your horse had died

and the dream sat in me
like a rock. Do you hear me? A rock.
gathered in layers, like silt
all over me; every inch of my damp skin
until it covered me. And I was a thing of black,
dark as a volcano about to spit
fire. The dream; a black mood.
and your dead horse weighed
on me like a deadweight, a body
that was not even mine to bury; but had meant
the world to you.

– your horse was dead. Brown mass
  of wet flesh, and the sea
    was lapping at the white stringy mane; messy tangle
      of dead-horsehair. Eating with salty lips
       at his wide-bewildered eyes. No one knew
        how the horse had died. Least of all,
         the horse himself; but there
        was a frothing at his thick lips bared
        to show long horse teeth: a horse
         that had eaten cocaine –

    O but you
  had loved that horse once. how much;
    only I knew.

So I, with burning arms,
began pulling that lifeless body
out to sea. O he was heavy; ten times
as heavy as me, but he was your horse.
and your horse was dead – so I
must give it a burial fitting:
a fitting burial
for something you had loved.

I pulled, I heaved
  and with limbs on fire,
    I pushed him gently out
      to his watery grave; and the seething sea
      took him gladly, with a rush: dragged him in

ceremoniously
and swallowed him whole. I felt a sear in my soul,
but I knew it would rest his bones.

what froze me
   was your response,
      when I told you your horse had died – and I
         had buried him alone –

      'so what?' in cold blood.
   your steely voice, eyes pin-pricks
of ice. 'just an animal.'

   just an animal.
it was the horse you loved.
  just a miscarriage.
it was your best friend's child.
  just a relationship.
   it was the song that had called you home;
the sea-bed where you'd rested your aching bones.

Sundowning

   I

A rose bled onto my lap
seeping through my skirt
and covered my thighs
with the faint rusted taste
of metallic,
dark loss

there was no closure in the sunlight.
    nothing explained what had happened;
      why your face
    was now just a yawning abyss,

into which I gazed too long
until the inky black
started shooting

its octopus jets of darkness
   into me.

II

we were swimming then,
in a lake of liquid red fire
now your mouth drags me
underwater;

the memory of it. your bones lit up
  like lava sparks

  my beautiful boy
  my beautiful boy,

come burn me up like brushwood.

KARUNAKARAN

(*b.* 1963)

Karunakaran was born in Iyakkachi, in the Northern Province, and works as a journalist in Jaffna. He joined the liberation movement as a writer in the early days of the struggle (he was 19 at the time) and was part of the editorial team of the journal *Pothumai*. From 1991 to 2004 he was editor of the magazine *Velicham* which was part of the cultural output of the LTTE and an important literary journal. Karunakaran has published six collections of poetry in Tamil and a collection of short stories. He survived the final stages of the war, the last four of his collections being written during this time. Poems were composed during nights of bombing and days of marching towards hoped for safety and sent to online magazines like *Thinnai* and *Vaarapu* when an internet connection was available. Karunakaran has written poems of witness, and his work, even in the 1980s, endeavoured to show the human cost (on both sides) of the conflict.

Along That Very Road

It was into that burning path
that I descended that day.
That girl, the flower-seller,
was there, and there too
were the soldiers firing off their guns;
the priest was saying his prayers
and children were playing.

The Catholic church stood there,
cattle were setting off to graze
and the radio was blaring
from the stall selling spicy rotis.
It was there, in that very road
where the mother was suckling her baby
and the army general was ordering his men,
that everything burnt down.
We stood there, all of us, while all around
everything burnt to the ground.
Day and night ended in smoke.
The Government vanished,
and so did the national flag.
Like smoke.

[tr. from Tamil by Lakshmi Holmström]

Burning Nests

the bird that flies up
out of the wound
takes along
its beautiful flower
its great fire
its sea
its space.

it has not even
the shadow of the thought
of returning home
to its nest.

along the way
it gives up even
its wings to the wind.

this journey beyond pain
fills the nest
with emptiness

in the bird's undampened heat
the nest burns, alone.

[tr. from Tamil by Rebecca Whittington]

The Warrior Who Could Not Part from His Shadow

when he could not part from his shadow
the defeated war hero
felt abandoned
in unguarded territory.

the closed doors
shut him up in fear
and the open doors
seemed terribly dangerous.

knowing the night to be well guarded
he was startled when the very next moment
it turned into
deep trenches of terrors.

when he saw
the keys glow red-hot as they opened the doors
working themselves into the locks
the keyholes
looked at him and smiled.

that mocking smile that said
in any lock
in any key
there is always a way to open
sank into him
like a sense of guilt.

unable to unite
with the shadow from which he could not part

he severed his own head
sweating profusely

in haste
in fear.

[tr. from Tamil by Rebecca Whittington)

U. KARUNATILAKE
(———)

D.C.R.A. Goonetilleke describes Karunatilake's *Kandy Revisited* (2001) as 'illuminated by [a] constant alertness of intellect', going on to say that in *The Kundasale Love Poems* (1999), 'he showed that love poetry can be wholesome, sexual and life-affirming'. (The poet's own note in that book explains that the poems were inspired by the death of his wife, Kusuma.) Karunatilake's poems appeared frequently in the *Lanka Guardian* and the *Daily News*. His published diaries reveal – to quote Ajith Samaranayake's review – 'a professional in the pharmaceutical industry' who is also 'a politically-conscious citizen with distinctly Marxist inclinations'.

Letter from Boralanda

They are planting new woods, Love,
Beyond that ridge of saplings
Which tittered as I passed,
Tall already, and graceful in wind.

The path cut through to slopes,
Fresh cleared of sparse bushes and wild hares,
To take the eucalyptus seedlings
On faint contours.

The forest overseer greeted me,
Slanting back his sun-bleached umbrella,
As his men moved slowly across the cleared patana,
Setting out the seedlings.

It was early evening,
We were on a heaving sea of low hills,
Westwards, high mountains held the sky
With the sun behind them.

185

The mountains were silent, but not aloof,
They know,
We labour antlike, to make the new woods grow.

Hometown

Not just one of those coastline railstops
(Single platform and two nameboards),
Mount Lavinia was a terminal
Where trains headed back, citywards,
Two platforms and a stairway bridge (to catch the Uptrain).

The rails curved round a hillock
To the hidden station,
With its post-box and buggy stand,
And the road looping back to town
(By buggy cart for five cents down).

The sophistication lent
By the hulk of the Grand Hotel
Was heightened in the War,
With radar finders and machine gun nests
Bristling the hillock beside sunken holes
And one lone anti-aircraft barrel
Pointing to the sky.

Being born here was just an accident
As in any other suburb,
Where fathers commute to office
And mothers keep house and the toddlers
Till old enough for school.

But the World broke in with this War
We had no say in,
Our school taken over for wounded from Burma,
And white men and women
Unrepressed on the beach
(Still imperially theirs).

We didn't quite grasp
What our schoolmasters meant,
Telling us to thank our stars
We were not in a column of refugees
Fleeing shattered homes, torn
From our parents.

Our Mothers still awaited us for tea and cake
(Honeyed sponge, fresh from the bake).

TIMRAN KEERTHI

(*b*. 1980)

Timran Keerthi received the 2015 State Literary Award for Sinhala Poetry, for his self-published collection, *Yannang Chandare*: 'Three people who loved what I wrote gave me money to publish the book.' Born in Rath Mahara, near Giriulle, he is a self-taught poet. He worked as a day labourer – at a clay plant, a coir plant, and as a well-digger – before getting a job at a garment factory loading and unloading containers.

The Forgotten Book

Then too I was a day labourer.
I loaded two lorries full of firewood,
was paid a thousand bucks
and went one September on a journey
I should never have gone –

To the big BOOK FAIR in Colombo.
That was a truly shameless thing to do.

My eyes hit on a Latino guy's book
It was one I had long been searching for.
If I get it, even to die on the road would be bliss
It was a book I had so long been searching for.

I paid for and purchased the book.
They gave it in a siri-siri bag.
Hugging my one book to my chest
I was reminded to take stock.

Book cost 500 /-
Trip expenses 200 /-
Balance 300 /-
Apples in the Fort are cheap...
I think as my brother's little one comes to mind.

Avoiding the eyes of poet-friends
carrying their mountains of books
I rush from the fair to the Fort
climb into a bus going home.

Like a thief, a step at a time, I enter
soundlessly, slowly, into the house.
My brother's little one as usual
rushes to my lap.

'What? Haven't you brought anything for me?'
Her eyes fell on the book.
'Did you bring me a storybook?'
There was nothing I had brought for her.
She grabbed the one and only book.

Clutching an unintelligible book
how she sobbed asking for a storybook.
I held her for an hour till she fell asleep,
then eased her soft fingers, took back my book.

My brother's family has long since left the village
no one knows where they are now.

A story stitched together in a 'book'
Life has no art more dispersed than that.

I too am a father now.
Have a little son who smiles in his sleep.
'Didn't you bring me a storybook?'
a little girl
crying in her sleep.
How it tears me up!

[tr. from Sinhala by Ranjini Obeyesekere]

GEORGE KEYT

(1901–93)

Modern Sri Lankan poetry in English was born between 1935 and 1937, when a painter forgot how to paint.

George Keyt, the Sri Lankan Cubist, published three volumes: *Poems*, in 1936, and *The Darkness Disrobed* and *Image in Absence* in 1937. (He stopped writing poetry when he began painting again, with a fresco cycle at Gotami Vihare.) 'My own life,' said Keyt, 'was confused and upset. There was a terrible tension in the world at the same time which also affected me, which seemed to be an extension of myself, of my own inner tension.' His long poem 'Kandyan Village' is an important Modernist work. He was friends with Pablo Neruda and Paul Éluard, but he also mentions as influences the poetry of Baudelaire, Mallarmé, Edgar Allan Poe and Dante. Deeply read in the classical literatures of South Asia, Keyt remarks that, at the time of writing, he was 'very taken up by the *sutras* on trance – the *Yoga Sutras* of Patanjali and much else Hindu'.

Kandyan Village

The stark look cannot be seen and the bones and the ants;
Despair has sagged and gone to seed and allowed
A denial of desolation in a glory of growth
Tuned and coloured to notes and tones never found
Anywhere but in dreams and the floating life of the drugged.
The twisted noise, clawing the sky so long,
Is a tune through long repetition, and with the winds
And the chirping of crickets and other rhythms has long found favour,

It is sunlight, the fence implanted between surface
And depth, sunlight sent to create the dust
That soils surface, the lodging room.
It is rain, the fence implanted between surface
And depth, to bind the dust to depth, plastered
In mud, so surface the lodging room could be clean.

Surface calls for evasive feelings and steady eyes,
Agility, toes that cling to the edge;
And that which is not of surface is depth, ignored,
And depth is simple and looks uncouth in surface.

The blank of surface must be kept alive,
So fabrication from below the smoothness
And also the grunts and chuckles and jargon of talk
From above, the screech of metal corroding.

But the homely moon is welcome, however, to moistening foliage
And is confident smiling the well known, if dated, beam of seduction
In lifting the covering cloth of night to drench out longing
And likewise the tread of the peasant is welcome to depth,
And spaces and tracts
Fall in a sudden rut,
In a void of thirst, but trusting to speedy dislodgement.
The spaces of depth, trodden, are clothed are being stripped, are naked;
Doffed dress is resumed in gaiety, after naked surrender;
There is clothing profuse inviting with prohibition
Announcing the flower intact.

There is also the broken tryst and the look deranged
The look in the saddened land of being overlooked
In having stripped for reception.

But the hills it seems, are hoodwinked, gazing around
With the scattering leaves of clouds when in season,
Withheld in deluded dreams from the play of the spaces below,

The hour and minute and the moment of indication,
The something that drips on a spot of time by conjunction of gods
Snail-like bearing their palaces, and trickles unnoticed like sweat
Through limbs in conjunction with toil, is theirs,
And a rite for most beginnings, a helpless gesture of heartening,
Help intangible,
So their heads may not feel the weight of the arches of time.
Surface tramples the smoke in depth, smoke inescapable,
Crowding in, filling the work of the women; the smoke is theirs
And reddened eyes watering in smoke and the fire on the floor
And the floor of cow-dust.

Ablution is theirs long drawn like the cry in the fields, and
Helpless in lust for water's eager descent, they keep
Submitting long hair and upturned faces and eyes agitated
And spluttering mouths and thrilling cavities
Damp with heat in the day's exertions.
And the gasp as it were of the trapped wind put into zigzag moulds

Of sound in winnowing, and the handling of rice growth in slush to the singing
Which clutches the heart of hearing and the rumble of hand mills, and
The ceaseless thud of the pestle.

And theirs the play, too, conforming with pulse of the blood,
Hands in assemblage upon the community drum,
A converging of hands in trance on the heated disc
Of rhythmical flavour to which they make the transfer of taste
The metrical patterns
The little designs from corners of scarves of feeling.

The fences fall before knees of intrusion and time,
The fences fall and arise, and men and cattle and clouds,
And the sky remains with the fence implanted between
Surface and depth, keeping time's features away and showing
A face not time's but an oval sound and notchless,
No pointing finger of nose, but smooth as an egg
Divined in an oval sound.
Nothing comes wandering in but the alien cry,
Sometimes of a straying need like a child in trouble
Thrust from the play of surface and sent to depth.
Nothing comes wandering in, nothing ever through stretch of time,
And time in denial of emblem cannot be seen as time,
And the years and the periods pass in a moment.

Nothing comes wandering in, living or leisured,
With challenge, or subtle, uninvited or called.
Bereaved the night and the sun in the door-frame;
No life of the outward dark or outward day that enters;
The night is as black as the sun.

Whatever may push through, parting the dark, is from within the threshold,
And it finds the dark collapsing again
Like walls of sand on the passage
Whatever relieves the monotonous day is from within the threshold,
And it finds its passage of shadow lost, submerged in the sun.

Imprisoned in spices of desolation, there is further the fashioning
Of the noseless face, of featureless time; and the thief of decay –
Detected ages ago, and that too on hearsay from mumbling sages –
Has long been bound over. So nothing goes stale and much less putrid;
And departure fades, as it were into reappearance,
And one's attention diverted a moment

Loses the pauses at times occurring
In ceaseless flow of a tune;
And freshness resembles time without emblem staring through spices.
The pointed alone seeks futility;
Endeavour of growth upon surface, outstripping companions in growth
Attempting to get at the sky, seeking futility
Depth, which is put among spreadings beneath all reachings and footholds.
With vision upon the performance only
And eyes never absent from limited hands
And never away in the taverns of heaven,
Is a stranger cold-shouldered in
Futility's saloons of uplift
Depth is pointless in saloons of privilege,
Thrust from seeking futility, screened from the sky.

A writhing stammer the need of surface, a pain and a problem,
Lost in attempt at utterance
Chasing the bits of itself that break and retreat
Or attempting embarrassed like a beast inarticulate
To capture expression
Never complete and never fulfilled,
And a dreary field without wall or fence exploited for ever
By dreary distinction digging the buried and digging up graves.

But the need in depth is fluent like nature or stain in water,
Debarred from seeking the stammering field, the pain and the problem,
The dreary distinction,
Absent in surface the sources of things that sustain;
So not inherent in surface are hunger and thirst,
Not relevant there.
But depth goes shadowed; and under the growth of fields reassuring.
The spectre lies lazily stretched, rolling its eyes,
And the hidden tentacles lie in wait in soothing foliage
Eager to feed, and the eyes of famine are lidless;
And in sap and moisture and damp and in all the patterns of water,
Heating the branding irons of thirst in hope of torture
The drought lies hidden.

Partition of surface and depth, division of world and earth,
Spirit and flesh,
Is a splinter hiding a bloodless wound, having struck at the flesh
A long while ago in events forgotten and followed by reasons
Fed on mystical lies regarding spirit and matter

Sources of sanction for pinnacled life with lives
For pinnacle, depth for bricks,
Mud in masquerade sitting on mud;
And remedy calls for release from the splinter; and shedding of blood
In payment for release from pain;
And depth strays staggering clutching the splinter, helpless in dreams
Entangled in cunning and aimless anger and servile gesture
Through trackless gloom and bewildering values of dreams.

The blinded continue to groan in a cell whose doors are open
And the splinter remains with the sky, the fence implanted between
Surface and depth,
And the fence of division, of rain to make mud and sun to make dust,
Of all the collected heaped up things without eyes
Like habits that clog,
Paralysing in surface its own result in aggression and greed
As much as in depth the victim preyed on in victimisation;
And the fence is a blight unchecked through countless sessions checking
All effort at sprouting features on leafless twigs of time.
A plague that insinuates, verminous,
Eating into rafters supporting the light;
A terminus, end of the line abrupt,
A road that leads without bridges and without a sign
Of a sudden end,
Suddenly signalling peril in further advance
And cutting communion.

So the hands of depth, the structure of earth,
The walls of wattle and mud which never get dwarfed
To eyes that never grow taller
There with the years outstripped –
As if stems of palms should be smooth where the branches fall –
The hands of depth embracing the life unweaned
There to eyes that never grow taller, are
Frustration effective, to childhood's abortive flight;
And through the long stretch of time, appearing
An inverted horizon with nothing vertical pricking
Complacent vision,
No limbs have ever known stretch
Restricted in walls of wattle and mud which never
Get dwarfed to eyes that never grow taller,
No limbs in depth have ever known stretch
And stretch of free action.

Remedy calls for the shedding of blood for release from pain
And the wound's exposure, calls for release from the splinter,
The flight of delirious fever, destruction
Of all the dividing shapes, awake or asleep.
Torture of shrieking darkness rooted in darkness,
Enlightened torture of darkness smiling and suave,
The drugged and the drugs and the thieves who administer mystical dreams,
The fence implanted between
Surface and depth.
The hands of surface are never free when away from
The venom injected inciting the fingers to feel for
The sifted and fugitive appetite set against nature
And foul as only spirit in segregation
Feeding on flesh could be.

So the hands of depth continue to lie unclasped in alliance
With surface, and all the potential splendour of depth is
In virgin condition, in waste, unenjoyed and unknown
To itself and the need in unconscious search of it;
And the hands of surface are fettered from hope of alliance
And surface is robbed of itself in something essential
And attempts to complete itself through limping vehicles
The impede like defection and call for defeat, vehicles
Out-dated, beyond repair,
Things that are doomed.

PARAKRAMA KODITUWAKKU
(*b*. 1943)

Parakrama Kodituwakku was one of the major (and controversial, experimental) Sinhala poets of the 70s: *Pody Malliye*, published in 1972, received critical praise, and was followed by *Otunna Hini Kumaraya* and *Rashmi*. A critic of the social order, he also worked as a translator, a novelist, and wrote short stories: many of his books received major awards. He worked as a teacher of literature and language for twenty years, before retiring overseas.

Court Inquiry of a Revolutionary

I   **(School Report)**

Doubts all teachings.
Questions continuously.
Thinks heretically.
Disregards rules.
Works as he chooses.

Conduct unsatisfactory.

II   **(Sunday School Report)**

Disbelief verily signifieth a sinful mind.
The horoscope too is inauspicious.
Choleric humours are become excited and turbulent.
Hath no knowledge of the Doctrine or the gods.
I take refuge in the Buddha. He should do so too.

III   **(Court Report)**

In the name of truth and nothing but the truth,
   (a) Attempted to break the law.
   (b) Destroyed the peace.
   (c) Should be ordered a whipping.
   (d) Be made into a good citizen

IV   **(Doctor's Report)**

Psychiatric treatment recommended.
Phobia, mania, paranoia, hysteria,
Neurotic, psychotic,
Abnormal – Criminal,
Behaviour – deviant.

Brain surgery recommended.
Demonic fantasies to be controlled.
Before going to bed
Several tablets of phenobarbitone.

V   **(Statement of the Accused)**

Do not turn me into a snail
My feelers chopped off.
Do not turn me into a coward
By preaching of gods.

Do not turn me into a buffalo
Burdened with false views.
Do not make me 'a good boy'
With hands and mouth gagged.

Allow me to question like Socrates
Doubt like Descartes
Crash like a rushing river
Cut clean as a knife.
Let me rise erect
Like a penis.

[tr. from Sinhala by Ranjini Obeyesekere]

An Unfinished Lesson

One by one each burnt out leaf
falls, fills the yard.
A blackbird cries a sharp tu...week
perched upon a mound.
Blackbird, is that a question
you too ask of me because you know me
for a schoolteacher?

A full half of my life I've spent
answering questions.
Now my white-haired head
has no more strength.

Those who asked me questions then
where are they now?
To questions that are posed to them
what answers do they give?

Children, you who walked to school by flowering forest trails,
you who brought the clouds with you, down mountain slopes,
you who stepped through cool stream beds to wash your feet,
tell O tell, where are you now, in what far place?

There was no playground for the school,
you trained on the bus route,

196

the hundred metres race was run
on the scorching road, barefoot.
While I stood at the bend, alert
for passing cars.

Where are you now, the lot of you?
Whether far or near
raise your hand for me to see
and answer clearly 'here'.

...Do you still, now, as you did then,
get drenched in the pouring rain,
trapped in the threatening storms,
wade across rushing streams,
see laughter in the sun,
run races on the road
see a winning post ahead?

A full half of my life I've spent,
answering questions
now my white-haired head
has no more strength.

[tr. from Sinhala by Ranjini Obeyesekere]

Little Brother

Little brother
busting birds
sling-shot in hand,
guarding fields
all day long
for fifty cents;

if your feet ache
take a rest
on the rock ledge
at the edge
of the paddy field.
The rock then becomes a chair.

When the noon sun strikes
its thousand cooking fires
and scorches your tiny face,
stretch out in the shade
of the spreading banyan tree
that stands at the corner of the field.

Its tender leaves will tremble
and fan you, little brother
beaks will quiver in the branches
you will hear birdsong, my brother.

When the sun turns red and dies
with your sweat and dirt and tears,
step into the river by the ford.
A hundred hands of soothing ripples
will encircle and embrace you
as the river flows on along its way.

Brother, brother when night falls
shades and shadows start to tremble,
then take the brown dirt road that heads for home.
The sand along the way
will become a white fur rug
to kiss your two small feet as they trudge home.

From far off beside the stile
what was it that the hen just said?
That she's laid for you a fruit without a stalk?

When you creep under your cloth
which scatters folds of moonlight
huddled in a ball on your rope bunk;
look, to keep you company –
flowers in heaven – flowers on earth
gleam with the colour of flame.

Brother, brother, stop a wink
before you fall asleep
think –
these are gifts the world bestows on you.
What do you
give in return?

So
do not beat your tin takay
right away
little brother,
let the birds get away
with at least one ear of grain.

[tr. from Sinhala by Ranjini Obeyesekere]

SENARATH GONSAL KORALA

Senarath Gonsal Korala began his career as a poet in the early 1980s and has published six collections of poems in Sinhala in addition to some books for children. He has worked as a school teacher, a director at the Ministry of Education, and a lecturer at a national teacher training college.

The Song of a New Shawl

The immense earth too suffers in this prolonged drought
The green shawl withers away
With its frills dropping
Yet with the rains return
It wears the green garbs again.

> Flowers bloom in the dry thorny bush too
> And get filled with the pollen
> The parrots and the Malithi birds
> Preen the new shawls with their beaks
> And fly in the blue skies above

Yet on a certain day
I saw my little daughter
Standing on the banks of
The Mahakanadara Tank
For a long time

> The tank too suffered
> Deprived of its green garb
> Yet with the rains return
> It wears its green garb
> Smartly again

But you wear
The same frock every day, daughter
To cover your modesty,
In it you step in
To the tank to bathe, wait till it dries again

These songs the cuckoo sings loud there
Are not songs of the spring only
Are those about you daughter
The sad songs that moist
The helpless bird's eyes?

[tr. from Sinhala by A.T. Dharmapriya]

SITA KULATUNGA
(1930s–2014)

Born in Bandaragama and educated both at home and abroad, Sita Kulatunga wrote poetry and fiction, in English and Sinhala. *Dari the Third Wife*, written while she was a teacher in Nigeria, received a Sri Lanka Arts Council award in 1988, and a book of her short stories was also shortlisted for the Gratiaen Prize. The poems included here were chosen from *A Godé Person and Other Poems* (2003), which collects work written over a long period of time. In their vernacular concision and her wit, Kulatunga's poems resemble those of the Indian poet Eunice de Souza. Her short story, 'The High Chair', became famous for its depiction of caste politics and was translated into many languages, including German and Japanese. She also translated several English novels into Sinhala, including *Wuthering Heights* and Kamala Markandaya's *Some Inner Fury*.

Pitu padam namamaham
(I worship at the feet of my father)

Nilanthi, my dear daughter,
I do not go for gold and fun.
I go to Dubai
to gather a few dirams
away from the red drunken eye
of your son-of-a-bitch

father
who kicks me, with his pada, of course.
How else?
Pitu padam nama maham.
Look after him my daughter
in my absence.
Beware of him in every way
not only of his foot.

Why

'Why, what is wrong with him?'
'Nothing', she said.
'Then? Good looking, rich and of good character
not bald headed or too old either',
said Jindasa mama in his mature, avuncular voice.

'Give us a reason, girl, give us a reason'.

Clearing her throat, she said,

'He drinks the tea from the saucer.'

NEETHA KUNARATNAM
(*b.* 1976)

Neetha (born Navaneetham) Kunaratnam, winner of the 2007 Geoffrey Dearmer Prize, was born in London to Tamil Sri Lankans, and has lived in both Japan and France. His debut, *Just Because* (2018), was highly commended in the Forward Prizes, and his second collection is forthcoming from Blue Diode Press. His work discusses structural violence, conflict and masculinity, living in the gaps between dual heritage and cultures, and climate collapse. Kunaratnam writes with sharp outlines, measuring every syllable: his work is clearly meticulously edited. *Just Because* was published in 2018 by Smokestack, and his second collection, *Cauc/asian*, is out now.

The Afterlife

After every war
someone has to clean up.
Things won't
straighten themselves up, after all.

WISŁAWA SZYMBORSKA,
'The End and the Beginning' (tr. Joanna Trzeciak)

And someone will have to clean up,
But this is no job for ordinary Joes,
Only specialists padded in moon boots,
Facemasks, and white chemical suits,

So someone will have to write out a cheque
For the foreign input, the expertise
And expensive equipment:
The mine detectors and nerve sensors,

Somebody will need to order them
From the front of the catalogue, ignore
The solar-powered, GPS models, plump
For the standard, remote-controlled breed,

As faithful and expendable as someone else,
Sought to cordon off the area, skirt the perimeters
On tiptoe, and mark out the dimensions
Of the operation with only sniffer dogs in tow.

Someone will need to believe the aggrieved can
Make a difference, pray in numbers, and petition
Our leaders to subsidise the farmers, who can no
Longer reap lest they're blown into thin air…

Someone will have to locate then collect
Any bright packages dropped in the interim,
Since the bombers droned off into the night.
Their black boxes still replaying screams,

And someone sort out the dried food
From the prosthetic limbs, filter out the notes
Of explanation, and decipher a rationale
From the mistakes made in translation.

Someone will have to point out
That mustard leaves might not survive the blasts,
And checking they've turned red might set off
A barrage of blinding and a cluster of regrets,

Somebody will have to teach the children
That these M&Ms aren't filled with peanuts
But pack a mighty punch. Explain that
A bomb as small as a battery can turn a sheep into a cloud.

Poppy

You see it can be undone,
rather than torn.
So we pick it apart
to see its four forms.

Its petal is an
overlap of lungs,
ridged radii
that my thumbs caress.

Its shard of leaf
is a disfigured hand,
frostbitten knuckles
numbed by shrapnel.

The plastic needle
gently pricks me.
Its sawn-off stem
slips in like a spine,

and latches on the collar
of the cotyledon.
The black button
that locks it all

is the perfect disc
of an exit wound,
a pupil dilated in
its bloodshot eye.

Beeline

When the engineer pins
the bee's wing down
to a blueprint,
delves and rips
into its secrets,

and Faust-like
trades knowledge
of the light-stitched,
pluck-tough surface

to a City conglomerate
raking it in from
an underground cache
of fighting machines,

When the hives lie abandoned,
apiarists now only landlords
of rotten honeycomb,

the poignant pleas
lost in the knowledge
that the mighty transmitter
deflected them far off course,

When the orchards' crab
and scrumpy lie barren,
with white nausea of pollen,

when the sprays we concoct
try to mate with the blossom,

and the high street bosses regret
the shortage of honey and coxes,
squashes and almonds;

When the queen abdicates her
brood chamber, sick of
the constant flux and bummed

by her poor ratings, flees
to hang in a hollow tree,
her solitude a slow dying,

When the smoke of
pine needles and hessian
no longer waylays them

from their path
as if they've homed in
unerringly on some God given

(Do any of us know where they're headed?)

LATHA

(*b.* 1968)

Born in Negombo (Western Province), Latha was forced, with her family, out of their home by the violence of Black July (1983), and had to move to Singapore. A highly regarded writer, she has published two collections in Tamil: *Theeveli* (2003) and *Paampuk Kaattil Oru Thaazhai* (2004). In 2008 she won the Singapore National Literature Prize for Tamil for her short story collection *Naan Kolai Seyum Penkal* which has since been translated into English and published as *The Goddess in the Living Room* (2014). Latha wrote her first poem when she was 20, and writes about race, gender, history and myth. Much anthologised in South and South-East Asia, Latha's poetry has been translated into English, French and German, and *Theeveli* is part of the undergraduate syllabus in universities in Tamil Nadu, India. She is currently News Editor of the Singapore Tamil daily *Tamil Murasu*.

from Untitled

1

The speeding mind
overtakes
past events
and races past the vehicle.

A journey of many years
for me and for the road.

The uniformed guide
standing on the first step
delves into the month of May
and rambles on about
artillery guns landmines
hand-grenades rifles
blood tears fear.

As it comes to a grinding halt,
he speaks of the time when
Tamil Eelam Welcomed You
here.

Face flushed by the harsh sun;
I shade it with a scarf.

The checkpost lies worn out.
Tamil lies under Sinhala
all along the way.

   3

houses blown to bits
in weird shapes
like an art fair.

in the middle of
the crushed vegetation,
wet footprints.

a young shoot peeps out
from the dead Tiger's Claw Tree
on which clothes hang out to dry.

the people have learnt
to pose for hours
clutching with ease
the barbed wire
without getting pricked.

in every nook and corner
of the razed city
flags of
banks with big money
reach out to the skies.

4

To the land that was done with triumphs and setbacks
comes the ancient wind,
drained now of its hues.
It speaks a new language now.
The flag it curls itself around it's also new.

As we move along
wheels kicking up the dirt,
the wind that blows
in one tight embrace
breaks the walking stick
of the old man.

[tr. from Tamil by Ra Sh]

SUNDRA LAWRENCE
(*b.* 1975)

Sundra Lawrence is a UK-based poet and writer, a second-generation Tamil. Her grandfather worked for the Colombo Port Commission and her great-uncle was a prison officer at Welikada Prison; they were Tamils working amid some of the earliest and bloodiest parts of the conflict. Lawrence is interested in the edges of identities and communities; histories undocumented, as well as the spectacular everyday: she is influenced by Seamus Heaney and Grace Nichols. Her poems and short stories have been broadcast on national television, radio and podcasts; her work has appeared in art exhibitions and has been published in numerous anthologies and magazines including *The Los Angeles Review*. She won the Aryamati Poetry Prize in 2021 for her chapbook, *Warriors*, which was published by Fly on the Wall in 2022.

Gold

(for Alan Kurdi)

The pull of the undertow eases
          your ring clean off,
                    while you shake your head laughing.

Our kids help comb the beach for gold,
          clouds of spume tickle their toes,
                    your pledge hidden in water's flesh

falls through tempers of current.
          On another perfect coast, a boy,
                    the same age as ours, is found

almost breathing low-tide lullabies,
          the sea no longer sick in his belly,
                    this island of child, feet

sore from the cut of new shoes,
          Mummy, I can't walk any more,
                    a silent tantrum; red-

soaked t-shirt and undone velcro.
          The detail of his name
                    smaller than the photograph –

Alan, not Aylan or *Aurum,*
          hands unclasped, fingers bare
                    on sand he cannot anchor.

Rassam

Mum would make it to dry our colds:
Icarus pepper, garam masala,
flesh of a soaked tamarind –
sealed with garlic, coriander,
mutton boiled clean off the bone.

You must learn Tamil, speak it!
The swell of heat claps the pot lid,
and sweats our yellow wall.
This is all the medicine you will need
she says ladling up to brim.

We sit balancing broth on our laps,
blow brown islands in each spoon.
She reminds us not to leave
anything behind. Our tongues burn
pepper hot with each sip.

MAHAKAVI
(1927–71)

Mahakavi was the pen name of Thuraisamy Rudhramurthy and means 'Great Poet'. He is celebrated for being a pioneer of modern Tamil poetry in Sri Lanka, who broke free from the Sangam model to concentrate instead on the ordinary speech and life of the ordinary 'Jaffna Man'. Yet, he did not champion free verse; instead his poetry is tightly written in the established Tamil yaapu metre, which makes translating his rhyme and word play almost impossible. Born in Alaveddy in Jaffna, Northern Province he began writing in his teens and was also a short story writer and a playwright; his output was phenomenal and deeply influential. Several of his works were published posthumously including *Veedum Veliyum* (1973), *Puthiyathoru Veedu* (1979) and *Mahakaviyin Aaru Kaaviyankal* (2000), although some of his unpublished manuscripts were destroyed when the Sri Lankan Army occupied his house in the 1980s. A substantial, three-volume collected edition of his entire corpus was published in 2021, edited by the poet, and a close friend, M.A. Nuhman, and organised by his son Cheran. An inspiring writer, he occupies a special position in the Tamil literary landscape and helped bring poetry to the ordinary people of Tamil Sri Lanka.

Ahalikai

From the Himalayan peaks
Indran descends;
the embroidered shawl
that hides his fragrant chest
reflects the rays of the waning moon,
and chirping insects abruptly cease.

209

The anklets silent on his floating feet
no pause in his majestic stride,
on grassy plains he touches the earth
and moves towards a warbling stream.

A bud that awaits the sun
he plucks,
then cups his hand and inhales deep.
This earthly joy
that blooms at morn and fades at dusk
he spurns but loves it too.

He reaches the stream and quenches his thirst.
Did this tasteless drink
defy the taste of celestial food?
A fleeting smile escapes his lips,
he flicks the flower and approaches the hut.

His shawl that glitters
like stars in that serene sky,
his sword, sandals, and bracelets
he hides with care
and treads once more the declining path.

His piercing eyes gaze and search
the maze of trees,
the line of shrubs;
he peers and sees the hut.

He steps across the thornless stile,
the fowls from branches
disturbed, stare.
He moves with steadfast eyes
blind to all but a tiny
crack, through which he peers.

Ahalikai moves her stalk-soft arms
across the hoary chest of Gothama;
he wakes, thinks it dawn
and leaves the hut – all these are watched.

The arm that slides to seek its joy
now comes back to rest

on half-seen breasts;
the lips curl with wistful smile,
she sighs and turns.

Gothama leaves for his well-worn seat
his eyes close in meditative pose.
Indran stands at the foot of the bed
eyes aflame with burning passion;
he sees her squirm with unfed love.

No beast of prey would dare approach
this hut the sage had made his own.
Now he stands with boundless lust
his body aches, he takes a step!

She gasps with pain, yet loves
the hands that hold with love;
he buries in her the passion he brought
her eyes closed she feels the joy.

Like one possessed his lips seek
the eyelids and the sensual frame,
his body hot, he makes her his;
she gently opens her eyes.

She sees, shudders, breaks out in sweat
and freezes as her breathing stops.
And as she stares
becomes a stone.

The lord of all celestial beings
watches in horror the woman he craved.
The sage returns and glances around
strokes his beard and turns away.

Indran flees
damned for dateless time.
His body erupts in a thousand sores.
Deserted by all, a senseless stone
she waits for the touch of a godly foot.

[tr. from Tamil by Chelva Kanaganayakam]

from **Birth**

The day dawned in the East
and the young buds raised their heads.
A cock jumped from the branch
of a mango tree and paraded up and down
Vellupillai's veranda. It then scratched
the dirt insistently.

There was no smoke coming from the chimney.
Was no one tending the cooking fire?
The front yard was empty. Usually,
through the open doorway, the smell of onions
cooking would tempt your nose.
Today things seemed out of order.

In the windowless room you could see
nothing moving; no shapes, no shadows.
But you could hear the sound of a woman's
low groans of pain. As our eyes became accustomed
to the dark, we saw Vellupillai's wife,
her clothes in disarray, writhing on the bed.

Her name was Valliamma.
Her belly protruded with new life;
her slim waist barely able to bear
the waves of agony engulfing her.
'The baby,' a voice said
as an older woman appeared.

Vellupillai arrived.
'Stay outside,' said the old woman.
'Boil some milk.' She went in search
of old sheets. Unable to help
in any useful way, Vellupillai stood redundant
wringing his hands. He paced up and down
the front yard, stopping here and there,
sitting down suddenly, springing up
just as suddenly, pacing again.

[…]

A storm arrived, the rain cooling
the ground. The sound of thunder
made him pause in bewilderment.
Soon, he resumed his pacing.
The older woman emerged
from the birthing chamber.
He trembled, dreading the news.

'A baby boy,' she announced.
On his face a new light was born.
She invited him in: 'Come and see.'
Her words were as sweet as sugar cane.
He rose with renewed vigour,
his body erect, his hair tingling.
In life's long story, this day
was one of victory.

That baby didn't stop screaming.
His father wiped away tears of joy
and raising his voice to the rafters said
'I name this child Muththaiyan'.
And thus the baby became bearer
of his father's name.

[tr. from Tamil by Shash Trevett]

from Excellence

The food cooked by Thevayaanai
was always delicious. Her touch
transformed plain aubergine
into shark curry. Words couldn't capture
the elegance of that good woman's
lentils when swelled with ghee.
Her fortunate husband's full belly
added inches to his waist.

On Fridays she nagged him
to go to the fish market.
He exhaled his reply.

He woke at eight each morning.
Was there anything he couldn't accomplish
in a day? Would they ever go without?
She cooked him delicious crab.
With thankfulness he gobbled it up.

[...]

Muththaiyan sent his mother's medicines
in a letter to his father.
He gave parties for his close friends
adding sparkle to their lives.
To prevent time from turning him
into a withered mango tree
he wandered the streets, searching
for newer, bigger houses to rent.

When he reclaimed the jewellery already pawned
he remembered the wise words of his father:
'Boy, you have only studied sufficiently
once tomorrow's lesson is over' –
His heart was overcome.
'Look to Shiva' his father had advised.
'Look after your health' – this had become
his mother's mantra.

[...]

Finishing work he would turn for home.
Waiting in a queue, his thoughts
circled around Thevayaanai.
If he had sufficient change in his pocket
he bought some laddus. Street after street
opened before him, but shutting his nose
to the distracting aromas he would hurry home.
Reaching the sari shop he would promise himself:
'After I get paid.'

[...]

[tr. from Tamil by Shash Trevett]

SUNANADA MAHENDRA

(*b.* 1938)

Sunanada Mahendra is an author, theatre director, poet, Sinhala Radio Play writer and a regular contributor to the Sinhala and English press in Sri Lanka. His book *Ogha Tharanaya* won the State Literary Award for the best Sinhala poetry collection in 2006. Many poems from the collection are now translated into English. He has won the State Literary Award for the best original playscript (1993), the best research work (2002) and twice for the best Sinhala novel in 1964 and 2002. His outstanding contribution to his field of expertise, mass communication, earned him a UNESCO Copernicus Award for Social Sciences in 1983. His play *Socrates* won eight awards including the state prize for Best Drama of 1991.

The Mountain

That tall mountain
Close to the little school,
We climbed with trepidation
As little children

There are miracles on it,
The elders used to tell us
Though we were never to see any.

The same mountain
Seen again in later years,
Why didn't it
Look so tall?
We grew into men
Brawny and big-made,
When I came
To the little school
Holding a son's hand
The tall mountain
Looked small to me.

[tr. from Sinhala by A.T. Dharmapriya]

IMAAD MAJEED

(*b.* 1991)

Imaad Majeed is a multidisciplinary artist based in Colombo, Sri Lanka. They are Director and Curator of the trilingual performance platform KACHA KACHA and part of the artist collective 'The Packet'. Their poetry has been published in *CITY: A Journal of South Asian Literature*, as well as the chapbooks, *Lime Plain Tea* and *Annasi & Kadalagotu*. Their work, influenced by language, documentary, and conceptual poetry, as well as projective verse and the work of Jean Arasanayagam, explores themes of identity, language, nationalism, enforced disappearance, late-stage capitalism, sacred space, xenophobia, ethnoreligious conflict and healing. Their poetry queers found language. Their documentary poetry zine *Testimony of the Disappeared* was exhibited in Dhaka at 'Chobi Mela: Shunno' (2021) and Colombo at 'Colomboscope: Language is Migrant' (2022).

arma christi

someone has placed a thorn
in a lion's paw, the lion must
not mistake it for a sword

this thorn has been placed, also,
in each of us, one hand, on a day
for one who wore a crown of thorns

let us remember this, whether
or not we believe, regardless
of faith, race, language
or whatever means by which
our kind-
ness is divided

each of us have, at least, one
hand by which to remove
a thorn, first from our own
hand, then from those
of others

but the lion, i fear
may have to use its other
paw to remove its thorn

for the lion has instilled fear
for too long, a state of terror
prolonged by the will to power

and the other was never truly
a thorn, just as the thorn
was never truly
a sword

April 21, 2019

'keppetipola mawatha'

i don't remember our last conversations
fragments of shadows, trees, branches
aerial roots, soft amber street lamp

a feeling of being
on the way, of leaving, arriving, but hardly
of being present

i remember the last time she visited
i did not speak to her. i stayed shut
in my room

i remember regret
i regret what i don't remember

a ceramic teacup, dipping marie biscuits
cigarette smoke in the air, my grandfather

distant

i remember her reprimanding me for raising my voice at my mother
i remember her confronting a cousin violating me
the only person to do so

terrazzo / cardinal red polished floor
i try to grasp what i've forgotten / what i've let go
kandos chocolate with cashew nut
walls painted cream / peach

                        a wooden stool with a swan motif

help me fill in these non-memories
these gaps between my fingers
        i grasp – ceramic teacup
        dipping half-memories
        holding on as they disintegrate
        afraid to touch my lips to taste

            i don't remember every detail of their home
            but – shut in my room
                    i remember their voices

                                                they echo
        ummamma / appa
                                                they echo
                whenever i raise my voice

                                i remember to lower mine
            soft amber

trees, branches, aerial roots

23 April 2021

SHARANYA MANIVANNAN
(*b.* 1985)

Sharanya Manivannan writes and illustrates fiction, poetry, children's literature and non-fiction. She received a South Asia Laadli Award for her short story collection *The High Priestess Never Marries*, and her books have been nominated for many other honours. In 2015 she was specially commissioned to write and recite a poem at the Commonwealth Day Observance in London. Manivannan grew up in Sri Lanka and Malaysia and has lived in India since 2007. Her family is Batticaloa Tamil, and her work – such as her illustrated Ila duology, consisting of the graphic novel *Incantations Over Water* and the picture book *Mermaids in the Moonlight*, and her novel-in-progress *Constellation of Scars* – brings into the English language the culture of this lesser discussed part of the island. Her creative worldscapes are often shaped by ecological, mythological and feminist themes, and her personal experiences of forced migrations and surviving abuse also influence her work across genres.

The Mothers

(Easter 2019, Sri Lanka)

A mother wearing glass beads looking for
another handkerchief, the melted candy
in the one she is carrying as sticky as
the nose being wiped on her arm, under
church fans too slow for this April heat.

A mother whose only existing photograph of him
was borrowed permanently by someone who
told her they could be trusted with her story,
praying to the saint who restores what has
been lost, on her knees again
– again, as many times as it will take.

A mother whose own countenance howls
in frames the whole world scrolls past,
captured by someone who did not care to
learn her name or the names of her dead.

A mother who is Amma, her other name forgotten –
the word a scream in the room at the morgue where
bodies beloved are identified by wedding-rings
and blood-splashed shoes on a projection screen.

A mother who wishes they could have gone for a swim
first, but they are so hungry she has to stand between
them in the buffet line so they don't break into a fight.

A mother with a baby keeping time
inside her body, a mother with a bomb.

A mother in the kitchen measuring the sugar
generously, preparing this Easter's feast,
waiting for the little ones who must just now
be saying grace in a circle at Sunday school,

waiting for the little ones
to come home.

River

When you leave, take with you the way light shimmered gold in the river,
how the weight of what you loved swirled into filigreed gold in the river.

That was how it felt to me, at the eventide of the annihilated dream,
when I first crossed into illumination at the threshold of the river.

There were mapmakers before me: their footfalls fade tender on the earth.
Like you, they brought palms of amaryllis, asked to be consoled by the river.

There's a pond in the forest whose water only ripples where you weep.
But here, all ruptures. Let your heart flood, uncontrolled, into the river.

Listen: the saga unbraids. Loyalties shift, fish-dappled in her surge.
You can no more submerge a story than you can hold a river.

Carry all you can into the world, a tributary. But pilgrim, linger a little.
Sit a while beside me. There are renderings still untold in the river.

ARJI MANUELPILLAI
(*b.* 1981)

Arji Manuelpillai is a poet, performer and creative facilitator based in London. Influenced by poets including Deborah Landau and Wayne Holloway-Smith, Arji continues to advocate for poetry as a tool for change. He was the Jerwood/ Arvon Mentee mentored by Hannah Lowe. His poetry has been published in magazines including *Poetry Review*, *The Rialto* and *bath magg*. He has also been shortlisted for prizes including the National Poetry Competition, the Out-Spoken Prize and the Winchester Poetry Prize. Arji's debut pamphlet *Mutton Rolls* was published by Out-Spoken Press in 2020, and his new book *Improvised Explosive Device* by Penned in the Margins in 2022. It was a Poetry Book Society Recommendation, was noted in *The Telegraph*'s top 20 poetry books of the year, and was named in *The Guardian*'s best recent poetry section in December 2022.

credit card

someone pretended to be me
filled my details out online
intercepted the card as it arrived
and went to Morrisons. Someone

in a red sweater, NY cap
black jeans, pink socks
spent 200 quid on
groceries I imagine, booze

toothpaste, noodles, coco-pops
definitely leeks and potatoes
for a leek and potato soup
(crème fraiche to stir in)

that someone then caught
the bus, the 343 perhaps, went
to that Peckham café
on the white side of Peckham

sat on a shared table
had a tea and carrot cake
read the paper, leant
back in their seat

so their hands fell to their sides
and the lady to the right
casual as breathing
pulled her handbag close

after the Sri Lankan bombing that kills 360
(after the 20-year war that killed significantly more)

after the news   my skin feels darker   prayers for   thoughts
for   texted condolence   but the majority of my relatives are
long dead   mostly from natural causes I'm only Sri Lankan
at weddings and funerals   or for inquisitive white people

Uncle Prithi is marked as safe   no damp tissues in this house
buffering   only slow moving heads   like watching slo-mo ping
pong   like when my brother had a splinter I knew wouldn't
come out on its own *downloading* everyone on the news
looks like my uncle or aunty   cousin or nephew   but poorer
or dead   'aahh back to the ol' days' Ammama would say
buffering   bathed in sun and blood   *Raj Kumar marked safe*
my uncle tells me   *typing…*   they don't need therapy in
Sri Lanka   they just get on with it   *typing…*   like taking out
the trash   *last seen 05.47*   or burying a body or detonating
a bomb in the buffet line of the Cinnamon Grand Hotel
from here (on the toilet)   it's all just a cluster of tiny red faces
wailing in a language I don't understand   in a country I can't
but look! that's where Mama and Appa first met

after being called a paki

        my father used to say
        the hardest oranges to peel
        are often the sweetest

        when he first came to England
        he worked double the hours
        took the jobs no one else would

        when his roommate was beaten
        outside Vauxhall tube station
        he hardly spoke for a month

        my father told him knuckle down
        the only answer was
        to work harder

        tonight when I tell
        my father what happened
        he covers his mouth

        with his hand
        an orange peel attaching
        back onto an orange

MISHAL MAZIN

(*b.* 1994)

Featured at TEDx, Colombo Fringe Festival, Annasi & Kadalagotu, Open Brain and WhiteBoard @ Black Cat Café, Mishal Mazin was born in the United Arab Emirates and moved to Colombo in 2012. He rides motorcycles, trains in MMA, writes in English, speaks broken Sinhala and feels disassociated from the language and culture of his own people. Neither here nor there, caught between two worlds of identity, Mazin uses poetry to anchor himself to reality, using it as his vehicle for dialectic discovery of self, society, and spirituality. His debut collection *The Slick Mongoose* was published in 2018; *Panic & Other Poems* appeared in 2022.

Rajagiriya

In one point in time,
        The only fresh air that ever existed,
        Came from the balcony behind
        The fox's room, in hometown Rajagiriya.

It had a stellar view, his balcony
        With oddly arranged roofs
        Of overly modest houses
        Peppering the dark green
        Marshes and dull flora
        Overlooking the capital Kotte.

And in the near distance
        Bright lights from the tall pillars
        Of success stories, lucky perseverance
        And executive tricksters
        Looked down at us
        Sprats, swimming pathetically
        In a pond, overpopulated
        With too many a fish bigger
        Than us.
        Feeding on their leftovers
        Like the unfortunate beggars
        That we are.

Here, some of us were still
        Hopeful, for when the frying pan
        Lights on, we'll get our chance
        To watch the big fish sear.
        Matara buth kadé lunchtime fantasy.

But for now, we are just stargazing
        Or cloud gazing, depending on the hour.
        Thankful that the sun and moon both,
        Bless the land on all ends of prosperity
        In our young town
        Rajagiriya.

Buth Kadé: budget rice-and-curry cafeterias.

Té Kadé

I sat once, at the most lowlife of places infecting
        The middle of a rich suburb in the city's arteries,
        To enjoy my tea the way a real Ceylonese does,
        Full of diabetes and stray dog love.

I saw one of your CMC fossils,
        Taking a break from his hellish shift,
        Sweeping up the fermented leaves on Barnes Place
        Thinking about the leaves of tomorrow,
        The leaves he couldn't take,
        Always the same work to be made,
        I saw his charred hands grasp the glass
        Watched him chug robotically
        What he probably settled for as lunch
        As he stared dead on at the wall in front of him,
        Thoughtless yet still thinking of something
        Just to keep sane in the science fiction of his reality.

Like I had been, before the interruption of my observance
        An ancient woman had come to sit across me.
        Haunting eyes are sunken at the end of her skull,
        A Saree draped one time too many,

Retelling a story heard one time too many
She asked me eighty for pills,
For her alleged blood pressure.
I didn't hesitate to give,
I knew spare change in my hands
Usually is just another cigarette,
But still, I checked her arms
For shots of dope, having stumbled,
Upon pages of stories of beggars
And addiction.
She had bought tea too,
Sitting across me, in this icky room,
Asking me where I'm from, why I'm here
And I, answering the best I can,
Trying to sound familiar,
Without using language,
Smiling, hopefully politely,
Cut the conversation in half,
Mostly due to my own
Comprehensive shortcomings,
More than hers.
I watched her telling the boys serving,
That the tea was good enough
For a second round, but I knew secretly,
Perhaps better than the others,
That she meant what she said.

In this concrete box, plastic furniture
    And red cement finish,
    Bizarre turquoise-walled
    And the greasiest of decor,
    I saw the Sri Lanka some of us ignore,
    I've seen how some of you
    Roll up your windows, seats
    In fat sedans, cuss complain
    About the beggar begging for change
    Bigoted to the bigot on shotgun,
    'THEY really need to do something
    About these beggars'

Who are they?

CIARA MANDULEE MENDIS

(*b*. 1991)

Ciara Mandulee Mendis is an Officer of the Sri Lanka Administrative Service. Her writing has appeared in the *Southeast Asian Review of English*, *Riptide Journal*, *Indian Review*, *Midway Journal*, *The Ekphrastic Review*, *Monograph*, *Anthology of Short Stories: Spring 2022* by Fenechty Publishing, and *Channels*, the journal of the English Writers' Collective in Sri Lanka. Both her collections of short stories, *The Red Brick Wall* and *The Lanka Box* were shortlisted for the Gratiaen Prize. Her poetry is inspired by Maya Angelou, Kamala Das and Sylvia Plath: she writes about collisions between people, concepts, ideas, cultures, and human relationships amidst it all.

The Dancing Woman at Embekke

I told him I do not like to dance and he kicked me
in the knees. I was broken and was crying
when they framed me.

And then he came with many men
to touch me. I was trying to stop them
when they framed me.

When I whispered it was cold he pinched
my breasts. They were swollen like coconuts
when they framed me.

When I told him I wanted a horse
he slapped me. I had a bruise on my cheek
when they framed me.

And you say I must have been
a courtesan for the way they have
carved and framed me.

SWOT Analysis on Marriage

They taught us SWOT analysis today
the lecturer got nowhere close to you.
I recalled the SWOT analysis you did
if we were ever to get married.

Strengths:
My ability to foresee rain
so the clothes on the clothes line
would never get wet.
And your knowledge of things
that matter like Brexit.

Weaknesses:
My idea of you and how
I waste an hour or two
on things that die like
flowers
and dreams.

Opportunities:
How we can finally post a picture –
me looking back but holding your hand,
a jasmine on my hair – with the caption
'couple goals'. A ring on my finger (finally)
and the house rent allowance added to your pay.

Threats:
All those women who adore
the Divisional Head, who have brains
and good looks. All those women
who 'mess with my head'
female writers, poetesses and lady lecturers
(writers, poets and lecturers, you meant).

TYRRELL MENDIS

(1934–2021)

Tyrrell Kingsley Mendis worked for Manitoba's civil service. A photographer as well as a poet, he captured images of both nature and pioneer churches and had over thirty exhibitions. He had professional qualifications in architecture, applied arts and librarianship, and was an Associate of the Canadian Association for Photographic Art. His books are *Broken Petals* (1965); *The Canned Think, Yours to Open* (1971), which won awards both for its poetic content and its innovative construction; and *Echoing Voices* (1986, poems and photographs).

Pivot

You. You are the fulcrum and your own time-swings
Beyond today's transience and tomorrow's hope;
Before yesterday's slips on oblivion's slope
Along the groove of cold predestined things.
The whirling planets in their orbits juggle
Dead moons in myriad galaxies; and we,
We pass beyond the utmost limits of the sky
But yours is the white problem to unravel.
Hour-glasses or the sun-dial cannot change it;
Nor can diurnal cycles ever know
The inmost secrets of your life-blood's flow;
Nor force – like mine – can seek at all to change it.

Spring Morning

In the patient weariness of the winds of the sea
And the muted voices of the buds of spring
There is remorse; the sudden rapture of a stolen thing
In the mixed branches of a winter tree.
There is also the silence of the crocus flowers,
The helpless anger of a frost-worn stone,
The unknown innocence of a day just born
And impotence in the tragedy of its hours.

CARL MULLER

(1935–2019)

Kala Keerthi (an honorific prefix, awarded 'for extraordinary achievements and contributions in arts, culture and drama') Carl Muller wrote journalism, poetry and award-winning fiction, including a trilogy of novels about Burgher life. His poems, resembling versified op-eds, are inspired by his impatience with cant, false religion and a spiritually bankrupt modernity. One of his collections is titled *Propitiations*, yet he's the least propitiatory poet one could imagine – his poems explain how and why things have gone wrong in Sri Lanka and globally, but also relish the contours of their own kvetching. He is a satirist who ascribes to the poet an important role, while asking his Sri Lankan reader to reassess what poetry is: 'I feel there is no necessity to elevate Nature and tell of those same old time-worn things like "Gossamer cobwebs" and "silver moon-shafts" and "golden daffodils".'

Deiyyo Saakki!

There was darkness on the face of the deep
because the CEB
reported a power station malfunction and said
they did not hear God saying let there be light.
The CEB said
that he could have the connection in eight hours.
God was annoyed when he got his bill and asked
who had read the meter. Anyway he called the light day
and then caused the water to bunk over in one place
and the dry land to appear which cost two lakhs a perch.
The dry land put forth grass and weeds and ganja
and the angels smoked the grass and got stoned
and one angel called Juana
was henceforth called Maru Juana.

God told the waters that were covering Ratnapura
to bring forth lots of fish and Araliya tinned maalu
and Keell's Fish Fingers and the angels went around
shouting *hurullo! hurullo!*
and *dan genapu maalu*
and God blessed them
and said it was good.

Then God made birds and beasts and pheasants
so that Queen Elizabeth could shoot them,
and monkeys that could be sold as *dada-mas* to those
on their way to Kataragama. Then he made cattle
and creeping things, and the government
made the Milk Board
and husbands said their wives were old cows
and became creeping things – that is creeping
into the beds
of the women next door.
Before he took a nap, God made man and was happy
with the result. 'I'll call him Adam
because he won't give a damn anyway,
and when I kick him out,
he can build an ugly walawwa and grow rambuttans.'
But God felt a tad sorry for this naked monkey
and gave him a woman, then told them:
'Of the durian tree
you shall not eat,' and when they asked why,
He did not explain.

So when God was in his bed and fluffing his pillows,
Adam and the woman called Eve – a name
she did not like at all – threw rocks at the tree,
knocked down a fruit that split and filled the garden
with a bad smell. 'Like farts of a brigade of angels,'
Adam said, and Eve dug out a bulb
and went slurp and said,
'Mmm – just like sucking something
I have not yet sucked,'
and told Adam to try it.
Adam liked it. 'Got a parliamentary flavour…
and it does things
to my mace.' And Eve said, 'I think I have
a place for that mace.'
And God got up for the smell,
wrinkled his nose and said:
'Eau de jiggyjiggy!' and, very angry,
he kicked the coupling couple out of the garden.
They retained a slimy lawyer to plead their case
and this made God furious.
He shot the lawyer in the knees and said:
'Go to Wolfendaal!'

and when the lawyer crawled around,
not knowing the way,
God said: 'Some lawyer! Go to hell!'
and he called an archangel and said,
'Cut down that bloody durian tree
and see that these two
don't creep in here again. And spray this whole place
with DDT.'
The lawyer cursed and swore.
'Look at what you have done to me,' he shouted.
'I shall appeal to the Society
for Prevention of Cruelty
to Animals!'

This is the first part of the Book of Genesis
and there are lots
of interesting things to follow – but Adam was very sad
and stood on one leg on Adam's Peak for centuries
because he didn't like the look of Eve who was getting
an outsize bundy. When she told him
she had a son called Cain, Adam hopped off the peak
and sulked in a cave in Gampola until Eve
came to tell him
there were lots and lots of Durian trees in the area.
So, by the sweat of his brow, he climbed
and knocked down
the prickly fruit and praised God and said:
'He has given us
prickly things for the prick, and henceforth can we do
whatever we like, wherever we like, whenever we like,'
and Eve seconded the motion.

'If we go on like this,' Adam said, 'we can surely win
the Presidential Award for Industry.'
Soon they had Abel
and Cain was jealous. 'All this fuss over a new baby!'
So Cain killed Abel and God looked down
from the trade tower
and said, 'Hey! What are you up to? Where's your
brother?' and Cain said, 'What brother?'
and God was angry
and took a madu waligé and chased Cain
over the Knuckles
and said, 'Don't you ever come back!'

and stamped his forehead with a big rubber seal
that belonged
to the passport office.
Cain stained in Bintenne and found a nice Veddah girl
and said he liked her dress of kos leaves
and that he had been punished by God
and was in the mood
to turn over a new leaf or two. He then began
to make and sell
testosterone pills because the durians only grew in season
and very soon men began to multiply
and there were queues
at all the co operative outlets
and some built maternity homes and pre-natal clinics
and God was appalled and said:
'What has this world I made come to?'

The angels also thought of applying for leave
and came down
to take Rodi women to bed although they complained
about the sleeping arrangements,
and out came a race of giants from Samoa
who began to play rugby and challenged the All Blacks,
and God shouted in a loud voice: 'Enough! Enough!
This whole world is corrupt. I'm going to wash out
this whole stable. Hasn't anyone told this lot
about contraceptives?' Then he told one good man
called Noah, to build a big ark
and take in a load of beasts
and Noah's wife was annoyed and said: 'For God's sake
open the portholes! This whole thing smells of horse shit
and cattle dung and there are lizards in the loo
and a hare in the oven
and a salamander in my knickers!'
And this surprised Noah for he always thought
it was salami.

When God sent the rain, every cricket match
was cancelled
and the Oval became a lake
and Premadasa stadium a sea
and at the university that was in Peradeniya
two history professors, sitting on the roof
of the Senate building,

said: 'So this is how the Sea of Parakrama was formed…
when the hell is it going to stop raining?'

So this, infants, is the epic tale that will ring forever
in the annals of Useless History.
Next time around, you will learn more.
The moral is: Never trust a garden. The strangest things happen in it.

God only knows!

Que sera, sera

In a small chamber beside a kovil
near Wanduramba, two men in dhotis,
red waist-sashes, dark-skinned and shifty-eyed,
throw fistfuls of incense on an open fire.
Cross-legged they sit, on a worn mat,
badgering the devas. People stand around
the bamboo altar piled with marigolds
and yellow alamanda and mounds
of jasmine. The men have asked for
six hundred and ninety-one rupees
to block the evil that will come upon
the headman. Great trial,
loss and bereavement of a loved one
is his lot – or so the astrologer had said.
Now the gods of the nearest heaven
must be summoned, told to counter
this fate that surely awaits him.
No one is there to point out that destiny
is a finished act, fixed and static;
that past, present, future
cannot be changed; that what is, is,
what will be, will be. Some say the universe
is in flux, that the act of creation
continues eternally, that what is, is becoming,
what may be, may be. Then, is the future
not fact but potential?
The ceremony continues, shadows
tossed by firelight against the faces
of they who watch. The men chant

of a constantly changing fate, its tendencies
and possibilities changed for the benefit
of the headman and his
six hundred and ninety-one rupees.
When it is over, when the headman
is draped in a dirty white cloth,
the men proclaim their triumph.
The fire burns itself out, the wind
moves the red curtain, puffs at the ashes.
The headman sleeps easy, confident
that the bad time will not come.

R. MURUGAIYAN
(1935–2009)

R. Murugaiyan was born in Chavakachcheri, Jaffna, and was one of the pioneers
of modern Tamil poetry in Sri Lanka. He had a masters degree in both the arts
and the sciences and worked in education throughout his life. He was Regional
Director of Education, Deputy Registrar of the University of Jaffna and was
an editor in the Educational Publications Department of the Government of
Sri Lanka. Murugaiyan began writing poetry in the 1950s and had published
over twenty publications by the end of his life. He was also a critic, a playwright
and a translator of Tamil poetry into English. A hugely influential figure,
Murugaiyan wrote highly intellectual poems which were Marxist in outlook;
his poetry championed the voiceless and the downtrodden.

Variations

Great grandfather opens
his toothless mouth
to tell them tales
of ghosts and demons:
hundreds of them
from his repertoire;
the tiny children
sitting around him
amazed and absorbed,
their toothless mouths
wide open
cherish the words.

He tells stories about ghosts
spitting embers of coal,
wandering in deserted spaces,
particularly on Fridays and Tuesdays.

He tells of the demon
climbing a tamarind tree
caught by Small Uncle, who
lived beside the huge jack tree;
he nailed the demon
by the scruff of its neck
making it captive.

Having been nailed
the demon now
sucks people's blood and sleeps
in regions full of shrubs.

Great grandfather knew
lots of strange stories,
the children never
tired of listening.

In time
the children grew up;
in their thoughts
the devils
now appeared sporadically.

The children, now adolescent,
pondered over the stories
and wondered:
maybe the ghosts, devils, and demons
have deserted our area
since the coming of electric street lamps.

The youth now thought
along such lines.

But one thing remains:
there are strange presences
haunting our land,
roaming at random

during day and night;
in the dark
and in broad daylight too.
Of course,
there are variations.

[tr. from Tamil by the poet)

Toil

In its grandeur
the chariot shines
reaching
towards the blue sky.

The bulls below, yoked to the chariot,
exhausted, panting
foaming at the mouth;
the chariot moves as the animals pull.

The glittering wooden horses
prominent above
frozen in galloping postures;
people do not see
the beasts below.

[tr. from Tamil by the poet]

Aboard a Van

Let's all
board a van
and be off.
Come, let's
attend the meeting
in the van
hired by the candidate himself.

He, an independent!
Does it matter?
He's shrewd and eloquent.
Even though defeated
he never was disheartened,
this hero.
Cars, Oh, how many?
The meeting place
a carnival ground
with a multitude
of earth-shaking jolting
vans of various sorts.
– Why does he stop midway?
Annai! Thamby! Ayah!
Away with questions, answers!
Here's coffee
drink it –
here, the snacks
– ah, that's what I thought!
Superb coffee.
– Board the van!
Let's proceed.
– See him straining?
He distorts –
with thundering effect.
He spews
words that come readily.
He screams.
His speech fiery
his bearing majestic
we could do nothing
but consent to vote for him.
Can we forget
this eminence's coffee and snacks?
– How was the meeting?
– A sea of heads.
What did they say?
– Something.
Think, vote
for anyone you like.
No one will ever know.

[tr. from Tamil by S. Rajasingham]

NEELAAVANAN
(1931–75)

Neelaavanan was one of the several pen names of K. Sinadurai, who was born in the village of Periya Neelaavanai in the Eastern Province, Sri Lanka. He was a teacher and of the generation of Tamil poets (alongside Mahakavi and Murugaiyan) whose work changed the literary landscape of Tamil Sri Lanka. He wrote two epics, plays in verse and short stories alongside his poems. He edited a short-lived literary journal called *Paadu Meen* and was president of the Writers Association of Eastern Sri Lanka; he cultivated a vibrant and supportive literary community in Batticaloa. Widely published in magazines and journals, a posthumous collection of poems was published in 1976 (*Vali*) and a collected edition of his short stories in 2001. Neelaavanan mined his surroundings for material, recording the lifestyle, rituals and customs of the people of Batticaloa.

Sleep

During the few hours
I happened to live in this world,
not even the smallest creature
because of my vile deeds
suffered;
this sweet assurance,
an elegant lullaby
that warms my heart

In that glow,
a little milk,
mixed with fruit;
I stretch my limbs, a blanket
covering me.

When, having surrendered myself
to that lullaby
I forget myself in sleep,
do not wail
or gather my friends.

I know well enough
what happens thereafter,
so, do you not try to wake me;
try to understand,
shut our doors

let not the drums
disturb my slumber;
do not dissemble with dirges;
I need no white cloth
for my long journey,
no guarded utterance
no eulogy.

Reach down if you will
into your silence,
draw from the depth of your heart
the hazy outline
of my feeble portrait
complete my image
in the pupils of your eyes;
light the lamp
and in the cradle
sing my story.

Later, with nature
laugh at death with derision.

[tr. from Tamil by R. Murugaiyan]

Murungaikaai

At the end of a long day
a poem hovered, promisingly.
I made a coffee and opened my notebook.
Then she called me. 'What is it?' I said.

'I bought some prawns for our curry
juicy as ripe tamarind.
But they really do need
murungaikaai to make them delicious.

'You know the tree by the entrance?
Right at the top hang
one, two, maybe three long, juicy
murungaikkaais.

'It's not too high.
You could reach it
standing on one leg.
Go, please, and gather some
for our curry.'

I could have refused.
But that would have curtailed
the promise of these nights.
So I complied.

I climbed the murungai tree
as she wished, but alas
broke it, and fell to the ground.

And the poem that had been hovering?
It disappeared somewhere within this bed.

[tr. from Tamil by Shash Trevett]

Faster, Faster

Faster, my dear driver, faster,
let's head for the new town
Before night falls.
     Faster, my dear, faster.

Love-drenched songs
resound in grove, field and flower.
Let's be done with journeying.
     Faster, my dear, faster.

Before the dew-tears' mournful curtain
glooms the path
before the sick moon's shadow dogs us,
     Faster, my dear, faster.

[tr. from Tamil by A.J. Canagaratna]

NILLANTHAN

(*b.* 1970)

Nillanthan lives and works in Jaffna. He is a poet, an artist and a political analyst, writing for various newspapers across Sri Lanka since 1990. He has published five collections of poetry in Tamil and his artwork ('Bunker Family Series', 'Ravana' and 'Pillaiyar: War Portraits') has been exhibited widely across the sub-continent. Nillanthan was a witness to the final days of the civil war in Sri Lanka: 'I am a product of war as well as the witness of war,' he has said, and his poetry is a lyrical dilution of horror through the examination of the ordinary. He interweaves memories of place, displacement and food, drawing on myth, folktales and legend, to juxtapose a historical past onto a dangerous present. The poems included here draw on his experiences during the final days of the civil war in 2009.

The End of an Age 2

They ran out of biscuits at Thevipuram
and coconuts at Ananthapuram.
From Valayanmadam onwards
there were no more green chillies or onions,
no more tamarind.
The coffins ran out at Irattaivaikal.
The morning they capitulated
they drank water squeezed from mud
and with three days grime on their faces
witnessed an age come to an end.

[tr. from Tamil by Geetha Sukumaran and Shash Trevett]

Kanji Song 1

In a village which had chopped its bullock carts
to make firewood, there was fire
but there was no cooking hearth.

On a shore thick with a thousand coconut
and palm trees, there was kanji
but there was no milk.

241

In the neithal land where one walked
by avoiding shit and corpses
there was the sea and boats on the sea
but there was no fish.

In a village which cooked every green leaf
except the banyan, the ironwood and the palm
there was kanji, there was vaipan
but there was no hunger.

In the final three days of a war that began
on water and ended by a lagoon
there was no water
but there was thirst.

[tr. from Tamil by Geetha Sukumaran and Shash Trevett]

The Mother of Two Martyrs

Before she was consigned to the slaughterhouse
this mother lived in a hell called
the security zone. In that particular hell
she kept her eldest child hidden
in the dark space beneath the cooking fire.
Yet, the motherland enticed this child away
until she was left with nothing
but a photograph. Her middle child,
while buying a candle of remembrance,
was then conscripted by the motherland.
On the day she escaped to that lagoon
with her youngest child,
was this mother shot in the face
or in the back?

[tr. from Tamil by Geetha Sukumaran and Shash Trevett]

Pina Koorai

The koorai is woven with textured meaning.
Bought after a careful search
it is patterned with joyful memories.
A prized possession
kept locked in a box of dreams.

At the end of this age
nothing remains which is sacred.
In three villages, the koorai sari
is now worth less than PP bags.

In a life surrounded by sandbags
where polypropylene is prized above treasure,
we use koorai saris to make sandbags.

We make screens out of them
we spread them on the ground
we wrap ourselves in them
we use them to make roofs.

The koorai make the most beautiful sandbags
but they have lost their meaning,
much like those used to shroud corpses.

Smoke covered the land when Ban Ki-moon
saw these sari-woven death slums
from the air.

Yet the threads of gold glittered
in the sun.

[tr. from Tamil by Geetha Sukumaran and Shash Trevett]

The koorai is the wedding sari, richly embellished with gold embroidery. Pina koorai is the practice of shrouding the body of a dead husband or wife in it.

PP Bags were in great demand at the end of the war in 2009. Being flame retardant, they were used to create makeshift sandbags by people herded onto beaches around Mullaitivu.

S. NIROSHINI

(*b*. 1984)

S. Niroshini is a writer of poetry, fiction and essays. Her writing centres stories of girlhood, trauma and the histories of Tamil women. She received a London Writers Award in the literary fiction category and won third place in the *Poetry London* Prize 2020 for her epistolary sequence 'Letters to Sunny Leone'. Her poetry pamphlet *Darling Girl* (Bad Betty Press) was released in 2021. Published widely, she is also a Ledbury Poetry Critic and writes the newsletter *phototaxis*.

Born in Sri Lanka to a family of South Indian Tamil origin – later she moved to Australia, and now lives in London – she studied law, history and Sanskrit at university, working as a solicitor before starting to write. Her work is influenced by A.K. Ramanujan, Toni Morrison, Anne Carson, Lucille Clifton, M. NourbeSe Philip, Saidiya Hartman and Arun Kolatkar; she also draws on photographic history and visual culture as well as Tamil and Sanskrit epic literature.

Neruda's Last Word(s)

to the woman who collected his shit

it was the dutiful ceremony of an indifferent queen

an ignoble routine never repeated she was right   to despise me

the most beautiful woman yet seen in Ceylon

completely unresponsive it was the coming together

of a man and a statute her eyes wide open all the while

tiny red dots   so very slim soon naked in my bed

she was another kind of existence a shy jungle animal a piece of silk

with the steps of a goddess strong grip on her wrist

stared into her eyes dark beauty solemnly toward the latrine

one morning no language I decided to go all the way

This poem uses language in its entirety from Pablo Neruda's *Memoirs* (1977).

Period Party / புண்ணியதானம்

a *big girl* now / fathers and mothers
rush / to tell the news to uncles and aunties
of her bloodletting / stories of a daughter's body travel fast /
otherwise unaccommodated /

*

I've been wanting to write a poem about the ritual
ceremony that girls in my Tamil community are often
made to participate in when they get their first period.
I'd been unable to write that poem, afraid to confront
the shame I still experienced in my own body. I was
naively optimistic that such things were no longer being
practised. Earlier this year however, I received an
invitation to attend the puberty ceremony of the child
of a family friend.

*

her skin is soft buttermilk / breasts
tender from the effort of first growth / walking
with hunched shoulders, nipples protruding / pink lace lines
her first bra / the brown stain on her cream nightie / changes
everything / nothing / she still watches *Neighbours* on
Saturday mornings / but doesn't want to hold her mumma's
hand any more / she tiptoes the aisles of supermarkets to buy
sanitary napkins / new emotional consciousness arrests her /
the false bravado of thirteen year old girls learning about
childbirth and sexual education / the physical response to the
sound of *men* and *rape*.

*

If you search 'period party' on Google, you enter the world of professional puberty celebration planning. This is particularly popular in parts of the world where there is a concentration of Tamil people, like South India, Germany, France and England. There are YouTube videos where girls of eleven, twelve, thirteen years of age are taken through a ceremony which resembles a wedding. Can a girl of twelve consent to the announcement of her period? It is confusing for me that some girls say they look forward to experiencing the ceremony. The ritual has its roots in a time when a girl's first period would mark the sign of the beginning of her sexual life and availability for marriage. If you look closely at the girls' smiling faces in the videos, it is like watching a strange mime.

*

the girl / the girl bleeds / the girl bleeds over and over / you live to see this girl bleed over and over / yet, she lives.

Girl, Ceylon

Albumen silver print photograph
Julia Margaret Cameron, 1875–79

I

Everything begins with a kiss   at the plantation   and then a disrobing

  she is sticky   in the hands   of a white woman   who lays claim to her body

    her body   dressed in pearls   like a lady   worked to bone   like a man like the sons

      who put her   to bed each night   who whisper words   of the good lord

        lord   they took her   on a dirt floor   exposed her cracked   feet

II

You asked me to write a poem about the history of indenture.

III

I am nine   and run in the wayward garden

I am nine   and pluck plumeria from undergrowth

I am nine   and catch butterflies in small boxes

I am nine   and my feet trip on swimmer crabs

I am nine   and my body is learning how to contort

I am nine   and my skin is beginning to absorb light

I am nine   and my eyes carry

all   the   water   in   the   ocean

IV

Who cared for the body of a little brown girl in the nineteenth century?
Who cares for the body of a little brown girl in the century in which I live?

V

Albumen print, a photographic process from the nineteenth century, was developed in 1850 by Louis Blanquart-Evrard. It involved coating a mixture of egg-white and ammonium chloride on paper sensitised with silver nitrate. Toned with gold chloride, it gave the photographs a sepia hue. The troublesome weather in Ceylon however caused many problems for European photographers who relied on this process as the surface was gooey and attracted the attention of insects.

VI

I think of the photograph when I'm at the doctor's clinic. The nurse,
a young woman with strawberry-blonde hair, inserts the speculum.

I see the face of my grandmother or her mother in the face of this girl.

VII

Daughter, let us play hide and seek

one last time:

one	*run run* as fast as you can
two	lift your frock to avoid dirt on its fringes
three	don't trip on the roots of the rubber trees
four	can you smell it? the ocean is not so far now
five	notice the light beyond the horizon
six	no one can tell you're just a girl
seven	you've made it! you've made it!
eight	strip off your dress, over your shoulders
nine	don't look back there is no time
ten	see the water and submerge

'Girl, Ceylon' derives its title from the photograph of the same name by
Julia Margaret Cameron. Reference was made to Julian Cox and Colin Ford,
Julia Margaret Cameron: Complete Photographs, 2002, Getty Publications,
for details about the albumen photographic process.

M.A. NUHMAN
(*b.* 1944)

M.A. Nuhman was born in Kalmunai, Eastern Province. He is one of the giants
of Tamil literature in Sri Lanka; a poet, editor, and translator, he was Professor
of Tamil at the University of Peradeniya until his retirement in 2009. He has
published over thirty works including several collections of poetry and works
of literary criticism. He was editor of the poetry journal *Kavignan*, and his
translations of Palestinian poets into Tamil has been hugely influential on
younger Tamil poets. Along with A. Jesurasa he edited and published the
groundbreaking *Pathinoru Eelaththuk Kavignarkal* (1984) and with Ranjani
Obeyesekere and Ashley Halpé produced *A Lankan Mosaic*, a book of English
translations of Sinhala and Tamil short stories (2003). His long poem 'Saluting
Heroic Vietnam' (written in 1975) is an extraordinary historical document.
Although there are several poems in this anthology written before the civil war
began, this is the only poem which, looking abroad with empathy for war's
victims, seems to anticipate the arrival of such violence in the poet's own country.

from Saluting Heroic Vietnam from the Silent Corners of Our Little Village

1

In a village library
I read this morning's news:
the war is over.

I came out,
saw heads bobbing
in passing vehicles.
Somebody stopped the bus, got in.
At the corner teashop,
somebody whisks the tea, metal on metal,
into a froth.
In the distance, but not far,
the sound of little boys playing kitti.
The fisherman, shouting out his wares,
disappears round that bend,
peddling on.
It is quiet in my village

Our village has not seen a war.
We have not seen bombs pierce
our land; we have not seen
craters burst open in the earth.
We have seen only crows fly in the air,
not bomb-dropping aircraft.
The growling armoured tank
the roar of the cannon,
are sounds we never heard.
War or peace, they are mere
snippets of news from elsewhere.

2

Heroic people
of the land of the far east,
where the earth awakes from its slumber,
your daily bath in flowing blood
we have not seen, or felt.
Babies die, their infant lips,
circling at their mother's breast,

blown apart by bombs.
We have not seen these sights.

In gardens and fields,
in the gaps in broken walls of the houses,
in the cracks on school desks,
under hospital roofs,
in worship places,
in the dust of the street,
bits of flesh, hang,
blown apart.
We have not seen anything like that
in our village.

Elderly bodies are burnt
to cinders in burning huts,
in the putt-putt-putt of machine guns.
We have not seen any of this,
this murderous dance of death.

It's quiet in our village.

(1975)

[tr. from Tamil by Sumathy Sivamohan]

Last Evening, This Morning

1

Last evening
we were here – just here

Through the crowded Jaffna streets
teeming with traffic
we wound our way, wheeling our bikes

We stopped for a while
at Poobalasingham Book Depot
riffling through the magazines

We gazed at the crowds
thronging at the bus-stand –
so many faces
so many colours
coming and going
climbing in, getting off,
going about their business

We strolled past the market
past the statue of Tiruvalluvar
went as far as the Post Office Junction
breathed some fresh air at Pannai

Just next to the Regal
at the tea-stall there
we drank tea, smoked cigarettes
We went in and watched a movie –
Jack London's *Call of the Wild*.

Then we rode our bikes home,
the wind ruffling our hair.

2

This morning dawns:
along the streets we walked
khaki-clad men patrol, guns held aloft
bullets rain
piercing bodies
drinking up lives

The bus stand is dead
the town has lost the smell of human beings
shops, gutted, lie smoking
the old market-place is shattered
on every street there are charred, blackened tyres

And this is how
we lost our evenings
we lost this life.

[tr. from Tamil by Lakshmi Holmström]

Buddha Murdered

In my dream, last night,
Lord Buddha lay, shot dead.
Government police in civilian clothes
shot and killed him.
He lay upon the steps
of the Jaffna Library,
drenched in his own blood.

In the darkness of the night
the ministers arrived, raging:
'His name wasn't on our list.
So why did you kill him?'

'No, sirs,' they said,
'No mistake was made. Only,
without killing him, it wasn't possible
to shoot even a fly.
So...'

'OK. OK. But
get rid of the corpse at once,'
the ministers said, and vanished.

The plain-clothes men
dragged the corpse inside
and heaped upon it
ninety thousand rare books
and lit the pyre with the *Sikalokavada Sutta*.

So the Lord Buddha's body turned to ashes
and so did the *Dhammapada*.

[tr. from Tamil by Lakshmi Holmström]

MICHAEL ONDAATJE

(*b*. 1943)

Michael Ondaatje is best-known as an author of fiction. *The English Patient* won the 1992 Booker Prize and the 2018 Golden Man Booker, and was made into an Oscar-winning film; *Anil's Ghost* (2000), addressing Sri Lanka's deep history as well as its war-torn present, was awarded both Canada's Governor General's Award and the Giller Prize. But Ondaatje – who is of Burgher descent – is also an essayist, editor, memoirist (*Running in the Family*, about his return to Sri Lanka, and his father, appeared in 1982) and a poet. Indeed his first book, *The Dainty Monsters* (1967) was a poetry collection, and his others include *Handwriting* (1998), which fuses memories of Sri Lanka with pieces of history and myth. His poetry is a multi-aspectual sprinkle of perceptions; he layers one perspective on another, and punctuation tends to disappear as we leap between startlingly concrete images. Besides his many literary awards, Ondaatje is also an Officer of the Order of Canada.

Letters & Other Worlds

'for there was no more darkness for him and, no doubt like Adam before the fall, he could see in the dark'

My father's body was a globe of fear
His body was a town we never knew
He hid that he had been where we were going
His letters were a room he seldom lived in
In them the logic of his love could grow

My father's body was a town of fear
He was the only witness to its fear dance
He hid where he had been that we might lose him
His letters were a room his body scared

He came to death with his mind drowning.
On the last day he enclosed himself
in a room with two bottles of gin, later
fell the length of his body
so that brain blood moved
to new compartments
that never knew the wash of fluid
and he died in minutes of a new equilibrium.

His early life was a terrifying comedy
and my mother divorced him again and again.
He would rush into tunnels magnetised
by the white eye of trains
and once, gaining instant fame,
managed to stop a Perahara in Ceylon
– the whole procession of elephants dancers
local dignitaries – by falling
dead drunk onto the street.

As a semi-official, and semi-white at that,
the act was seen as a crucial
turning point in the Home Rule Movement
and led to Ceylon's independence in 1948.

(My mother had done her share too –
her driving so bad
she was stoned by villagers
whenever her car was recognised)

For 14 years of marriage
each of them claimed he or she
was the injured party.
Once on the Colombo docks
Saying goodbye to a recently married couple
my father, jealous
at my mother's articulate emotion,
dove into the waters of the harbour
and swam after the ship waving farewell.
My mother pretending no affiliation
mingled with the crowd back to the hotel.

Once again he made the papers
though this time my mother
with a note to the editor
corrected the report – saying he was drunk
rather than broken hearted at the parting of friends.
The married couple received both editions
of *The Ceylon Times* when their ship reached Aden.

And then in his last years
he was the silent drinker,
the one who once a week

disappeared into his room with bottles
and stayed there until he was drunk
and until he was sober.

There speeches, head dreams, apologies,
the gentle letters, were composed.
With the clarity of architects
he would write of the row of blue flowers
his new wife had planted,
the plans for electricity in the house,
how my half-sister fell near a snake
and it had awakened and not touched her.
Letters in a clear hand of the most complete empathy
his heart widening and widening and widening
to all manner of change in his children and friends
while he himself edged
into the terrible acute hatred
of his own privacy
till he balanced and fell
the length of his body
the blood entering
the empty reservoir of bones
the blood searching in his head without metaphor.

The Cinnamon Peeler

If I were a cinnamon peeler
I would ride your bed
and leave the yellow bark dust
on your pillow.

Your breasts and shoulders would reek
you could never walk through markets
without the profession of my fingers
floating over you. The blind would
stumble certain of whom they approached
though you might bathe
under rain gutters, monsoon.

Here on the upper thigh
at this smooth pasture
neighbour to your hair
or the crease
that cuts your back. This ankle.
You will be known among strangers
as the cinnamon peeler's wife.

I could hardly glance at you
before marriage
never touch you
– your keen-nosed mother, your rough brothers.
I buried my hands
in saffron, disguised them
over smoking tar,
helped the honey gatherers...

When we swam once
I touched you in water
and our bodies remained free,
you could hold me and be blind of smell.
You climbed the bank and said

                this is how you touch other women
the grass cutter's wife, the lime burner's daughter.
And you searched your arms
for the missing perfume

                and knew

                what good is it
to be the lime burner's daughter
left with no trace
as if not spoken to in the act of love
as if wounded without the pleasure of a scar.

You touched
your belly to my hands
in the dry air and said
I am the cinnamon
peeler's wife. Smell me.

House on a Red Cliff

There is no mirror in Mirissa

the sea is in the leaves
the waves are in the palms

old languages in the arms
of the casuarina pine
parampara

parampara, from
generation to generation

The flamboyant a grandfather planted
having lived through fire
lifts itself over the roof

unframed

the house an open net

where the night concentrates
on a breath
            on a step
a thing or gesture
we cannot be attached to

The long, the short, the difficult minutes
of night

where even in darkness
there is no horizon without a tree

just a boat's light in the leaves

Last footstep before formlessness

S. PATHMANATHAN

(b. 1939)

Somasuntharampillai Pathmanathan, also known as 'Sopa', has been a stalwart of the Tamil literary scene of Sri Lanka for a very long time. He is both a poet and a translator of Tamil poems that have appeared in the *Journal of South Asian Literature* (1987), *Penguin New Writing in Sri Lanka* (1992), *Lute-song and Lament* (2001), *A Lankan Mosaic* (2002), *Mirrored Images* (2013) and *Uprooting the Pumpkin* (2016). He has won three State Literary Awards, five Provincial Awards and the Governor's Award. He has translated Sinhala poetry into Tamil, his own work has been translated into Sinhala and he was part of the Goethe Institute's 'Poets Translating Poets' in 2016. Sopa has three books of translations forthcoming, working between Tamil, Telugu and Malayalam.

See Through

Look at the range of handbags!
symbols of fashion!
some can be classed
'see-through'
no need to open them
ICs and passes are visible
you can pass through
check-points without delay

Shouldn't we wear
see-through clothes as well
to facilitate a passage
through check-points?
Our pockets will reveal
tickets and tags

There won't be any
groping or probing
patting or petting
searching or trespass
into my person!

Like see-through bags
and see-through clothes
if we are blessed
with see-through hearts

how grand would it be!
If your hearts have nothing to hide
won't it mean the end of all falsity
deception and hypocrisy?
or
will man
shamed by his 'nakedness'
hide himself
like Adam and Eve?

[tr. from Tamil by the poet)

A Thorn in My Flesh

Manonmani akka
was our neighbour
a diminutive woman
fond of children
She was childless

I used to marvel
how she observed
the skantha sashti fast
without solid food
for six days!

Mano akka had been stung
by a venomous scorpion
The native physician
had prescribed urine
(simple you might think, not quite!)

'Urine of a child
who had not lost
his milk teeth!'
I answered that specification
Mano akka, mug in hand
was after me
'Rasa, like a good boy pee into this!'
I was a very, very shy boy of seven

I started running around the house
Mano akka begging me
for the miracle medicine.
I didn't relent

When childhood memories
swell within me
the urine incident irks me
like a thorn in my flesh

[tr. from Tamil by the poet]

VIHANGA PERERA

(*b.* 1984)

Vihanga Perera is a poet and novelist from Kandy, Sri Lanka, who is also a
commentator and literary critic. Perera has published four collections of poetry
including the 2014 Gratiaen Prize-winning *Love and Protest*. His poems and
stories have been featured in numerous international platforms and are taught
in universities in Sri Lanka and India.

The Playwright

As they say: is there some suburban avenue
That I will not tread just to win your favour?
Will I lock horns with a cart-bull and bray like an ass
If that makes your temper any much the wiser?
Most probably I will. Not that, in life and in love,
I haven't had my kill. But, I will.

On the second day, the bread is hard,
Love is harder:
How to maintain what with effort was got?
Would s/he bat an eyelid at a bastard?
Trip over the paint? In spite of the Beach Boys' singing
Send out all the wrong vibrations?

There it begins. You hear the curious sound
Of wings flapping out the
Back door of your memory floor:
That is the unmapped path through which the once frostbite
Romance will go.
Knowing all these would come to pass, I yearn for more.

And with an undying chalk/choke, on a hopeful wall,
I cross out the number of times you
Touched my heart.
In your life's great romance you are the playwright
Of that suspenseful script. In the line next after
I should be kissed. Or whipped.

The Memory of Fragrance

The wood which makes my coffin will
Remember my fragrance
– But you wouldn't –
For you will remember only my final minute,
A moment in which I am all but gone,
And already you would have lost me
Among other real complications,

And then, I would be buried
On my own.

KASRO PONNUTHURAI
(b. 1995)

An emerging talent, Kasro Ponnuthurai writes in Tamil. He was born and lives
in Jaffna, in the north of Sri Lanka. His work has been published in local
newspapers and magazines, as well as online and he is influenced both by the
landscapes of P. Ahilan and the feminist writings of Indian Tamil academic
Perundevi. A queer artist and activist, Kasro is interested in fostering networks
between poets and artists and founded the Jaffna Queer Festival, an annual
festival featuring queer excellence in creative and cultural sectors.

Amir's Lover

Amir,
It has been
A week today
Since I last saw you.

A crow
Has been cawing
For three days now
On the branch
Of a plumeria
In the backyard.

Last Sunday
As I returned home
After Salat
My neighbour Fathima's
Fighting rooster
Its eyes reddened
Lay dead
Beneath that same tree.

'An evil omen'
Anar had said…

*

A stretch of sea
Beside the Kabristan.

An octopus
Removed
From the push and pull of the estuary
Clings tightly
To a slippery
Moss-covered rock
With its purple tentacles.

Amir,

We withdrew
From the core

Of this crushing life
And clung to love.

Yes,
We are
Deviants.

*

The way Anar gazed
At Saleem
When he boarded his boat.

The way Mulla gazed
When she saw
Her first menstrual blood
Stain her hands.

Amir,

What more can you expect
Of a man, in the first
Moment of knowing love,
Except to gaze at
You?

*

Every grain of sand
On this Kabristan beach
Is cursed
By the tears
Anar shed
As she spread the salted fish
To dry
Thinking of Saleem.

One after another
Every wave
Tries
To wash it away
And cannot.

Amir,
This
Is a cursed shore
Just like our love…

*

I have never seen
On these Kabristan shores
The red-legged
Flamingos
That fly
From the Caribbean
To the southern lands.

When they told me
Saleem's eldest son
Abdullah
Saw a pair of flamingos
Perched on Rasul's boat
And that in awe
He called them 'birds of the sun'
It was only you
Who pervaded
My soul.

Amir,

I thought
Of our dream
To see the doves
Of Bombay's suburbs
Through the window
In your room.

Yes,
This sea
This sky
These birds
None of them are meant for us…

[tr. from Tamil by Nedra Rodrigo]

S. PORAWAGAMAGE

(*b.* 1993)

Introduced to the socially and politically conscious world of poetry by the monthly gatherings of Poetry P'lau, Samodh Porawagamage's poems deal with the 2004 tsunami, the civil war, poverty, colonialism, and Sri Lankan history, among other things. These poems are from his manuscript *Becoming Sam*, a political bildungsroman in poetry. Writers such as Jean Arasanayagam, Bertolt Brecht, Richard de Zoysa, Rita Dove, John Keats, Philip Larkin, Karl Marx, Philip Metres and Lakdhas Wikkramasinha haunt his work, some of which has appeared in *Annasi & Kadalagotu*, *Ceylon Daily News*, *Mantis*, *Stoneboat*, and *The Sunday Observer*.

My Kinda Name

It's February. Too lazy to cook, I've ordered
Free Delivery! App pings and he knocks.

The poor guy's in a parka. Two feet away,
I can't see his face. The food's steaming.

He's just made my day. 'Sorry, I'm a few minutes
behind,' he says. 'The roads are crazy with snow.

I saw four accidents today.' He tries
my name on the bag: 'Jeez! Zamudd, Sha-

mouth, Chamoth, no, Saa-mutt, right?
Haha! See, I can. But dude, seriously!

where in hell… what kinda name is that?'
'It's a Vedic mantra the ancients chanted

for rain, but also means I'm the king,
can lead well, or be vicious: "it's actually

a Fuck-off kinda name." Thanks anyway
for asking.' Then I take the food.

Step inside and lock the door.
Skip rating the service. Tip ten dollars.

The Wings

Nobody comes here to be alone.
Some birds kept watch, but they
too have flown away for the winter.

I lie on the grass, aim my Celestrons
at the sky. Nothing moves. The world
is no longer alive. Campus police

drives by. She waves. She's used to
seeing me here. I move under a tree,
prick my nose to a smell so familiar:

torture and blood: under a thick bush,
a pair of wings strewn from each other.
The grass has perked up with dry blood.

The claws are curved into a ball as if
they grabbed the air against the pain.
The feathers are intact, not a speck of blood.

I want to bring the remains home, give
a proper burial or let them display his pride
well after death. Campus police kneels beside me.

The wind picks up. The wings sway to fly,
but the claws keep them grounded.
We reflect on the precision of violence.

The First Name

What is drawn in water
doesn't survive

the full circle of a letter
with a stick.

What we draw
on the beach in evenings

doesn't last
the next day's light.

When the wave
came too far into the land

it only left
names with us:

My cousin couldn't make it
to seventh grade,

his name was the first
in the register.

The teacher called *Sapurnal* –
once every morning,

it bounced off a wave
onto the wall and fell

on us like
an absent funeral.

We bent our heads
and breathed deep.

One day I stole
a glance at the book

and saw him
marked ✓ for every day.

PRAMIL
(1939–97)

Pramil was one of the pen names (he derived them from numerology and astrology) of Tharmu Sivaram, who was born in Trincomalee in Eastern Sri Lanka. He left Sri Lanka to move to Tamil Nadu, India, in 1975. Pramil's poems are tightly crafted, minimalist and symbolist in nature; he is considered one of the finest imagist poets in Tamil (earning him the title 'Padimak Kavignar'). He was also a critic, wrote plays and short stories, was a talented artist and sculptor, and translated several English works into Tamil. Pramil believed in a unified Sri Lanka with an intermingling of both Sinhala and Tamil cultures and traditions. His work remains relevant and popular even after his death, with 21 posthumous collected editions published to date.

The Desert

This vast stretch of sand
Golden in all directions
Is a soothing view, but
Burning underfoot
And ever on the move
Is a fistful of desert
In search of a shade.

[tr. from Tamil by the poet]

(your) Name

Looking to swallow
its own head
a deranged word
slipped into me

The Name began a slow
invasion.
Trembling, my heart
wrenched away.
The Name backed down
I looked up, relieved…

Having crashed on the moon, the Name echoes.

Today, your relentless name
pours down from the crescent
makes my blood surge.

[tr. from Tamil by Janani Ambikapathy]

The Great Wind Tamer

A seven year old
Tames the wind
With a kite.

[This poem was written in English]

SHIRANI RAJAPAKSE
(*b*. 1967)

Shirani Rajapakse was born in Colombo. She started writing about 15 years
ago, and has published three books of short stories: *Breaking News* (2011), *I
Exist. Therefore I Am* (2018), and *Gods, Nukes and a Whole Lot of Nonsense*
(2021). The last two won State Literary Awards. Her books of poetry are
Chant of a Million Women (2017), which won the Kindle Book Award, *Fallen
Leaves* (2019) and *Samsara* (2022). Rajapakse has also won, or been shortlisted
for, several other awards. She counts Keats, Frost and Dickinson as early
influences and enjoys reading modern American poetry. 'Much of my writing
concentrates on women, conflict, animal rights and the effects of development
on the environment.' She currently lives in Sri Lanka and is the co-ordinator
there for the 'World Poetry Movement'.

Unwanted

You placed me
on a shelf and left me there
to dry. I was forgotten.

Like the old newspaper you
spread on your
writing table to protect
the wood. It turned yellow in time
and you threw it away
one day, not so long ago.
I too have faded.
Would you
throw me out too?

Chant of a Million Women

My body is a temple, not
a halfway house you enter for
temporary shelter from
the heat and dust swirling through trees.
It's not a guest house to book a room, spend
a night on your way to someplace else.
Not a transit lounge
to while away the hours until
your next flight to fantasy seeking
greener pastures.

My body is my temple.

Enter with reverence.

Keep your shoes at the door your
hat on the step. Bring flowers as offering.
Garlands of jasmine wound tight, pink
lotus piled up high on a tray, petals opened,
lips inviting, alluring.

Place oil lamps on the floor.
Let the light guide the way, chase away
shadows trying to hide in gloomy corners.

Burn sweet incense, let the perfume linger
on the air, climb on the tail of a
gust of breeze
and travel unhindered.

Murmur sutras to supplicate.
Sing songs of praise.
Call out my many names amassed
down the ages.
Place those trays of fresh fruit,
succulent, ripe and oozing, at the side.
My body is my own.

Not yours to take
when it pleases you, or
use as collateral in the face
of wars fought for your greed, or zest to own.
Not give to appease the enemy, reward
the brave who sported so valiantly in the
trenches, stinking of blood and gore.

It's not a product.
Not something to bargain, barter for goods
and services, share with friends,
handed around the table,
a bowl of soup, drink your fill,
use and abuse as you please.

Don't adorn me in expensive silks and gold,
and gift to the Gods, or
wrap me up in a shroud,
imprison me, maim my thoughts
that shout to get out.
No religious decree, no social pressure,
you have no right to own.

It's mine and mine alone and you have
no authority to take it away from me.

S. RAJASINGHAM
(*b.* 1927)

S. Rajasingham has taught in Nigeria and has worked as a lecturer in English
at the Technical College in Jaffna, Sri Lanka. He actively promotes English
studies in Jaffna and has translated poetry and fiction from Tamil into English.

Lizards

You African lizards of assorted colours and sizes
descendants of primordial giants
scions of royal lineage
erstwhile masters of the world
decimated almost, dwarfed but not destroyed
you shall inherit the earth
if only you stand up on your legs
instead of lazing on boulders, culverts, walls and whatnot
and scrambling for cover ungainly
into disused holes abused
when biped homo sapiens
you spy.

You don't realise
despite his cockiness
he lacks tenacity
lives forever in fear
his treachery machinations
will sell no more

He will fall
as surely as Adam and Eve
if only
you catch him
flatfooted
unawares.

Then yours the kingdom here on earth.
You'll once more be masters of the world.

[tr. from Tamil by the poet]

T. RAMALINGAM
(1933–2008)

T. Ramalingam was born in Chavakachcheri in Jaffna Province, Sri Lanka. He was a graduate teacher at Meesalai Veerasingam Maha Vidyalam, eventually serving as its Principal until his retirement in 1993. He started writing poetry in the 1960s and his first two collections, *Puthumeik Kavithaigal* (1964) and *Kaanikkai* (1965), were among the earliest collections in modern Tamil poetry in Sri Lanka. He was committed to fighting societal divisions, especially around caste prejudice in Tamil society, and his poems (in common with other writers of his generation) were preoccupied with this.

The Future

Today, in the salons,
the barbers' scissors
enjoy a respite: no more agony;
we shaved our faces
everyday, and
broke our spirits!

Hereafter, youngsters,
let your hair grow free;
rejoice of your own accord.
Mud and mire have gathered
in work;
the single track
we followed
now useless.

As for the classroom,
expositions in white chalk
cover the blackboards –
like charcoal graffiti
on lavatory walls.

Once we played outside
wandering where we pleased;
but kites, having lost their tails,
come hurtling down
with broken strings
tangle among the trees.

Be careful now, our feet are slipping,
all our calculations
proved to be false.
Youngsters, don't you know
those who would lead us to freedom

273

only the teeth they display are
white?

These are times
when the wind blows hard:
do not go into the dark
trusting only your hand-lamps;
If we think it is our fate
to drown in a single downpour;
if we shrivel and remain helpless,
if we crave to marry
with only the gutter to offer
our heirs –
beware, youngsters! –
a whirlwind might arise,
felling tall trees, carrying
the roofs of the houses we inhabit.

Youngsters, don't throw away your energies
but gather together, here.
These are times when the wind blows hard;
do not trust your hand-lamps
do not go out into the darkness.

[tr. from Tamil by Lakshmi Holmström]

ANNE RANASINGHE
(1925–2016)

Fleeing the Holocaust – the only survivor in her Jewish family – Anne Ranasinghe studied in England, worked as a nursing sister, and, marrying a Sinhalese physician and professor, lived in Sri Lanka for over sixty years. She later obtained a diploma in journalism, which helped launch her literary career. Her poetry, interlaced with memoiristic prose, concerns atrocities – she dares bravely to compare the events of Black July, 1983, when Tamil houses and shops were looted and burned, and hundreds killed, with what happened to her own Jewish family. She expresses a saddened knowledge of how tenuous the bonds between different people and their communities always are. 'Well I'm sorry,' she writes, 'I have no answer to your questions. There is injustice, hatred and war / And equality is only a slogan.' Yet her luminous resilience also suggests the work of Eastern European poets like Czesław Miłosz, who do not give up in despair the idea of the poet as a witness and a preserver of vanished histories.

Judgement

I had noted this particular crow
For several days because it looked
More like a caricature than a crow –
Its feathers thin and beak more hooked

For the lack of feathers. And its neck
Extraordinarily elongated, naked, frail
And scraggy. The moth-eaten back
Ended bluntly; there was no tail.

Its eyes seemed larger than the eyes
Of other crows, with an expression
Of wicked intelligence. One had the impression
That in spite of what seemed otherwise

A complete misfit among the choice
Aristocratic crows of our neighbourhood
Here was a chap who counted. – His high voice
Sharp-rasping like a saw on wood

Could easily be recognised.
And watching the other crows – so prim
In their glossy opulence I realised
They were mortally afraid of him.

The afternoon was heavy and still –
I was reading propped high on my pillows
When I heard a tip tipping on the sill
And the eager clicking of hard sprung toes

On tiles and ledges and telephone wire;
The air was full of a fluttering and whirring
Of thousands of crows, their wings black fire
As they pushed and jostled; and nothing else stirring.

Yet in spite of the stillness the air vibrated
With a tensing of claw, of predatory beak. –
Then I saw. On the ground totally isolated
The misfit caricature, a pathetic freak

With ruffled feathers and head tucked low
Flattening into the unopening ground
As if to ward off the expected blow,
When suddenly there was a sound –

The authoritative caw of a veteran crow
And all the others as with common assent
Rose from their perches, and diving low
Converged on the one who was different

With outstretched talons, all ready to tear,
There's a wild confusion of wings in the mud –
Then, in elegant flight they swoop up in the air.
Below – a heap of feathers, a few drops of blood.

At What Dark Point

Every morning I see him
Sitting in the speckled shade
Of my blossom laden araliya tree
Which I planted many years ago
In my garden, and the branches now
Have spread into our lane.
Under my tree in a shadow of silence
He sits, and with long skeletal hands
Sorts strands from a tangle of juten fibres
And twisting twisting twisting makes a rope
That grows. And grows. Each day.

Every morning I pass him. He sits
In the golden-haze brightness under
The white-velvet fragrance of
My tree. Sits
On the edge of his silence twisting
His lengthening rope and
Watching
Me.

And seeing him sit day after day,
Sinister, silent, twisting his rope
To a future purpose of evilness
I sense the charred-wood smell again,
Stained glass exploding in the flames
(A fireworks of fractured glass
Against the black November sky)
The streets deserted, all doors shut
At twelve o'clock at night,
And running with animal fear
Between high houses shuttered tight
The jackboot ringing hard and clear
While stalking with the lust for blood.
I can still hear
The ironed heel – its echoing thud –
And still can taste the cold-winter-taste
Of charred-wood-midnight-fear.
Knowing
That nothing is impossible
That anything is possible
That there is no safety
In words or houses
That boundaries are theoretical
And love is relative
To the choice before you.

I know
That anything is possible
Any time. There is no safety
In poems or music or even in
Philosophy. No safety
In churches or temples
Of any faith. And no one knows
At what dark point the time will come again
Of blood and knives, terror and pain
Of jackboots and the twisted strand
Of rope.
And the impress of a child's small hand
Paroxysmic mark on an oven wall
Scratched death mark on an oven wall
Is my child's hand.

July 1983

I used to wonder
about the Nazi killers,
and those who stood and watched the killing:

does the memory
of so many pleading eyes
stab like lightning through their days and years

and do the voices
of orphaned children
weeping forlornly before dying

haunt their nights?
are their nights sleepless –
has the agony and anguish and

the blood and terror and pain
carved a trail in their brain
saying: I am guilty. Never again...

Forty years later
once more there is burning
the night sky bloodied, violent and abused

and I – though related
only by marriage –
feel myself both victim and accused,

(black-gutted timber
splinters, shards and ashes
blowing in the wind: nothing remains) –

flinch at the thinnest curl of smoke
shrink from the merest thought of fire
while some warm their hands at the flames.

ARIYAWANSA RANAWEERA

(b. 1942)

Ariyawansa Ranaweera is a prolific poet, translator and freelance critic from the south of Sri Lanka, who writes in both Sinhala and English, and is acclaimed for what he can do with what seems ordinary language, and ordinary landscapes. He studied at the University of Peradeniya and at Kelaniya University, and works in public service. He has published more than forty Sinhala books, fifteen of which are poetry, and has won the State Literary Award several times for poetry, poetry translations and translations of prose works; he has also won several other awards for both poetry and drama, and was recently awarded an honorary degree from Sabaragamuwa National University in recognition of his contribution to Sinhala Literature.

Today's Lion

With sword in right hand
Swinging its lordly head
It flutters in the wind
Our logo, the lion-king

*

Maha Vamsa (The Historical Lion)

The forehead of the elephant he splits
The Lion King, the lone wanderer
His mighty roar comforts his own species;
When his kind is in adversity
To save them from calamity he marches forward
Gives leadership at times of tranquillity
He harnessed the waterways
And built great lakes that baffled the ocean
To grow fruits and crops

*

Daughter's Zoology Book

Lazy and sleepy
With his eyes closed day and night
When he sprints a few fathoms fast

He fags out
And abandons his own pride

But runs back to it
To live on the prey
Fetched by the lioness

*

Post-Script

The lion flutters in the wind
Rising now and then
As if to check,
Whether there are historical lions
Left among the lions zoological

[tr. from Sinhala by E.M.G. Edirisinghe]

The Giraffe

With golden stripes
You glitter amongst the rest
Elongated neck reaching up
To the branches atop
The towering trees

But tell me, have you ever tasted
The savoury grass that sparkles with dew
That you crush under your hoof
As you gaze upward

[tr. from Sinhala by E.M.G. Edirisinghe]

Paintings at Gothami Vihara

Siddhartha
Alive again through Keyt's brush
In the Lumbini Sal garden
Renounces the world's pleasures
Disgusted with the golden maidens
And rides out on horse back
Defies the wiles of Mara
Attains enlightenment

All this blossoms
On the long outer wall

Along the corridors
Round the shrine room
Urchins nibble gram
Unconcerned

Inside the shrine room
Running about the place, the young kids
Play hide and seek

The virtuous rub their foreheads
On the floor
Turning their back on the murals

In the sky above
The moon buries itself inside a cloud
In anguish

[tr. from Sinhala by E.M.G. Edirisinghe]

The Intersection

I love that intersection
where one path leads
to a certain little house.

A few dwarf stores
their old plank doors half closed
break the deserted loneliness
and stray dogs
with mouths down on the ground
sleep here and there.

It's just an intersection
with nothing special about it.

Yet
I love
that intersection
with one path leading
to a certain
little house.

[tr. from Sinhala by Liyanage Amarakeerthi]

EVA RANAWEERA
(1924–2010)

Eva Ranaweera was a poet, novelist and journalist (she was the first editor of the newspaper, *Vanitha Viththi*) and wrote in English as well as Sinhala. She studied at the University of Colombo, travelled to Switzerland, Russia, China, India, Vietnam and Egypt, and was a feminist activist. She won three state literary awards and was shortlisted for the Gratiaen Prize several times. Her five books of poetry in English include *What will you do do do Clara what will you do?* (1994), *With Maya* (1997) and *Ending with beginning* (2001).

In the Street of the Pearl Tree

In Shagaret-el-Dor under the Pearl Tree
Who sits and waits for the Mamelukes?
And who comes riding in a golden chariot?
A thousand suns gleam on his head.

Who sits and waits with the fellaheen
Queueing up for American chicken?
The game'eyya overfills and spills onto the
Street of the Pearl Tree.

The golden leaves fall over me
And the waiting is so long.
Who is crying for the broken bags of rice
Scattering the tarmac?
Oh! Shagaret-el Dor who picks your Pearls?
The Pharaohs are passing under the Tree.

Someone dozes in the midday sun.
The little donkey resting by its garbage cart nods and nods.
The zebalin smiles in his dreams.

The leaves pile up and they are dead.
Dead of the yellowed old age.
Agouza the woman wandering by
Mutters, another is waiting like me.

The Pharoah, he rode by yesterday.
Don't you know that today is another day?
Spill the dhall and spill the rice and pour the oil over me.
They fight for subsidised cheese in the game'eyya.
But someone will always wait.

Cairo, 28 November 1982

CHALANI RANWALA

(*b*. 1991)

Chalani Ranwala is a writer, artist and communications specialist based in Colombo. She has published her poems in the *Economic and Political Weekly* (EPW) as well as the collection *No one is listening: A selection of new poetry from Sri Lanka*, curated by the British Council of Sri Lanka. Her first short story, 'Let it be', was shortlisted in the Wachana 'Write & Win' competition and published in 2020. She is a board member at the Lakmahal Community Library in Colombo, a community space built to encourage interest in the literary arts. Ranwala also writes as a communications specialist, publishing on international platforms such as *On Think Tanks* and the LSE Impact Blog.

The in-betweeners

Poured into this painful mould,
its expectations fill me with fear
as I slowly abandon my desire
to escape from this unforgiving
assembly line of rituals.

Sinhala, Buddhist
Sinhala-Buddhist
A hyphen that takes away all
that was meant to be in-between.

Lost is the hope of creating a new path –
the kind that makes others curious.
For sometimes, when we find solitude
in the unknown, it makes us happy.

And then there is the hope
that this is all just a precaution,
a hand that will touch but not push,
follow us from behind
but not lead us from the front.

For we yearn to be in-betweeners
don't we, you and I? To be caught
between two worlds and someday
to tell ourselves that we grew
into our own skin,
made our own mould and thrived in it.

A.M. RASHMY
(*b*. 1974)

A.M. Rashmy was born in Akkaraipattu, Eastern Province, Sri Lanka. He worked as a journalist at the Tamil newspaper, *Sarinigar*, in Colombo between 1995 and 2000, before fleeing the country as a refugee. He has been living in the UK since the mid 2000s. He has published four collections of poetry in Tamil with presses in India, France and Canada, including, *E Thanathu Peyarai Maranthu Ponathu* (2011). English translations of Rashmy's poems have appeared in various journals and anthologies.

Recently Rashmy has been branching out into short fiction, although his forthcoming collection, *Adaivukaalatthin Paadalkal* (2022), contains poems written during the Covid-19 lockdowns; we have chosen three for inclusion here. Influenced by the Tamil poets who preceded him (N. Aatma, Cheran, Jayapalan, Shanmugam Sivalingam, Solaikili), Rashmy is also inspired by poetry from Palestine (translated into Tamil by M.A. Nuhman) as well as Pablo Neruda. An artist as well as a poet (Rashmy has designed the covers of numerous Tamil, Sinhala and Malayalam books), he delights in experimenting with form when writing poems of love, longing, separation, war and life.

from Songs in a Time of Confinement

1

On the second floor, a full-length window
Beyond the window, three rows of trees
In the trees, an effusion of leaves
More than leaves an abundance of flowers
Flowers scattered, spread, and beyond, a stretch of pasture
In the pasture, the creeping, rising day
The day turns, from there it retreats
As it retreats, a cool spread of breeze
In the breeze a shedding, dying summer
Summer unfelt in the passage of a lost day
What day, what week, an oblivious wasted season
The season ends and trees shed
Where they shed, they begin to leaf
Leaves bud at the threshold, and still the birds…

2

It takes the span of a hundred days
For a tender green to appear on the bare branches –
Between two shades of green two hundred
And a hundred hundred hundred times the sun must rise
That the shades of green, sapling – dense – dark may unfurl.

It takes a thousand nights
Between the eruption of the branch
And the emergence of the season's first flower –

The waiting of a thousand nights
Between a beginning in purple or in pink
And an ending in a shade of lilac.

No magic
Happens within a single day.
No era
Is contained within a single flower.

3

Within his poem –
He discovered the root of the forest
He knew the wellspring that erupted into an ocean
He spoke of the four pillars that held up the skies
He revealed the core where mountains swelled
He unearthed the skull
Thought to belong to Adam
He planted the remains of the ancient apple
He tested the alchemical combinations of fire
He learned that women like
A surprise kiss on the nape
Seeking to escape death, he hid –

Death
Was there before him

[tr. from Tamil by Nedra Rodrigo]

SAHANIKA RATNAYAKE

(*b.* 1989)

Sahanika Ratnayake was born in Colombo. Her family emigrated to New Zealand during the immigration boom of the late 90s. 'In many ways, it was an idyllic place to grow up. Then they did something very strange for migrants – they went back.' The family lived in Sri Lanka for a few years during the civil war until they moved to Australia. She eventually emigrated to the UK to do postgraduate study and has remained there. Her writing is memoiristic and driven by an attempt to 'meld and interrogate this mishmash of identities, and the sense migrants have of being from manywhere and nowhere at once, particularly when you are not entirely a creature of the west'. She researches mental health: 'The obsession of my work is the increasingly clinical language we use to describe our personal experience.' Her poems have appeared primarily in Australasian journals and she has also written for *Aeon*, *Vice* and *Slate*.

from Murmur

I know a boy with a heart murmur. Murmur.

Murmur murmur. It is a ludicrous word, both in sound and spelling.

Sometimes I think I can hear it hiding under the pounding of his heart. It is not a skipped beat or an 'irregularity'; it appears impulsively, surfacing occasionally to interrupt the normal pattern.

Idly, he wonders about the benefits of having two hearts, not knowing that this is already so. One is the relative of the heart that lies in my chest, separated from his only by the dual layers of our respective skins. I question the benefits of the other.

If I were to open him up, with the ease with which I would open a cardboard box, I would not find the two hearts lying side by side in the jam of his insides. The second heart lies hidden, nestled inside the first; a Russian doll motif.

I am enthralled by its childish unpredictability. It appears struggling inside the chambers of the first heart, scraping at its walls. It flutters under the base of my palm, fragile and tender. It is a 'double take'. At its cruellest, it reassembles his anatomy at whim and forces the heart to retreat so that I can hear it best not from his chest but the back.

When I attempt to roll away, it follows. Afterwards, I continue to hear its pounding in the memory of my skin.

I know this is not how the qualified men would describe it, the ones with stethoscopes and powerful pens.

But trust ME, no one else has pressed themselves so intently upon his chest.

from **Case Study #1: Vocabulary Lesson**

I am instructed to seek refuge in the present. To nail myself to my breath.
I am prescribed a little something for cognitive distortions. To untangle, what is tangled.
I am directed to repeat what ails me, over and over, until the words are merely sounds.

Once upon a time, there was a man with a self like a house frame of dark wooden beams. High ceilinged and sparse. I did not know what the years, or life, had done to make such a thing of simplistic beauty, sunlit and holy.

I did not know then that it was possible to maim oneself like this.

There are the things we do to ourselves. The things that are done to us. The things that are.

With a thin bladed chisel, I delicately tap, then prise apart the building blocks to examine each piece. Under advisement, I attempt to polish sharp corners to the smoothness of river stones. I arrange and rearrange, group and regroup, but comprehension fails to emerge.

When I am done, will the blackred stickiness of the self well between the gaps and seal me closed? Or will I gaze upon what once was, unable to reassemble what I have disassembled?

Tell me though, is it actually possible to know oneself better than this: to lie on the floor, cradling yourself for comfort, to watch the sunlight leech out of the day through your salty fingers and your matted hair, not black, but brown and faded henna red, to know the taste of your skin bitten in despair, the exact size of your shoulder joint as you cup it in your palm from the embrace you give yourself.

Well?

Case Study #3: Chariot

Materials and Methods

Place, on an IKEA white surface, a semicircle of cough syrup cups. On this altar, pour into the crystalline plastic, the subject's:

        1) Blood.
        2) Last view of the sky.
        3) Thoughts.
        4) Feelings.
        5) Behaviours.

Discussion

When it is asked,
'Are you: your blood or your last view of the sky or your thoughts
or your feelings or your behaviours?'
It is said that,
I must answer 'No'.

When it is asked,
'Are you: your blood and your last view of the sky and your
thoughts and your feelings and your behaviours?'
It is said that,
I must answer 'No'.

When it is asked,
'Are you something besides: your blood and your last view of the
sky and your thoughts and your feelings and your behaviours?'
It is said that,
I must answer 'No'.

I tire
i am so tired
of
observing myself
as if i were a misbehaving dog.

VIDYAN RAVINTHIRAN

(*b.* 1984)

Vidyan Ravinthiran was born to Sri Lankan Tamils in Leeds, UK, and now teaches at Harvard. He is the author of two collections of poetry: *Grun-tu-molani* (Bloodaxe Books, 2014), and *The Million-petalled Flower of Being Here* (Bloodaxe Books, 2019), which won a Northern Writers Award, was a PBS Recommendation, and was shortlisted for the Forward and the T.S. Eliot Prizes. His study *Elizabeth Bishop's Prosaic* (Bucknell University Press, 2015) won both the University English Prize and the Warren-Brooks Award for Outstanding Literary Criticism, and *Poetry* gave him the Editor's Prize for Reviewing. In 2022 Columbia University Press published *Worlds Woven Together*, a collection of essays, and *Spontaneity and Form in Modern Prose* came out from OUP. *Asian/Other*, a fusion of poetry criticism and memoir, will be published by Icon in the UK and Norton in the US.

Uncanny Valley

I had been walking further and further into a desert
of yearning silicon – the air shimmered

in oblongs already, you could hear voices
crying out softly

from thousands of viewless windows.
Life without walls ™ – well you need walls,

load-bearing and beautiful, to fix
the windows in, and you know her hair

is never so beautiful as when she's crying out

from the window and letting it down

so you can scamper up. So much hair, so intricately
braided and pinned that its sheer brushfire

exerts little to no pull on the skin of the scalp,
so you could go on climbing forever

toward the mirage crashing and burning in the air
and her entreaties would never be those of pain.

Ceylon

– the word's on the tip of your tongue
(or, as you say it, *tong*), as we take tea.
Waiting for you to speak, I sip mine:
Tetley's tastes of nothing, but I suppose
it's good to know true flavourlessness,
the prose of life we sugar over with verse.
*Cey*lon you say – a trochee not an iamb –
referring to the drink I drink
with two spoonfuls at home and, here, none.
Though by 'home', I mean the house
my parents live in and where I grew up;
like and unlike them saying 'back at home'
when they intend Sri Lanka, and not Leeds
where they live and I haven't, not for years.

The Annupoorunyamal

(or Florence C. Robinson)
– a scaled-down copy of a
'full rigged New England clipper';
or, 'a direct descendant
of an early
19th-century British naval brig';
that Valvai thoni

plied long-known
Tamil sea routes; made port
from Cochin to Vizhakapattinam, Aden to Rangoon;
carried rice, spice, tiles and timber
(sandalwood, teak),
tobacco and dried fish;
was purchased, for as much

paper money
as filled the back
'of an ancient open Buick';
sailed the Pamban Channel
to Colombo;
arrived in Gloucester, Mass., in August 1938:
her pilgrim crew,

'turbaned, beskirted', clomb the yards barefoot
– 'a fine lot of men, too,
if you treated them right and respected their beliefs' –
singing 'lusty sea chanties
in an in-
congruous' – fine word, *incongruous!* –
'biblical English'.

MONICA RUWANPATHIRANA
(1947–2004)

Monica Ruwanpathirana is one of most acclaimed modern Sinhala poets. She wrote twenty-three books, including nineteen collections of poetry: three won a State Literary Award. In 2005, she was awarded the title of Kala Keerthi, for her contributions to the arts. Born in Matara, she graduated in 1967 from the University of Colombo and joined the Plan Implementation Ministry where she worked for eleven years before departing for an NGO working to alleviate poverty. During this time she arranged programmes to improve literacy and mitigate the effects of globalisation. Madhubashini Ratnayake describes her style: 'She writes to a definite metre and more often than not, each line ends with a rhyme. Since the verses are usually quatrains, they have much similarity with Sinhala folk poetry.'

My Grief

When you analyse my poems
acclaim their various merits
my heart hurts
as if denied the praise I sought.

I hide from the world
guard in my heart
a tender affection;
you are not aware of it, friend.

Except for an occasional sigh
my love does not show itself
it is reborn as a poem;
you are not aware of it friend.

You've read and analysed
a thousand of these poems
they have one meaning only – you –
that alas, you do not see.

[tr. from Sinhala by Ranjini Obeyesekere]

Wife Lamenting

Like my possessions
All burnt out
The black smoke spreads all over the country
Blood shivers, nerves and muscles tingle
Before the flames that burn my husband

The croaking of frogs by the canal
Seems like the chanting of pirith near the cemeteries of night
With the devils around preventing all else
So the branches and the leaves falling down
Alone can pour the redeeming water

No white flags or garlands near
The only offering the smell of kadupul flowers at night
My heart's faith confined to my head
Under the light of only the moon in the Western sky

The fond memories of our past weigh on my heart
No permission for relief through drops of tears
Instead of mourning, I find relief
As the sounds of thousands of cicadas rise
Mimicking grief through village and mountain

It is not a dream of midnight
I see my husband dying on the road
God, turn your eyes to this suffering land
Which the Buddha enlightened
Through compassion

[tr. from Sinhala by Ranjini Obeyesekere]

from Your Friend She Is Woman

In a distant city,
one evening,
as you return from work,
look, son,
a hundred mothers begging on the streets.

The children have grown up, left,
scattered in a hundred directions.
The look in their sad listless eyes
is in my eyes too, son.

In the sun or rain
they linger in alleys and gutters
I too loiter, alone,
in my decaying house.
See my image in the midst, son.

From far away you send me money.
If you want to know how I feel

when it comes,
drop a copper in their palms

you'll see it on that face.

You may find me in their midst
one fine day.
Don't be alarmed, my son.
There is nothing that I'll ask
when we meet.
If you only recognise me
It's enough.

[tr. from Sinhala by Ranjini Obeyesekere]

PUBUDU SACHITHANANDAN

(*b.* 1980)

Pubudu Sachithanandan was born in Colombo and currently lives in the Netherlands. During the anti-Tamil riots of 1983 his family house was attacked and they were forced into hiding in a small hill-country town, Hatton, for several years: 'Those few years in the early 80s, in many ways, shaped me, my sister, and my parents. When I look at myself now, the memory of violence and a childhood spent in the countryside, climbing guava trees and playing hide-and-seek in the tea bushes, are trapped within me like the dark and light paint inside a tattoo.' A prosecutor at the International Criminal Court, Sachithanandan has been published in several anthologies and is working on a novel about migrants and displaced persons from Sri Lanka, Central America and East Africa. He cites Seamus Heaney, Pablo Neruda, Richard de Zoysa and Han Kang as notable influences on him as a poet.

Anthem: The war is over

Blogs, newspapers, my gmail inbox alive
with bravado. Only patriots and traitors now.
Ripe jackfruit juice, sound of tabla music
feel of milk rice wattalappan after breaking fast,
sound of Tamil guttural to my ears

but full of memories – my father's friends
trips in the rickety old van with a loose seat
through tea estates. Big chariots wheeling
deities in a Kovil with the hundred
(thousand?) steps in Hatton town.

I was in a Sinhala version of *Macbeth* once
on an island the bard had never heard of.
Like the wooden stage of the Lionel Wendt
the soil in Madinnagoda is full of the past,
warm between my toes, through my fingers.
Memories: a young priest in the Wattala temple
didn't shave too often chewed betel-leaf giving
sermons in our living room. My college team-mate
praying prostrate three times a day towards Mecca.
My father struggling to explain children's stories
in Sinhalese, my mother treating an injured man
on Hatton estate with Dettol, gauze & broken Tamil.

I'm angry. Trying to hold on to dreams of rainbow
nation (s?) fusion, compli-cation, inter-racial marriages
hybrid island at a cross-roads, time to forge, (iron's-hot),
grab this chance for a melting pot, enough monoliths,
scarred lathe, enough tin-pot-monarchy-math, time
to play with our United-Colours-of-Benetton-clay,
mix-match-make hay before the sun fades to a mono-
chrome mono-tone 'with-us-or-against-us'.

There's no disloyalty in refracting light, no necessary
treachery in devolving might, no need wipeout
(by-white-van) lives because they turned a flashlight on
the maggots in the machinery of state. Seamus Heaney
wrote a poem once, about a Republic of Conscience,
whitens my knuckles yearning for a benign Babel,
a home, an anthem, of many tongues, many songs

MINOLI SALGADO

(*b.* 1960s)

Minoli Salgado has written four books on the Sri Lankan civil war: the critically acclaimed study, *Writing Sri Lanka: Literature, Resistance and the Politics of Place* (2007); the novel, *A Little Dust on the Eyes* (2014), which won the first SI Literary Prize and was nominated for the DSC Prize for South Asian Literature; a collection of short stories, *Broken Jaw* (2019), shortlisted for the Republic of Consciousness Prize and longlisted for the Orwell Prize for Political Fiction; and a book of narrative non-fiction, *Twelve Cries from Home: In Search of Sri Lanka's Disappeared* (2022). She is Professor of International Writing at Manchester Metropolitan University where she directs the Centre for Migration and Postcolonial Studies (MAPS), and taught for many years at the University of Sussex where she was Professor of English.

Blood Witness

After the screening of the Channel 4 documentary 'Sri Lanka's Killing Fields'

There is some dispute
about the quality of film
the pixelated grain, the date, the provenance
genetic code and splice of voice in camouflage.

The President's men demand forensic proof
of pedigree, the producers rage new wars
while the West calls for the justice of anger avenged.

The barrel of a lens jolts
the barrel of a gun
fires the final shots
again and again
naked figures fall

bound, blinded by a darkness lashed across their eyes, they
fall into the replay of enquiry in a spray of spreading blood.

When the twin towers fell pristine, I wonder
how many contemplated the angle of the lens?

Telegraph

Point Pedro and Dondra Head mark two poles of loss

one who crossed the bridge of bodies
clutching a shruti box
the instrument that tunes her voice
kept close to her heart
the scars on the box
rippling up her arm
her song untangled
flung into the open beak of a bird

another who was carried
by the third and final wave
that beat her children from her
before swallowing them whole
twists her head like a bird
as the water stole her hearing aid too
still hears her children cry
through a swelling permanence of sea

the connection between them
as tenuous and slack
as a tapped telegraph wire

A. SANKARI
(*b.* 1948)

A. Sankari is the pen name of Chitralega Maunaguru, a Tamil poet, critic, feminist and activist. She has been a crucial figure in the women's movement in Sri Lanka since the 1970s, working for organisations such as Poorani Illam which provides support for women affected by the civil war. During the war years she was active in travelling around the country documenting the stories and trauma of the Tamil women she met. She was Professor of Tamil at the Eastern University at Batticaloa until 2013. She has edited four groundbreaking anthologies of poems by Tamil women including *Sollatha seithigal* (1986) and *Uyir veli* (1999).

Living and Dying

I never knew you
before this.
You might have been
anyone at all; one
among three thousand students.

You might have come and gone,
not seen in any play,
nor in student association activities,
never part of a strike,
not interested in any of this.

We might even have met,
you and I, some day –
perhaps under the shade
of the wide-spreading vaagai tree
or on the steps of the library.

Or again, perhaps,
I might have seen you
in the university foyer
or behind these buildings
somewhere in Palaly Road.

But I didn't know you then.
Today when I saw
the notice of your terrible death
on the library walls
and the science faculty entrance
I was struck to the heart.

Young man,
all day today
your features
and your just-learnt name
have slowly eaten into me.

That notice of your death
also told me your name
and your town,

told me of your life.
How we must grieve for a life
known only through death!

[tr. from Tamil by Lakshmi Holmström]

In Their Eyes

I have no face, heart, soul.
I have, in their eyes, two breasts
long hair, slight waist, broad hips.
Cooking, spreading beds,
bearing children are my tasks

They'll talk of chastity, its power
to make rain thrash down on command,
and of Kannaki endlessly. While they talk so
they'll keep on gazing at my body.
This is habitual from shopman to husband.

[tr. from Tamil by Sumathy Sivamohan]

DIPTI SARAVANAMUTTU
(*b.* 1960)

Born in Sri Lanka, Dipti Saravanamuttu is both a poet and an academic. She moved with her family to Australia in 1972, and studied at Sydney University. She worked as a journalist with the *Tribune* newspaper and wrote two film scripts with the Migrant Women's film group. From 1988 to 1991 she studied and taught at the University of London. Her poetry ranges from everyday conversation to literary theory with an emphasis on issues of social justice. Her three collections are *Statistic for the New World* (Rochford Street, 1988), *Language of the Icons* (Angus & Robertson, 1993), and *The Colosseum* (2004), which won the Age Book of the Year Dinny O'Hearn award for Poetry. She has also published a novel, *Dancing from the Edge of Darkness* (2000).

Among the Icons

Sri Lankans are diligently sending
their brains out to beg.
Western Europe gets its next increment
of shrewdness, a new generation's
investment bankers.
For the exiled Tamils,
Benelux nations feel like climbing mountains
each one its own particular kind of defeat.

Others find a private sentry-box
in keeping their hearts collapsible.
Facing the piggy presence in
a less patient age than Barchester Towers,
without resorting to either's weapons.
You try to speak to anyone –
while the pirate eyes over the fence
keep the volume of anxiety beating
when you stumble over
those uncontactable emotions.

Then the dashing pirates
turn out to be your helpers
as you plot the nature of icons –
the way they can stand for
everything they are not.
You love the controlled intensity
of Richard Jordan's paintings –
like some ritual
both devotional and precise.

You run out of money in Norway, just
before the Arctic Circle.
That's sad, but not getting tea
in the Vatican café
made your morale founder badly.
To the Italians you're on some frontier
between an adventurous foreign woman
and an illegal immigrant with
an enormous battered bag, that you
heave around adeptly. Other women,
you notice, find this hilarious,
so you cheer up.

In Venice, you tell Salvatore
that you've taken yourself
so far away from contentment
it's as though you'll never recover.
He flashes a look at you, and comments
that you're exactly the same, and
you wish that were true.

Landscape Art

In '88, the Sri Lankan civil war
is your permanent backdrop
to reading eighteenth-century novels
and theorising the (gendered) subject.
'Sinhalese subversives… Tamil terrorists'
someone reads to the meeting, from
a conservative newspaper.
Listening to this stuff feels like
an exercise in learning how
the enemy thinks –
'Rhetorical indoctrination' you say
grimly, and everyone laughs.

You realise it can't be said exactly,
how it is to be here, stuck
between carnage, and theoretical commitment.
You'll do without Saturday night –
(drunks and lovers everywhere) but
some things never let up, as if
still wanting someone who's dead.
It's not so much altruism as
that you can't resist paradox, ever.

In a world from
which to nourish yourself
you can read your poems to the ocean.
Meanwhile in the Angels' kitchen
Kristeva in an ankle-length white fur
and high heels has just created
caviar on toast.
And it's okay, she knows

that the food you brought here
had no sexual significance.

The Sri Lankan security forces are absolved
of any blame for the kidnap
and murder of my cousin Richard.
More feasibly, Kristeva explains
that the celebration of love
as absence, as in the *Song of Songs*
had its earliest expression in Tamil
devotional poetry of longing
for the return of Krishna;
the truth-principle, pacifier,
translucent god with the sky-blue skin.

You're gratified to discover
that the tradition exists, even if
you write yourself out of it.
When Kristeva gets her style right
she's very methodical and precise
while hinting unmistakably
of strongly emotional elements.
You're as determined about
other people's freedom as ever
but on mapping these
mostly personal songlines
you know for certain
there's no such demon-dance
across her lucky heart.

You go for a morning run, while
it's still misty, and tell me
how the lake was frozen.
I see you sprinting across a
Sylvia Plath landscape.
Leaves on the grass outside
our squat in East London, like
the dead white bellies of small fishes.
I sit working, waiting, expecting
you to take up where we
left off fighting, and you
walk in with the loveliest, most
loving smile I've ever seen you smile…

and ask me how I'm feeling…

For Maia, 6 December 1989

Line Drawing

A close relative of that supposed
myth of the romantic
artist, the original portrait of the witch
with swollen, fallen dugs. Framed
on the wall of this homely café, it
sits above the wholesome ethnic food
we have perfected, as though it were
a death wish, with incidental, bitter
and haunted dark eyes. How to eat,
or whisper to your lover on the phone,
beneath such insistency and silence?

The usual target looks like she'd give
anything to get away, out of the picture
with a good line for the next poem about
life choices, it's still too much love and trouble
like an Alice Walker novel re-living the face
of even its darkest days. Racial features
are not rendered distinct, although
we can always read the lines, and she
looks the absent-minded type who trusts
her dreams of a happy ending and therein
is their chance for spite. She'll wear honour
tied around her belly like a secret charm
that's proof against the evil eye, the delicate
and fragile metal as cool as her skin.

Crazy fingers and paranoid eyes, she forgot
and just smoked the whole joint; eeny-meeny
monster-face, telling of my love; how everything
new needs the goodwill of others allowing it,
of what our grandmothers lived through before
us, the sound of the sea, the feel of water,
the scents of our careful and discordant earth
and all other casual instances of found art.

The maps we have for beloved landscape,
the space for faith and other flowerings
of the unpredictable and savage heart.

Flying North in Winter

I start to go out again, like a phoenix
rising out of the ashes of a good book.
How did they burn you?
I think about connections between
spirituality and economics, as refugees
climb onto the roof of the Woomera Detention
Centre, to chant 'We love you' at protestors
marching toward them across the desert.
I stand grey as a weevil in a fresh pure slice
of bread. Who could
be the frog that was stung
by the scorpion who drowned,
to stamp out dancing from the world?
Who could be as creepy as leeches,
and steal people's unread love-letters?

My name is such a difficult word.
Full of repeating vowels,
and someone tells me I should write
a poem about how difficult it is
to say it. I said 'Why don't you
just learn to pronounce it?'
Perhaps there's no such thing as instinct
and our feathered friends have all been had,
socially programmed to dream
of warmer skies in winter.

Beekeepers and makers of silk
have their secrets. Perchance
the endangered Honeyeater's sunlit
acres are not the best green clover.
Bees being bees, they get on with it.
Silkworms meanwhile, sleep snug
in their soon-to-be unbearable chrysalis.
Longing to re-kindle their hearts

in iridescent colours, as we
extract each silken thread.

PETER SCHAREN
(———)

Peter Scharen was born in Sri Lanka and emigrated to Australia. His poems appeared in *Poetry Peradeniya*, *Ceylon Daily News*, *Ceylon Observer*, and the anthologies *Twelve Poems to Justine Daraniyagala* as well as *New Ceylon Writing* (1970 and 1971). His PhD thesis (University of New South Wales, 2000) was on 'Famine and Prophecy: General Sir Arthur Cotton and the Poverty of India, 1844-84'. His books include *Twenty Four A.M.* (1972), *Southern Village* (1974), *Signs and Seas* (1980) and *Rain Blows* (1981).

Landscape

I know a people of nightmarish self-sufficiency,
who have faced, for a moment or a century, their landscape,
the wooded ranges that from the eye
recede and give no more than the sky
that's already given, the desert in which survival
is only of the toughest species –
the sea is hardly considered for the terrible expanse
of the burning land.
In the town that turns its back on
land, poet and mythology,
I listened to the endless verse that had not begun,
a language hooped together, grey strips of wood,
a voice that hides its energy from the sun,
and cringes before a Surrealism too vast to explore.

Winter Lines

Home fires bathe our faces with light.
The child sleeps early, a small
mountain of curled-up warmth; when we call
out to the deer wandering the waste of snow,

the dog, from his place by the fire, looks up.
I hope the old leaning willow will not break
under snow; ice covers the lake.
Ah, bells: a stranger makes thin traffic
on the single road of cold Cooper Valley.
Tomorrow sunlight will hit the hardened back
of three nights' snow; no sign
of deer, rider or howling wolves to be found.
And look, our little garden, swollen with the snow,
is like a memory of early love.
It has grown bigger, but where are its nooks,
its colours and scents and bird-foliage in season?
Lighter steps have filled our steps in the snow.

Transitory

Images are vast,
subtle and strong.
I leave them aside for a little.
I want to rest
in the common dust, the roadside
of the people,
the flowering garden of my love.
I am plucking grains
from an old sieve,
I am setting birds free
for the open sky.

MAHAGAMA SEKERA
(1929–76)

Mahagama Sekera was a poet, lyricist, playwright, novelist, artist, translator and filmmaker. A significant figure in Sinhala poetry and literature, he played a role in the artistic renaissance of the late 1950s, inspiring generations of writers. Drawing on folk traditions, he tried to articulate modern experiences in a diction and style that was both appropriate and innovative, and was influenced by Japanese poetry as well as English and French free verse. Several of his songs are still widely popular in Sri Lanka, and his poems are still quoted almost thirty years after his death. His more introspective works are shaped by Buddhism.

The Moon and New York City

Only black competitively upward-thrusting
concrete walls,
no iridescent blue-green sky,
leaf, tree, or view
to rest the eye.
In this city named New York
atop a hundred storeyed closed-in tower,
a cell – doors and windows sealed –
a bed – a chair – a table –
me.

On the other side of this huge earth
loved ones –
parents, kinsman, friends,
children, wife –
they come to mind.
To drive out dead desolation
I sing out loud a verse.
The sound
rebounds
my voice on my own ear.

I know not where to go.
I open the window and peer
deep into the abyss.
Sharp piercing thorns of cold
rush in, claw my face.

Caught in a flood of electric lights
vehicles, howling rush in all directions.
Stunted ant-like man-machines
impatiently run here and there.
Is there not one
to stop a moment
look at me kindly, ask how I am?
Some passing acquaintance?
Nobody. Not here.
I forget.
They are all on the other side of the earth.

In despair I gaze upwards.

Shining, shining in the sky
a golden plate,
the moon!
One I know well.
The moon that shines above our village rice-fields.
The moon that every poya night
lights up the Bo tree in our temple yard.

[tr. from Sinhala by Ranjini Obeyesekere]

No.16

Like an unwritten poem
you itch
inside my head.

No. 24

The dew drop
on the lotus leaf
addresses the pond thus:

'Friend
you are only
a slightly bigger
drop.'

[tr. from Sinhala by Ranjini Obeyesekere]

See Yourself in My Poetry

Don't search for me in my poetry.

You and I and everyone
Whether we know it or not
Are travelling in the same direction
To see the morning star appear
At the edge of the black sky.

On that journey
One day you will also reach
The edge of a steep cliff
Like I face.

When the path is blocked
You slog through rubbish
And when your body is covered with
Scattered lies and disgraceful scandals
You will be hit with a spiked club
And clutch the earth with a weak hand.
When you helplessly cry out that day as I have
Then the poem I wrote
Will belong to you also.

Friend! In that moment, in my poetry
Don't look for me, see yourself.

On the path I walk, the thorn bushes
Prick my feet and make them bleed.
If you avoid the thorny path, understand the proper path,
        and complete your journey.
If you see, before me, the morning star
That we are looking for
Then the flowers of benediction
Will bloom at your feet.

See me within those flowers.

[tr. from Sinhala by Garrett Field]

SELVI
(1960–91)

Tamil poet Selvanithi Thiyagaraja was born in a village just outside Jaffna in the North of Sri Lanka. An ardent supporter of women's rights, she had been active in feminist circles since the early 1980s. She founded the feminist journal *Tholi* and was a prominent member of Poorani Illam, a women's centre offering support to those traumatised by the war. In 1991, when a third-year student of Theatre and Dramatic Arts at the University of Jaffna, she was abducted by the LTTE. Although never loud in her condemnation of the Tamil Tigers, Selvi's work was often critical of their practices; she was held captive alongside fifty other writers, artists and playwrights. In 1992 she was awarded the PEN/Barbara Goldsmith Freedom to Write Award, yet despite the publicity gained, she was never seen again. In 1997 the Tigers confirmed that she had been executed. Selvi's clear and strident poetry is full of concern for the freedom of women to be able to live, dream and flourish despite repression and war.

Summertime

A red sunset consumes the sky.
Large waves embrace the shore.
The tips of the grass by the pond
appear singed as the fire spreads
from the west, and the empty fields
look on the sky in silence.
The soft breeze sweeping over
is tinged with warmth.

The red earth of a newly laid road
irritates the eyes. From a fruit-laden
mango tree, a songbird intermittently
sings its song. The sharp stones
littering the road have learnt
the taste of blood.
Stones cast by the wayside
laugh mockingly.

Memories spread.
Suddenly, as the wind turns cold
the heart aches.
The green of the gum tree,
the beauty of the water flowing

with abandon from a brimming pond,
are telescoped into the future.
Time now long past
presses mutely on the mind.

[tr. from Tamil by Shash Trevett]

Raman, like Raavanan

I am very weak. Please, don't anyone
disturb me with questions.
My heart is hanging by a thread.
It could fall and break open at any moment.

Raavanan's pleasure gardens were not destroyed.
This house itself, is like one
filled with Ashoka trees.
But my captor is not Raavanan. It is Raman.

There were moments, during Raman's reign
when I witnessed him changing masks
and become like Raavanan.
My heart missed a beat.

Who will come to release this Sita from prison?
For how long will the Ashoka trees prevail?

[tr. from Tamil by Shash Trevett]

Within Me

The warmth and the dust brought with it
the tonsure ceremony.
One evening, my mother took me
to my room. Criss-crossing the floor
she looked at me intently. Oh.

My little sister peeped through the door.
'Are you coming to play Akka?' she asked.

After that, dreams which had grown
to touch the heavens, shrank back to earth.
The bars on the window and the walls of the house
now contained my existence.
My hands sought to stretch out to claim the sky.
But my feet were earth-bound
buried deep, rooting in the underworld.

Like lava boiling at the centre of the earth
my mind too seethed. I want you
to see my anger. One day, I will rise
like Vaamanan and crush all your thoughts –
pulverise them to powder.
I will erupt, an angry volcano.

And then all knowledge will explode.
Then your rituals will wither and die.
Your sacred literature containing the rules
of life will be consumed by fire.
The heavens will open in a deluge,
rivers of lava will flow out of volcanoes
and I will swim in them.
The forest, the pastureland, the mountains
I will circle them all.
Whether you have a good evening,
or a productive morning
will depend on the life-force
of my breath.

[tr. from Tamil by Shash Trevett]

In Hindu practice, the tonsure ceremony is performed on both girls and boys when they are 4 years old, in order to teach them humility and devotion. A child with a shaved head is seen as innocent and holy.

Vaamanan: One of the incarnations of Vishnu used to defeat the demon king Mahavali.

G.B. SENANAYAKE

(1913–85)

G.B. Senanayake was born near Colombo and had to abandon his schooling
due to economic difficulties. In his later teens he made use of Colombo Public
Library to educate himself and submitted his first Sinhala short story to a
newspaper when he was 19. These early efforts caught the attention of Martin
Wickramasinghe, who gave him a job at his newspaper. In 1946 Senanayake
published a short story collection called *Paliganeema* which he called an experi-
ment between prose and poetry; he was one of the pioneers of Sinhala free verse,
borrowing from both Western poets and Sinhala prose writers to create a new
poetics. He published more than fifty books of poetry and prose, and although
he became blind in later life, carried on writing with the help of family members;
twenty books were written after he lost his sight. Senanayake won numerous
awards and his work is studied in schools and universities in Sri Lanka.

Philosophers and Pundits

Around the bed are philosophers
Poets, historians and other learned men
With hands folded behind them
With hands folded on their chests
Heads bent, pensive, eyebrows raised.

> Lying motionless in bed
> On the spreading white sheet
> He is seriously ill.

The lamp that's hung from the roof
Lighted with its scented oil
Showed to him their familiar faces
As he opened his eyes from time to time.

In all his adult life
When fear or pain arose
When his heart leapt with joy
It was to them he said everything
The way he ran to his mother's lap
To tell everything when he was a child.

His life story flows before him
In his mind's valley as he watches

Then someone started whispering to him.
>'Who is it?'
'It's me, your heart.
>That which you dismissed with disdain
>Insultingly, listening only to what the philosophers,
The poets, the historians and
Other pundits said.'

In fear he looked at them
The philosophers and pundits
Lest they heard the words of the heart.

>Death embraced him in that instant

When one philosopher said
'Our friend lived in wisdom and virtue,'
As he left the room
Others following him assented
Nodding their heads all the way.

[tr. from Sinhala by A.T. Dharmapriya]

DISHANI SENARATNE
(*b.* 1986)

Dishani Senaratne was born and raised in Sri Lanka. She is a PhD candidate at the University of Queensland, Australia. Previously, she taught English at the Sabaragamuwa University of Sri Lanka. Dishani is also the Founder and Project Director of Writing Doves, a non-profit initiative that employs a literature-based approach to enhance intercultural understanding of young learners in Sri Lanka. She has a BA (Hons.) in English from the University of Peradeniya and was a recipient of the E.F.C. Ludowyk Memorial Prize for best performance in a course on Shakespeare Studies. In addition, she has a MA in Linguistics from the University of Kelaniya. Dishani's poetry has appeared in *Write to Reconcile* and she has published research articles in international peer-reviewed academic journals and edited volumes. Her debut children's book *My Best Friend Next Door* was published in 2019. When she is not seen navigating between the two realms of reading and writing, she can be found baking magic in the kitchen or talking to her plants.

Dreams

A flickering lamp-post
at the junction,
a howling dog
in the distance.

The young man,
stringy and curly-haired,
dark as a nightmare
lies naked on the road.
Thousand of ants
in his open mouth
as if feasting on
the honey of his words.

He attended the five classes,
dreamt of wiping away
the tears of the poor.
'Never got married,
laboured day and night
for his family,'
the village folk murmured
not daring to go retrieve him.

His cherished red wristband
given by a sahodaraya
lies torn apart
under his broken wrist.

Lament

I will never forget the day
you decided to join the army.

Running your fingers
through my hair that night
you promised to attend
our doni's indul kata gama.

At the village temple,
under the murmuring Bo tree,
you promised to build
an upstairs house with Italian gates.
Carrying our doni, your eyes twinkled
just like the pahans we lit.

Because you were buried
in that sealed coffin,
I could not touch
your rough hands
I could not run a finger over
that raised birthmark on your chin
which I would stroke
as we lay together.

Now I show our doni
where your tomb is.
Yet to me you are not
in this tomb, you lie
elsewhere far away.

GAMINI SENEVIRATNE
(———)

Gamini Seneviratne worked for the Ministry of Agriculture and Food, as the chairman of the Coconut Development Authority. He studied English at the University of Peradeniya, and, alongside his wife Indrani, cultivated in his children – including the poet, Malinda Seneviratne, and the novelist, Ru Freeman – a profound appreciation of the arts. *Twenty-Five Poems* was privately published in 1974.

Tune for Ariel

Rediscovering dialects
in the train
after three years
lost to memory.
Strange world;
I have migrated, it seems, into another generation.

The young
dress a little differently, the boys
slip into long trousers sooner than we did
the girls stay
a little longer in short skirts;
and all are a little bit bolder
and somewhat more aimless.

We used to play cricket too
hatless at high noon
and till the night came on;
very often, having no other sight-screen,
we'd turn the wickets around
to catch the twilight as it passed
from cloud to cloud till the last faded
and the dusk gathered our dark heads
and the sweat and the white shirts
but friendship failed to dissolve.

Friendship and home and beauty,
much later, the don told us,
are virgin and Anglo-Saxon and have survived
inviolate, the heart of the English tongue;
the new Odysseus too
would argue in inebriety
that connotations will survive
every fresh description of the denotation.
(Home is still home
though we eat out every day
and cleanse the bath with antiseptic care
since at night there still remain four walls
and a double-bed, and a door to close.)

The years have passed
gathering mementoes from other tongues
while the full moon barking deafened the last bus home.
The bright sun finds us
ducking in cars from roof to roof
and evenings come with children
and sensations of a breeze
blowing past the chemist's, through the market square,
the traffic thick on the street and a cradle
falling in the wind.
So with children I've relapsed

into an age I have no memory of
with a faint appreciation, if that be memory,
of my father's fears for me.

And now I discover again
so casually,
what I wonder I had at all forgotten
now it comes to mind again,
although my limbs ache, strap-hanging in the train,
and this language jostles me
so thoughtlessly,
the tap-root of our tongue
in this dialect which survived our passing
from that tribe to this society.

Nangi

And you, my daughter, for whom
I have had so few words, survive
the collapse of my lungs.
There will be voices
sweet with singing, voices sweet
singing in the garden, through a high window
as now, in my mind, for you, as you lie asleep.

Arjuna

(A portrait of Dorian Gray)

I can see the charm of my figure
in your face, son.
Time
will invest your figure
with the changes that time brings.
Let growing up, for you,
be as a seasoning of hard wood,
the hardwood that
my face in your figure sometimes sees
which your eyes on me
must less and less detect.

MALINDA SENEVIRATNE

(*b.* 1965)

Malinda Seneviratne is a poet, critic, journalist, translator, political commentator and activist whose opinion pieces are widely read in Sri Lanka – as are his books of poetry and his translations from Sinhala. He has won the Gratiaen Prize and also been shortlisted several more times. His books include *Epistles: 1984-1996*, *Threads*, *The Underside of Silence* and *Edges*. In 2011 he won the H.A.I. Goonetileke Prize (also with the Gratiaen Trust) for his translation of Simon Navagattegama's Sinhala novel *Sansaranyaye Dadayakkara*. Seneviratne studied at Royal College, Colombo, the University of Peradeniya, and during the JVP insurrection in the 80s, he looked abroad and won a scholarship to Harvard, returning to Sri Lanka in 1991. His poetry is influenced by Neruda, García Márquez and Eduardo Galeano, as well as by his childhood encounters with Western literature, music and elocution.

Nangi

She was tiny
that's my first memory of her:
tiny,
and over time
she grew smaller and smaller
not by the distancing of time
or continental shifts
tinier
for reasons of proximity
order of both
tiny enough to command
pandered to, she was
indulged
but perhaps feared
I could hold her hand
or hold her in my palm
but maybe
that's what she wanted me to think
she holds me too
in a heart-palm
made of mother
and friend,
but she's tiny
this sister of mine.

Oil-bullets

When you can't take to sea
you take to the street
when you can't take the sea
you take the street
and for all explanations
of agent provocateur
cat's paws and tweaking of proportion
for all narratives of the law and lawlessness,
destabilisation beyond provocation
all that matters is someone wrote a number
someone didn't see the numbers
someone didn't care
someone wondered but discounted
left one less head-count for enumerator
and emptied the universe of a little girl.

Mitsi

There were pick-me-up times
in profusion
and so too 'put-me-down',
but in all the years of carrying
you did not know
(or did you, I wonder?)
who carried whom,
but I know,
girl of butterfly-winged thoughts
that I was more of let-you-down
than by-your-side,
for there were times
when my eyes were so full
of other tears
to see yours,
not even when they cascaded
fell from petal to petal
of your many booked universe.
I am ignorant, but this I know:
Amma varun pamanai mathu budu wanne.

SENI SENEVIRATNE

(*b.* 1951)

Born in Leeds and currently living in Derbyshire, Seni is a writer of English and Sri Lankan heritage, published by Peepal Tree Press. Her books include *Wild Cinnamon and Winter Skin* (2007), *The Heart of It* (2012), and *Unknown Soldier* (2019), inspired by her father's experience as a signalman in the Second World War, which was a Poetry Book Society Recommendation, a National Poetry Day Choice and highly commended in the Forward Poetry Prizes 2020. She has been widely published in several anthologies and magazines, most recently in *100 Queer Poems* (Penguin), *Where We Find Ourselves* (Arachne Press) and *Wretched Strangers* (Boiler House Press), *The Rialto* and *New England Review*. She has collaborated with filmmakers, visual artists, musicians and digital artists and is one of ten commissioned writers on the Colonial Countryside Project. She is a fellow of the Complete Works programme for diversity and quality in British Poetry, is currently working on an LGBTQ project with Sheffield Museums entitled *Queering the Archive*, and is completing her fourth collection, *The Go-Away Bird*, which will be published by Peepal Tree Press in Autumn 2023.

Dear Mum

Not a word from you until today. I was pegging out
the washing and it was as if you were there next to me,
reaching to fasten a sheet in loops on my washing line.

You were always a say-it-like-it-is, speak-as-you-find,
no-nonsense – some might call it sharp-tongued –
kind of person, so your silence had surprised me.

And there's no criticism implied. I'm grateful to you
for teaching me to speak my mind and for the cushion
of love, the space for comfort in the crook of your arm.

I've been wondering about your war years, how it felt
to be the one he left behind in 1941 and all the waiting.
You wrote letters, your sister helped you with the spelling.

Not your fault you were taken out of school at 13 to be
the one who helped at home – what with my grandma
having her mother and a sick relative to look out for.

That bout of TB when you were six can't have helped.
Nearly two months alone in a sanatorium, you told me,
no visitors allowed. Looking out for them every day.

Must have been five years before you saw my dad again
and not knowing whether he'd survive. Not to mention
the posting to Ceylon – the worry he'd decide to stay on.

It was a long engagement for sure, but the wedding photo
tells its own story. Head held high, you're looking round
at all the guests as if to say, 'See. He was worth the wait!'

I'll write more soon. Glad you came to break the silence.
I can still hear your voice, those broad Yorkshire vowels
asking me, 'Why is your dad getting all the attention?'

Opus Tesselatum

Diminutive tesserae, bright shards of marble
and glass paste – copper, cobalt, nickel, gold
and lapis lazuli. My fingers, sticky with Pliny's
mortar, three parts sand to one part lime,
bind the fragments of my shattered history.

Terracotta cones play geometric games
with pebbled stone and random shells,
in landscapes of enamel, where a flax dresser
combs the bark of Linum trees, lays it out
on grass to bleach its yellow fibres linen white,
breaks and swingles with the swipple of his flail.
Ready for the loom, it makes a canvas for
the seamstress, embroidering familiar gardens
with her alphabet of stitches, who takes the pen
from the fingers of the registrar and holds it,
like a needle, above inky swirls of red and black.
Her eyes close to the paper, she copies
a cross-stitch to mark her name.

Tessellated tales of agate, boiled in sugar,
stained as black as onyx, pave the path
of a sea-captain, landlocked by grief,
who trails three motherless daughters,
across the Pennines, to Yorkshire,
where a boot finisher, eighteen years old,
abandons his waxing wheel to join
a Regiment of Foot, and wear out
thirteen pairs of regulation army soles
to defend the British Raj.

Pictographs in amethyst and turquoise
set at angles, catch the light in the courts
of Seethawaka. A Mudliyar strokes
the gold of his brocaded sash and dreams
of grazing water buffalo in the hills of Rakwana,
where a mother, haunted by a vision of an upturned
rickshaw, bows her head before the wisdom
of the astrologer's charts, to save her unborn son.

Ochre-tinted grout smooths the rough edge of
voices in the family of a lawyer's daughter.
She discards her Burgher name for love of
a Sinhala, a poet buried under
too many letters of the law, a barrister
paid by the poor with sacks of mangosteens.

The stories coil like ammonite, are etched in epitaphs
sealed in unmarked graves, stamped on soldiers' passbooks
released from faded photographs, whispered through the centuries.
I gather every bright shard, collect every broken piece,
wash and polish, press them into place.
The mortar is damp and yields to the touch.

Slave Lodge, Cape Town

She is the woman who, after disappearing in the curse
of a ship, finds herself newly arrived under the mountain.

They call her no name, then a new name in another language,
they write her name on page 472, Slave Lodge Census 1714.

Maria of Ceylon, counted, accounted for in the roll call,
in a pebbled courtyard where she counts stones,

digs at the dirt in cracks between the stones, marks hours
until the hour when the doors are opened for the pleasure

of free men. No, in any language, should be understood,
but she is the silenced goods and worth three inches of tobacco

to the man who's trading her. When men with strange voices
fall on her in turn, she is the woman with numbers rattling

behind her teeth – eka, deka, tuna, hatara, paha, haya, hata,
ata, navaya, dahaya – counting stones, counting shapes

in the red of her eyelids, who is unravelling threads of herself.
She pulls them out, lays them warp and weft, on the stone floor,

reweaves the fabric of her flesh. She is the woman who is waiting
for the rain, waiting for the Yala Monsoon to uproot her silence.

Slave Lodge was built in 1679 to house the slaves of the Dutch East India Company at the Cape. The doors of the Lodge were open to free men between eight and nine every evening, to be used as a brothel.

NATCHATHIRAN SEVVINTHIYAN

(*b*. 1974)

Natchathiran Sevvinthiyan is the penname of Arun Ambalavanar. He was born in Jaffna, Northern Sri Lanka and lost his parents at the age of eight. Raised by his grandfather he left Sri Lanka when he was 17. He has published two collections of poetry in Sinhala, *Eppothavathu Oru Naal* (1994) and *Vasantham 91*, along with political and literary essays published in various online magazines. Natchathiran Sevvinthiyan's poetry negotiates exile and identity; he now lives in Sydney, Australia, and is working on a collection of short stories.

Until My Wineglass Was Empty

One evening, early in winter
in a bar in small town Eastern Australia
I saw D.H. Lawrence playing billiards.
With his long, sharp nose, his red-flecked beard,
his nineteenth-century-sailor-eyes
piercing the souls of young women
I saw D.H. Lawrence playing billiards.

Tall, thin and dark, surrounded by men
of a generation who knew how to gamble,
he walked between tables littered
with wineglasses, and tables on which
billiard balls bounced off cushions
and I watched D.H. Lawrence play billiards
until my wineglass was empty.

[tr. from Tamil by Shash Trevett]

Kokkatticholai 166

It means nothing to me.

Today's headline.
166+ Thamilar killed in
A gruesome massacre.

Tomorrow,
I have an examination, again.
Tonight, I will study.

[tr. from Tamil by Sumathy Sivamohan]

SHARMILA SEYYID

(*b*. 1982)

Sharmila Seyyid is a writer and social activist who was born in Eravur, in the Eastern Province of Sri Lanka. A journalist since 2001, she has fought for women's rights in the district of Batticaloa, founding the Organisation for Social Development in Eravur (working with minority women in the region) and Mantra Life, working to reduce the gender gap in Sri Lanka. Forced into exile due to her writing and activism, she is currently based at the University of Nebraska's Leonard and Shirley Goldstein Center for Human Rights and the Sam and Frances Fried Holocaust and Genocide Academy, where she is in receipt of an IIE-Artist Protection Fund Fellowship.

Seyyid has published nine books in Tamil, winning awards for her collection *Siragu Mulaitha Pen* and her novel *Unmath*, which is available in English from HarperCollins. Seyyid's poetry centres on the multiple burdens faced by Muslim Tamil women in Sri Lanka.

Three Dreams

The first dream…

An island surrounded by a green, green sea.
Everywhere, trees yielding heavenly fruit.
Golden-yellow sand drifts.
Fisherman at rest.

The second dream…

Pale blue fields.
Pomegranates, lit up by the sun's rays,
weaver birds' nests, hanging down,
under the shade, women opening
their bundles of food.

The third dream…

A crimson sea.
Gardens caught up and drowning
in a vortex.
Sand drifts lost in the waves.
Fishermen's wrinkled necks.

Burnt out fields.
Sun's rays swallowing up the fruit.
Empty nests, broken, torn.
Women's corpses, naked.

[tr. from Tamil by Lakshmi Holmström]

Keys to an Empty Home

There. That was my home,
the house where my mother gave birth to me
where my father carried me on his shoulders
and played with me.

They broke up this house;
we don't know why.
Yet the keys to the house we locked up
are still with us.

It was in the courtyard of that house
I wrote out the alphabet
for the very first time.

There, that was my home.
That neem tree you see by the side of the well –
it was there I played on my swing.
Look, a scrap of the red rope
from which the swing was hung
is still suspended there.

I have no idea why they did it,
what use my house was to them
I don't know;
but they broke it down.
Yet the keys to our locked-up house
still stay in our hands.

After the house was broken down
my father wept constantly
gazing at the keys
to the locked-up house.

Until he died, all he yearned for
was to lean against the walls of his house
peacefully, for one last time.
His love for his own house
was an empty dream.
Now my father is gone
and so is the house where
I clung to my father's shoulder.
Yet, the keys to the locked-up house
are still in our hands.

[tr. from Tamil by Lakshmi Holmström]

Fire

The day before yesterday
when I ran toward the street
some chased the fire that bounded
like a peeled papaya.

This illusory fire cannot be cradled in your hands,
nor does it abide in your focus.
It does not have the habit of impinging on you
it does not burn
it does not adhere.

The fire escapes its pursuers somehow,
enters through the back door into the house
to stay.
I am sleeping in a fire-lit room,
embers I secretly keep hidden in my bag.

Three times a day,
half hour ahead or behind my meal time,
I eat a handful of embers.
In the coming days,
scientifically, change will become visible.

[tr. from Tamil by Pramila Venkateswaran]

ALFREDA DE SILVA

(1930–2001)

(Rachel Lilian) Alfreda de Silva worked for the Ministry of Education in Sri Lanka and also wrote poems for children, short stories, and feature articles and made television and radio broadcasts for the BBC and the Sri Lanka Broadcasting Corporation. She also published in 1990 a prose memoir, *Pagoda House*. She became a Fellow of the Trinity College of London in Speech and Drama in 1956 and won the 1993 Zonta Award for her contribution to fine arts in Sri Lanka. The beautifully wrought, yearning poems of her two collections, *Out of the dark the sun* and *The Unpredictable Blood*, deserve to be back in print. She writes of frustrated homecomings, vanished homesteads, in measured rhythms and with exact, stinging word-choices.

Grassfields in Sunlight

Now at one end of them the squatters' shacks
Hurt the eyes with their tin-white roofs,
And the stench of rotting dirt
Piled on the tree-roots
Disturbs the old images.

Once these were fields
Turned into seas or mountains
By childhood, and the wind's cries
Were horses' hooves and the whining grass
A tale one listened to in the moth-brushed night.

I remember the sun over these fields
Like a fisherman netting
In green water, shocking everything with its
Scathing radiance,
On a day that fell in the reeds
And was irretrievable.

Cormorants and Children

The wing-tips of cormorants
are silver, like bells
on the water of our coral island.
They dive for their wriggling dinner
while the pampered tourists on the tank-bund
watch in the rose montage of evening.

Further on, unexpected spindly
children from the squatters' shacks
lift themselves naked
out of the water
like sombre islands,
and scramble for leftovers
of rice on banana leaves,
and a hash of bread and meat
thrown there by picnickers.
Later, much later,
fat cormorants and hungry waifs,
together they share the moon.

The End of Something

The emptying café is ready for its nightly death.
The orchestra suddenly goes dumb.
They start turning the chairs upside down
on the stripped tables,
putting out the lights.

In the moody drizzle outside,
the street lamps wear haloes of mist
under the branches,
where our words are unsaying themselves
in cruel caricatures:
our hands unknotting,
our bodies moving apart
towards the loneliness of separate destinations.

The night is a sick landscape
of small wet moons,
bilious yellow
and neon blue –
a sustained despair
that spreads over the quick, wild rage
and regret of irrevocable decision.

I drift like the aimless leaves
on the inscrutable side-walk.
I don't want to go
anywhere
except into myself.

Kotmale

A century hence, perhaps,
some parched and hostile season,
a man standing
on the dark tongue
of a dry spill-way
may see the uncovering
of this village
in the valley.

Strange blue and yellow
gods will rise,
their dark faces
surfacing from
a buried temple,
and all those drowned roofs
like splayed fingers
will move into focus
above the granite floor.

But only till the next monsoon
will the past stir
and memories return.
Then the rains will come
bringing back the turbulence,

the roar in the tunnel,
the flood-tide in the valley,
the abundant consummation
of the land.

LAKSHMI DE SILVA

(*b.* 1936)

Lakshmi de Silva is best known as a translator – her version of Martin Wickremasinghe's *Ape Gama* was published as *Lay Bare the Roots*. She writes poetry in both Sinhala and English and has published it in *New Ceylon Writing*, *Poetry Peradeniya* and various Sri Lankan newspapers. She was an English Honours graduate of the University of Ceylon at Peradeniya and lectured in English Literature at the University of Kelaniya. An inspiring teacher as well as a critic and poet, she received the Gratiaen Prize and the State Literary Awards and has been honoured with the Sahithyarathna Lifetime Achievement Award. De Silva's poetry is traditional in form and personal in content.

Tangalla, 9th April 1971

That too was real; the evening sun
Dripped like slow honey through the filtering leaves
Gilding the dried grass cropped by the pied goats
Foam lit blue sea, cloud lit blue sky; and peace
Dawned with clear morning, loitered by our eaves.
Flocks of shrill parrots dangled upside down
Nibbling the fat thorn-pods; the Kohas lay
Fanned on the sunwarmed hill with songless throats.
Mongooses slid low shadows as they passed
Stars lit the sky, as fireflies lit the grass
That too was real as this night we lie
Silently, listening to the crash of guns.

Addition and Subtraction

There are two kinds of failures; those that press
The high wind down, keep unregretful calm
And these the wind rides – proud and violent men
Whose minds are helium-driven. Those suppress
The wind and reap sound profit. These shall reap
The force that whirls the irised manyshape
Of cloud and brilliant vapour. Those escape
The cry of wind within the drumming breast
The restless urgency that longs for roads
To lead to tasks sufficient for its strength
While they accomplish only what the length
Of reason and good sense can measure well.
But these, unfortunate winged creatures, swell
The surge's cry and breast the clamorous dark
And beat the thick-glassed wire-protected panes
They call and call to the unanswering light
Nested beyond them. Born to their unease
They cry its anger and its fierce delight.

S.J. SINDU

(*b.* 1987)

Born in Trincomalee, S.J. Sindu is a Tamil diaspora author living in Virginia. She has published two works of literary fiction (*Marriage of a Thousand Lies*, which won the Publishing Triangle Edmund White Award, and *Blue-Skinned Gods*, which was an Indie Next Pick and a finalist for the Lambda Literary Award) two hybrid chapbooks (*I Once Met You But You Were Dead*, which won the Split Lip Turnbuckle Chapbook Contest, and *Dominant Genes*, which won the Black Lawrence Press Black River Chapbook Contest), has two graphic novels forthcoming (*Shakti* and *Tall Water*), and one forthcoming collection of short stories (*The Goth House Experiment*). Sindu holds a PhD in English and Creative Writing from Florida State University and teaches at Virginia Commonwealth University and Vermont College of Fine Arts. 'I'm interested in the margins, liminal spaces where accepted norms and identities blur into the queer, the outsider, the weird. I want to find the nuance in experiences of trauma, war, and immigration.'

Gods in the Surf

I envy my American city friends
their impractical swimsuits
made to be seen not touched by sea
unable to stand in weak Florida surf
I was born by the ocean an island child
the core of me salt water and seagulls howling
we wade into the Gulf the ocean holds us
amniotic fluid shot with jumping mullets
jellyfish constellations too small to see
worming their stinging tendrils into skin
waves spitting shark eggs and tangles of seaweed
pelicans strafe the water we gorge on chips
chug shitty beer under a rainbow umbrella
my city friends tell stories innocent childhood
beach trips Florida vacations coconut sunscreen
back home people saw gods in the surf
watery limbs and hair made of dirty foam
fishermen went out to sea came back
nets full of prawns to bombed out homes
children tried to hide in the sand
evading military planes only to shatter on land mines
I never saw visions in the waves but I knew
a boat with no motor and no lights
could take me across a lagoon at night
and if I heard a helicopter
I should sink my body into the ocean
and trust it to hold me

For Sale: 1997 Christmas Barbie, $600

before puberty twisted my body
I was everything they wanted
I looked like a doll
the kind that closes and opens its eyes
my skin a perfect translucent honey

as a child I cut all the hair
off my donated Barbies

the free ones I found at the laundromat
or bought for two dollars at yard sales
three-for-five deals
discarded Barbies, grimy skin
and decades-out-of-fashion clothing
I snipped their shining blonde hair
with safety scissors, combed Elmer's glue
through the strands styling each one
into a permanent dyke pompadour

when I was seventeen at the mall
a middle-aged man told me I was perfect
like a doll and had I ever posed for photographs
and he just happened to be a photographer
looking for models
his skin was inflamed from the dry Nebraska winter
little red patches peeling off his cheeks
his hands jittery in his pockets
he had me cornered in a Yankee Candle
my back against the shelves
the smell of cinnamon pine all around us

an older lesbian on YouTube
calls us pillow queens
the girls who like to lie back and just get done
the other word is power bottom
we're all power bottoms now
plastic cocks in a drawer
are so much better than a real one
how awful when it's attached
and I just think masculinity is better served removable
when you can boil it clean

in Sri Lanka during the war
there were no dolls in our house
we made play food out of the red clay in the backyard
an uncle of mine brought back a doll from the capital
smuggled it wrapped in his lunch of rice and pickle
my grandmother washed the smell out of her hair
she was perfect and blonde
though her plastic yogurt-coloured legs were hollow
not filled through like a real Barbie
I squished her legs and watched them fill back up
the plastic returning to the shape it knew how to be

I used to love movies about dolls coming to life
and having to reckon with this world
they're perfect outsiders
to show us our absurdity
made in our own image
though I never had a doll that looked like me
and I can't help but wonder if I did
whether I would've slathered Nair all over my arms
until it burned off not only my hair
but also five layers of skin
third degree chemical burns
just to look plastic and new

remember when we left our skins
for the tingle of electric being
floating ad infinitum in the cloud
finally reduced to our likes and timelines
finally immortal electrons?

REGI SIRIWARDENA

(1922–2004)

'Regi,' writes A.J. Canagaratna – who taught with him at the University of Jaffna in the 70s – 'was interested not only in literature and the arts. He was multifaceted: a human rights activist, one of the founders of the Civil Rights Movement, a keen and knowledgeable student of politics, especially of the Soviet bloc, a perceptive and witty lobby correspondent, a keen student of astronomy and a champion of the equality of all races, multiculturalism and pluralism.' In his political prose he aspired to the clear democratic style of George Orwell; analysing literature, he was an adventurous comparatist; as a poet, writes Canagaratna, he was precise rather than effusively emotive, an 'Apollonian rather than Dionysian'. He also wrote fiction and drama, won in 1995 the Gratiaen Prize and in 2004 the Distinguished Service Award for his contribution to English letters at the State Literature Festival.

Birthday Apology and Apologia

1

To have existed while the planet made
Eighty revolutions round the sun is no

Achievement, but I must confess I am
Rather surprised to find myself still here.
It's scandalous at eighty years to walk
The earth where younger, better people now
Are dust and ashes. Thinking only of those
Who died of violence and had much more
To give – Rajini, Richard, Neelan — makes it
Embarrassing to be alive. However,
I never hungered for longevity:
My mother's family's sturdy peasant genes
Must have prevailed, although my father left me
A diabetic legacy – a nuisance.
But I shouldn't complain: to compensate,
I have acquired immunity to some
Infections – post-modernism, for one,
And free verse, for another. I'm glad, too,
I never caught, as my late brother did,
The Sinhala nationalist flu. An early shot
Of Marxism, perhaps, took care of that.

2

When I was young, I said to my friend Herbert –
A fine designer of stage-sets, a cook
Of creative genius, a treasury of lore
Of all things Lankan – 'If you'd only stuck
To one thing, Herbert, you'd by now have been
The top of that tree.' 'But, putha, how boring
To stick to one thing!' Now, at eighty, I know
I've been, like him, a fickle butterfly
Flitting from field to field, from flower to flower.
The kindest word they'll find to say of me
Is *versatile*. But do I really wish
It had been different? What a bore to be
The sovereign of some scholarly half-acre,
Crowned for a thesis on 'Semiotics of
Consonant Clusters in Six George Keyt Poems'!

To change the entomological metaphor,
I'm Grasshopper, not Ant, in the old fable
(Or *Gracehoper*, in James Joyce's version).
Writing, I have enjoyed myself, laid up
No masterpieces to outlast the winter,
But hope I've pleased somebody now and then

With a poem here, or a play there, and if
My tombstone is a footnote in small print
In literary history, that's okay.

3

By time's mere flux, I'm called to play the part
Of patriarch I am unfitted for.
But not for long, I hope. When the time comes,
Ajith, Prince of Obituarists, will write,
I know, a graceful piece – measured, as always,
And free of flattery or fulsomeness.
(A pity I shan't be there to read it, though.)
I don't believe there's judgement after death,
Or penal court of Yama: if there were,
And I were called to account, what could I say
In mitigation of sentence, but stammer,
'P-please, sir, I tried not to be p-pompous ever,
P-pretentious, sir, incomprehensible,
Or b-boring.' Would the judge pronounce severely:
'A frivolous trifler! He deserves no mercy.
I sentence him to fifty years of torture
Translating into Serbo-Croat the texts
Of Gayatri Spivak and Homi Bhabha!'

4

When you are old, you find that simple things
You took for granted are no longer simple.
Climbing the three steps to the office door
Is now an Everest-scaling feat; crossing
The street, a perilous odyssey. However,
Age has its compensations. You have grown,
Perhaps not wiser, but at least more prudent.
You can admire a woman's charm and beauty
With no possessive demons plaguing you.
Books and CDs that you once cherished dearly
Are burdens now you're glad to shed: even
The sight of the half-empty shelves is pleasing.
And so, to quote a poet I never liked,
'Port after stormy seas.' To all those friends –
Too many to be named – who've helped me past
The whirlpools and the rocks, my heartfelt thanks.
This makes eighty pentameters. THE END.

Colonial Cameo

In the evenings my father used to make me read
aloud from Macaulay, or Abbot's Napoleon (he was short,
and Napoleon his hero; I, his hope for the future).
My mother, born in a village, had never been taught

that superior tongue. When I was six, we were moving
house, she called at school to take me away.
She spoke to the teacher in Sinhala. I sensed the shock
of the class, hearing the servants' language; in dismay

followed her out as she said, 'Gihing ennang.'
I was glad it was my last day there. But then the bell
pealed; a gang of boys rushed out, sniggering,
and shouted in chorus, 'Gihing vareng!', as my farewell.

My mother pretended not to hear the insult.
The snobbish little bastards! But how can I blame
them? That day I was deeply ashamed of my mother.
Now, whenever I remember, I am ashamed of my shame.

To the Muse of Insomnia

Lying awake in the dark, while a poem forms
slowly in the spaces of the mind, like a crystal growing
molecule by molecule, I remember Akhmatova, who bore
her poem within her for many years, knowing
it was too dangerous to betray to paper, nourished it
with heart's blood, agonies, terror, tears
(husband in the grave, son in prison), carried it
through the womb-dark silence of the terrible years,
till the first gleams showed of the approaching dawn,
the moment was come, her daughter ready to be born.

SHIRANI SITUNAYAKE

(*b.* 1957)

Born in Katunayake, Shirani Situnayake is a Sri Lankan-British dual national: 'I try to go home every year, a crucial breathing out for my spirit, without which I begin to feel hemmed in.' She started writing in her teens as a way of 'making sense of my world and discharging distress'. Her writing is preoccupied with identity, dislocation, nature and rage – 'the rage more muted now but still very present and an aspect of the struggle for belonging and community'. She loves the work of Pat Parker, Audre Lorde, Chrystos, Rohinton Mistry and Eve Ensler. She has worked for the last twenty-three years as a therapist, and lives in Derbyshire with her wife Maya and three horses. 'I am always seeking the wildness of nature, a hunger for rawness and authentic presence – something imprinted on me in Sri Lanka so many years ago.'

Beginnings

The weather into which we are born
is what we live with all of our lives.
Elements that speak our name
and outline our nature poke through
and reveal themselves. But many of us
are set adrift and find ourselves grown
in places where our skin doesn't shimmer
nor our feet skip. Then we must find
our way home called by the imprint within,
whispering our name in forgotten tones.
Our eyes caught by certain glimpses,
our senses tuned to small vibrations
that release a shiver of recognition.
Here we are unmasked, undone
heart songs set loose. Sitting deep
in the hollow of ourselves, we move
in a gait that our feet already knew
but had forgotten how to dance
and sing ourselves back home.

SHANMUGAM SIVALINGAM

(1936–2012)

Shanmugam Sivalingam was born in Pandiruppu, Eastern Province of Sri Lanka. One of Tamil Sri Lanka's major poets, he was a teacher of science and began writing poetry seriously in the 1960s. His outlook, in common with many of the intelligentsia of the time, was Marxist and his poetry addresses issues of caste, poverty and later, the civil war. A prolific contributor to literary magazines, he only published two books of poetry: the first in 1988 (*Niir Valaiyangal*) and the second, two years before his death in 2010 (*Citaintupona Thecamum Thoornthupona Manakkukaiyum*). Yet his influence is still felt by emerging poets today.

Nowadays

Nowadays, cats stalk narrow alleyways
their young clamped in their mouths.
Nowadays, hornets do not build
their hives on the sides of houses.
Instead, they pour molten lead
into the cracks of rocks
and secure themselves in the forest.
Nowadays, the weaver bird also
has retreated to underground holes
to brood over its eggs.

And thus, at least, these will survive.

[tr. from Tamil by Shash Trevett]

Unsung Songs

Once a plant has been pollinated
its flowers wilt and die.
Sometimes something goes wrong
and life burgeoning in the womb
ends with a flow of blood.
Sometimes within an egg, a chick,
its wings barely formed, dies.

Yet, you tell me to sing.

The streets are filled with the stench
of dead bodies. When bullets tear open doors
doves tumble to the ground, their wings broken.
Boys leave without saying goodbye.
They tell us to search by the shoreline
for bodies dumped at sea.
But still, you tell me to sing.

My songs are soaked in blood.
They are songs about rotting corpses
songs dark as the jet black smoke
swirling around my head.
Songs stunted, deformed
that have not been expelled
in a flow of blood.
Songs which break your heart
that catch in your throat.
A time will come when these songs
will disintegrate on our tongues –
ask me to sing then, not now.

[tr. from Tamil by Shash Trevett]

In Memory of Our Songs

Dear Jesus,
In this time of penance we worship you
with your holy hymns.
They tied your hands behind your back.
Yet my Lord,
did they hang you from on high by those bound hands?
While hanging there did they force you to breathe smoke?
Did they insert a piece of wire into your penis?
Blow chilli powder into your eyes and your anus?
Did they rape you?
Did they force you to rape another?

343

My sweet Jesus,
They tore off your clothes
adorned you with a crown of thorns
and whipped you till you bled.
Into your sainted hands and feet
they hammered nails
and raised you on the cross.
They split open your side with a spear.
Yet my Lord,
Did they cut you to pieces and suck on your blood?
Did they pluck out your eyes?
Did they taunt you with fire?
Did they throw you on the flames?
Did they shoot at you like a stray dog?
Oh my Lord,
by your cross you have saved this world.
With our crosses how many worlds
were we able to save?

Father,
They knew not what they did.
These people, here too,
know not what they do.
They do not know that their torture
and cruelty will lead us surely
on towards liberation. Amen.

[tr. from Tamil by Shash Trevett]

SUMATHY SIVAMOHAN
(*b.* 1959)

Sumathy Sivamohan was born in Jaffna, Northern Sri Lanka, and is an inter-
national scholar, filmmaker, poet, activist, playwright and translator. She has
been involved in the women's movement in Sri Lanka since the early 1980s
and is Professor of English at the University of Peradeniya. Her poems and
translations have been published widely and her work with theatre and film
have won her much recognition; she has been a visiting fellow at universities
in Europe and the US. Sumathy has written widely on gender and the nation
with emphasis on Tamil and Muslim polities in Sri Lanka, and almost all of

her poems deal with the painful and the humorous found in situations of political violence, ethnicity and postcoloniality. In 2020 she co-founded the Kuppi Collective, an activist academic initiative of intervention in contemporary educational, political and economic affairs. Sumathy was awarded the prestigious Premchand Fellowship by the Sahithy Akademi of India in 2011. She is a 2022 recipient of a Global South Translation Award from Cornell University for her translations of Sri Lankan Tamil poetry into English.

on reading the astonishing novel 'mm' by shoba shakthi

when he said m, i said, hmmmm,
immm, as in 'a little', wits we have not
for medicine even,
and also, as in nihilism, the tamil-way, yes,
then of course, thaam, theem and thom,
as in thesam and thamil, thaam and tham,
we the tamils, a nation, sit tight,
talking through the night,
in mumbling murmurs of mmm
and mmm, dreaming of
all, dreams all
in ell_am in eelam,
seeking
am in
ammmerica,
and asylum, talking,
mmmmmm, mmmmmm, hmmmm and
immmmmm, of 'em,
ahem, and hee and haw.

of course, ma as in amma and marxism and
m as in men and women and feminism,
and then oh, as in whore, hmmm,
yes, nice, some one cries, hmmm,
need, asyl_um@aaaamm.yes.uk
a photo, of a woman-in-green
card, aha, hooo, ooooommmmm,
dowry, im-material, dole-can-manage-fellah
no? go? illegal? legal-sex-free, thammmmm.ma
thamil_an@yalpaaaanam.ohm
mmmmmmmmmmmmmmmmmmmmmmmmmmm

345

the boys said, naaaam thaaaam, no way,
and the leaders said,
aaammm_aaammm,
nodded vigorously, numb and dumb,
yet the a_im of the pistol
did not falter,
straight on the pottu-spot, all
'em leaders, six feet under-oh!

Poet's Note:
i fell in love with the novel mm when i first read it. this is a love poem dedicated to the novel. i do not wish to spoil for anybody the pleasure of reading mm by reducing it to a paraphrase. i shall for the sake of clarity of my own poem, 'translate' for the reader [Shoba Sakthi's] dedication of the novel submitted here with his permission.

my people, this story is for you,
who, after,
listening, listening,
to all the long tales and short ones
the stories and the epics,
told and retold, again and again:
     a war of thirty years,
     a cruel war,
     a hundred thousand persons killed,
     fifty thousand persons maimed,
     twenty thousand widows
     ten thousand persons, taken crazy
     boosa, magazine, kaluthurai,
     massive displacements from homes, lands,
     (liberation) movements, great hero-oes,
     the proscription of thamil eelam;
     the prison camps of thamil eelam,
     traitors (tamil)
     (peace) talks
     reunion (of men, persons),
     pongu thamil or thamil overflowing,
     and so many, so many others,
(merely) say, again and again:

mm

S. SIVARAMANI
(1968–91)

S. Sivaramani was born in Jaffna, Northern Sri Lanka and became well known for her feminist and political poems while a student at Jaffna University studying English Literature, Political Science and Linguistics. An outspoken critic of the LTTE, Sivaramani was often harassed by them; a possible contributing factor to her decision to burn all her poems before committing suicide. She was 23 years old. A prodigious talent, the twenty-two Tamil poems we have by her had either been published in journals and magazines between 1985 and 1990 or were in the possession of her friends. Nothing survives from the final year of her life. Her poems were published posthumously in a collection called *Sivaramani Kavithaigal* by the Women's Study Circle in Jaffna, which she had co-founded a few years earlier. Chitralega Maunaguru (see A. Sankari, p. 298) compiled and prepared them for publication in Sri Lanka, India and Canada.

Oppressed by Nights of War

Oppressed
by nights of war
our children
become adults.

Across the pathways
of their bright
fledgeling-mornings
faceless and bloodied
corpses are flung;
their quick laughter
is shattered
by crumbling walls.
And our little ones
are children no longer.

Even the faint sound of a lone gun
shatters the silence
of a starry night
destroying forever
what children's stories tell.

In these foreshortened days
they have long forgotten
how to play hopscotch
and to make temple-carts from palm-fruit shells.

Now they only learn
to shut the gate in good time
to listen when dogs bark strangely
never to ask questions
to be silent
when they get no reply.
These they have learnt like dumb animals.

They pluck away
the wings of dragonflies
they shoulder sticks for guns
their friends become their foes.

Oppressed by nights of war
our children
have grown up.

[tr. from Tamil by Lakshmi Holmström]

[Untitled]

At evening times
all burdens lie upon us
more heavily.

Now
when the heat and the light
which cannot be stopped
from falling upon dead days
are gone at last
like scribbles disappearing from a slate
it is not just to pass the time
that I count each breath I breathe.

Flying insects fall, one by one,
by the light bulb.
Which would it be wiser to count?
The flying insects?
Or the stars
whose messages are as inscrutable
as the eyes of the dead?

I do not know the truth.
Nor is it an easy matter, in this darkness
to make out the lies.
But I cannot tell my sister
hard at her lessons
to look only for meanings
that match her practice.

Everyone, it seems, is in a hurry.
With me,
memories alone remain.
Outside,
the trees stand silent and fearless,
with ragged shadows beneath.

At this hour,
when dogs bark in fear
when people look again at locked the doors
before going to sleep,
I cannot think
of the sun that will rise
tomorrow.

Night is important to me.
This darkness in which
– like last night –
another friend might disappear –
this darkness is most precious to me.

[tr. from Tamil by Lakshmi Holmström]

S. SIVASEGARAM

(*b.* 1942)

S. Sivasegaram was born in Inuvil, Northern Province. He was Professor of Engineering at Peredeniya University until his retirement in 2008, having gained an MSc and PhD in Engineering from Imperial College, London. A poet as well as a translator, he wrote in Tamil as well as English and has published over twenty books including nine collections of poetry in Tamil and one in English. He has also published four plays, a collection of short stories and two volumes of literary criticism. A Marxist in outlook and an astute political commentator, Sivasegaram has also published widely in the social sciences field; his poetry was critical of nationalism, ethnic chauvinism, violence and war.

from Faces of War

2

He claimed that the face on the identity card was his.
It was not they said.
He pleaded that the card was ten years old,
but the face was his.
When his body floated in the lake
its face was not his.

3

When the child who wore the face of a fighter
met the fighter who wore the face of a child
they could not exchange faces.
The fighter sobbed like a child
for the child who died in a shattered mirror.

6

Some said that her face was her mother's.
Others said that it was her grandmother's.
Her face wore the fire of the smoke
worn by the faces of her mother and grandmother.

7

They killed the fathers of the children and
drove away their elder brothers.

When the children took to arms
they wore the faces of humanism and
shed tears for them.

8

He is a trader.
He wears the face of a recruiting officer.
He does not trade in goods –
he buys people, sells death.

12

The lines on this face are not wrinkles of the skin.
The lines furrowed by poverty are deepened by war.

17

I went to the vihara to see the Buddha.
'Why have you lowered your eyes?' I asked.
'I haven't the heart to see anything that's done in my name,' he said.
'Is it right to remain with arms folded?' I asked.
'The state would place a gun on unfolded arms,' he said.

18

The mosque where they pray here is just like
the mosque where they prayed there.
Why are they unable to pray here
the way they prayed there?

19

The task of implementing the peaceful solution
was assigned to the armed forces.
The earth soaked up the blood
of those who could not understand
the words of peace spoken by bullets.

22

I asked the artist
'Why do you paint the face of this land in yellow and red?
Don't you know any other colour?'
'Poetry speaks of war and death.
When martial music from musical instruments ceases

I hear the lament of the funeral.
What colours do you want from me
while I live between the burning and the burnt?'
The touch of the brush dipped in colour set the canvas afire.

24

The people left bag and baggage
when the soldiers came to conquer.
The people left bag and baggage
when the soldiers came to liberate.

29

Q: Why are the faces of the dead always identified as
those of combatants, terrorists and the enemy?
A: Because bullets and missiles shall always be on target.

30

Ghosts do not come to gulp blood in the battlefields of our era, nor
demons to consume flesh.
The ghosts and demons that consume us from afar have faces like
yours and mine.

31

We could talk of peace, we could talk of war.
Those talking of peace could peacefully
sell arms to those who talk of war.

32

The bombs of that side descend from the sky.
The bombs of this side, walk down the street.
Is this a wrestling match or a game of chess
for us to lecture on rules of engagement?

34

He went away because he could not stay in the village.
When he decided to return the village had gone away.

[tr. from Tamil by the poet]

SOLAIKILI

(*b.* 1957)

Solaikili is the pen name of Uthumalebbe Mohammed Atheek, who was born in Kalmunai in the Eastern Province of Sri Lanka. An important Muslim Tamil poet, he began writing in the 1980s and has published fourteen collections of poetry, of which *Kaakam Kalaittha Kanavu* (1991), *Paampu Narambu Manithan* (1995), *Paniyil Molli Elluthi* (1996) and *Munn Kolli* (2018) have won Sahitya Academy Awards; he has also been honoured by the Japanese government. Solaikili was forced to flee his home in 1989, and his poetry rejects all kinds of ethnic and nationalist ideologies; he writes about life, nature and spirituality instead. He edited the literary magazines *Iruppu* and *Viyookam* and he is a great influence on the younger poets who followed him. Solaikili has been translated into English, Kannada and Sinhala and his poetry is part of the syllabus in schools and universities in Sri Lanka.

The Story of a Golden River

Sun, have you finished bathing?
And did the fish bite you?
There's a special beauty about you
when you fall among the lotus and bathe.

This is a river awash with turmeric;
yes, it is a golden stream.
Even the buffalos bathe here at all times
like gorgeous, gilded figurines.

Once, in this very river
a golden buffalo and a beautiful white stork
fell in love! Yes, in this very place.

So what then?
Well, the stork never looked for fish again;
it would only fly round and around
this stretch of the river.

The golden buffalo too was the same –
unhappy and lost
when the stork didn't fly.

Then one day –
a day when the lotus bloomed densely
and the frogs raised this song –

the white stork swooped down
and carried off the buffalo.
As for the buffalo,
it stuck like a leech
to the Stork's feet –
all for love.

[tr. from Tamil by Lakshmi Holmström]

A Refugee Poet Talking to the Moon

Moon, I won't write poems today
in this temporary house
I have no doors of my own
no plant to pluck, to smell my own flowers

You are an alien moon to me
the light that falls on my courtyard
and your light now on this alien courtyard
are not the same, they trouble me

I am a refugee for three days now
my only relief to preserve this life
and the poems that spring from it

Those who saw my house tell me that its face is broken
the flower plants I loved were eaten by cattle
and have turned to dung

Here I do not have my own sky
and the air that I breathe
seems too to belong to others

Moon, how can I write poems when I have lost
my nine hundred thousand stars
I have lost you and the sky
my butterfly and the lizard that lives under my bed?

Cover your face with a cloud
if a poet sighs
for even the cold breeze will be charred

[tr. from Tamil by M.A. Nuhman]

ISURU CHAMARA SOMAWEERA

(*b.* 1981)

Isuru Chamara Somaweera was born in Colombo and currently lives and works there as an entomology officer with the Ministry of Health. He is a Sinhala poet, short story writer and a freelancer for several newspapers, including *Rasa*. His poetry collection *Suda* (2005) received a Godage National Award and *Malak kathaa karai* (2015), his book of short stories, another. His other books include *Apa dhedena meda maha muhuda* (poetry, 2017) and *Gahanu pirimi mal palathuru* (short stories, 2019). Ten of his selected short stories were published in Tamil as *Thirumadi Perera*. 'I have been writing since I was a small child. It's the space where I am free and where I talk to myself. My father was in prison when I was young. We had problems. I had no one to talk to. So I wrote. It's addictive. Writing makes me wonder and understand. It is an honest revelation with oneself.'

The Little Fellow

Vomiting,
sipping a plain tea
at a roadside-shop
to rid the fever-taste in my mouth
from that never-ending
longest-ever bus journey
with mother
to Boosa
in search of father,

when boys grabbed the green mango
I broke with such effort
biting my lips.
How I stifled sobs
not having father there
to teach them a lesson.

Seeing mother
who never openly cried
secretly weep,
pretending to be asleep,
how I bit my pillow
and cried.

Watching river-waves break,
Idda flowers bloom,

stars fall from the sky
in the darkest dark –
– alone.

However much I try
to drive him away
that dark, small, skinny
little fellow
is still there.
Sometimes
he wakes in the middle of the night –
sobs alone.

[tr. from Sinhala by Ranjini Obeyesekere]

My Pillow Is Wet

Where is he?

The cricket sings
all night.
His high-pitched tone
grates on me.

When I complain
that I could not sleep
my friend laughs.
'How can there be a cricket
in the middle of the city
in a high-rise tower?'

He sleeps soundly
snoring softly.

One moment in my ear
next instant from afar
he sings never-endingly.
His high pitched tone
keeps me awake.

[tr. from Sinhala by Ranjini Obeyesekere]

Mother's Actress Friend

Every time she saw
the actress perform
mother would say

'When we were in school
we were best friends
sat in the same class
on the same wooden bench.
In those days
she was not that attractive.'

Then my mother would look
at her own hands
the broken nails
the thumb scarred
by the fine slicing of mallun greens.

Afterwards she would look at us
my face, my brother's face.
Then, eyes narrowed she'd laugh
the wrinkles on her face disappearing.

[tr. from Sinhala by Ranjini Obeyesekere]

The Meaning of Life

In a scrub jungle village
near Kahatagasdigiliya
in an abandoned temple
that no monk visited
seeing an old farmer woman
observing 'sil'
alone,
I asked her the meaning of life.

Taking my hand
in both her knobbled hands

she stroked it affectionately
'Son your hands are still very tender,'
she said giving a childish smile
from a toothless mouth.
I asked her again
what she saw as the meaning of life

'Son, let us sweep away
the dried leaves scattered around this Bo tree...'
she said, her soft childish smile continuing
not answering my question.

[tr. from Sinhala by Ranjini Obeyesekere]

SANDARESEE SUDUSINGHE
(*b.* 1984)

Sandaresee Sudusinghe is a poet, archaeologist, journalist and published author. Her collection *Gini wadunu Piyapath* (2022), written in Sinhala about the burning of the Jaffna Public Library in 1981, won the Vidyodaya Literacy Award from the University of Sri Jayawardanapura and the Rajatha Pusthaka Award. She studied at Mahamaya Girls College in Matara and read Archaeology at the University of Peradeniya. She completed an MA in Journalism and Mass Communication at the University of Mysore in India; an MSc Archaeology at the University of Kelaniya in Sri Lanka; and a Diploma in Library and Information Science at the Sri Lankan Library Association in Colombo.

from Gini Wadunu Piyapath

105

Dear Library of Jaffna –
who sacrificed your life
right next to the ruling wolves
that plant springs of war
between the North and South,
those who signed for your death
are no longer at peace
on this earth.

358

Justice Nature
has gifted the adjudication
to a lawsuit that was never filed.
Stay alert
as to not let those shadows return.
And into the pages and plates
that record human doctrines
we must etch this as
'the secret that must never repeat
in a history infested with black holes.'

[tr. from Sinhala by Chamini Kulathunga]

27

The blue sky turned black
even the god Nallur left
the smell of humanity dried
and for a second, the wind stopped right there.

Even Tusita heaven up above
melted and wept
in a garden of jasmine flowers
creeping lilies bloomed.

[tr. from Sinhala by Chamini Kulathunga]

30

The universe's rhythm
stopped for a second
even the eyes
of gods
moistened.
That memory of fire.

[tr. from Sinhala by Chamini Kulathunga]

PIREENI SUNDARALINGAM

(*b*. 1977)

Pireeni Sundaralingam was born in Sri Lanka, grew up both there and in the UK, and currently lives in San Francisco. Her poems have appeared in over 30 literary journals and numerous anthologies, and have been translated into five languages. Also a playwright and cognitive scientist, she co-edited *Indivisible*, the first anthology of South Asian American poetry, winner of both the Northern California Book Award and the PEN Oakland Josephine Miles Book Award. She is also the winner of a San Francisco Arts Commission Individual Artist Award, the PEN USA Rosenthal Fellowship, and fellowships from Djerassi Arts Center and the Headlands Arts Center. She explores the nature of erasure and the loss of language, and the silencing that is born from fear, political censorship, or the desire to forget past trauma. She is College Poet Laureate at University College, University of Oxford.

Lot's Wives

We stood,
as women before us have stood,

looking back at our burning cities,
watching the smoke
rise from our empty homes.

It was quiet then. And cold.

We heard their cries, the caged birds
clawing at their perches, our daughters
naked in the hungry mob.

Such death. The smell of justice
drifting on the burnt wind.

We saw it all,
saw the fire fall like rain,

saw our tears
track stiff, white veins
down our bodies,

saw the brine crawl
through salt-cracked skin.

Now, turning in the restless night,
we dream we stand there still,
alone on the hill's black belly.

We, the forgotten,
whose names were swallowed by God.

Fugue

(after Paul Celan)

We were born, we were named,
we were schoolgirls dressed in white cotton.

There were bells, there were lessons, the light
a mirror, breaking over the lagoon.

We learned dates, we learned names,
we tied up our braids with long ribbons.

There are bells, there are lessons,
we march in white lines
and the priest takes our confession.

We hear soldiers, checkpoints,
our brothers trapped between sandbags,
the drum roll of boats across the lagoon.

We learn dates, we learn names,
fill kerosene in bottles, douse the white cotton.
We are schoolgirls in white, our braids in long ribbons.

We are suspects, we are names,
we are women sheathed in white cotton,
the bells in the schoolyard,
bodies wrapped in white cotton.

We were born, we were named,
we were schoolgirls dressed in white cotton.
We tied up our braids and wove them with ribbons.

Times Two

found poem based on reports on Sri Lanka from *The New York Times*
and *The Times* (London)

Vacationers can lounge

                                   inside one camp

on poolside hammocks

                                   for five hours

under palm trees

                                   queuing for food.

Or they can order

                                   urgently needed

cocktails

                                   medications

                                   food and clothing.

Teeming with stylish guest-houses,

                                   forced internment

four-poster beds

               where more than a quarter of a million ethnic Tamils are detained

A place where the Queen of England might stay

                                   guarded by the Army

  Boutique hotels

                          tents fraying after 6 months use

       mango courtyards

                       the controversial barbed-wire enclosures

         with private terraces.

                       There were deep craters

miles of sugary white sand

                     where the lagoon had been bombed

                a pristine coastline
                                        a waterway strewn with mines
Snorkel its crystal-clear waters.

While a few military check-points remain

                                        where refugees are being forced to strip
                rich in natural beauty
                                before they are allowed to pass
elephants roam freely
                        children snatched from the camps

        monkeys swing from trees

                        minors being taken
                        with the tacit support of the Government.

        Water buffaloes idle in paddy fields.

                Among the most scenic
                        ground-impact mortars
                cultural splendours
                        1,000 civilian deaths each day
                flanked by bamboo groves
                        reduce trees to burnt stumps.

                The majority perished under government guns.

                Like one big tropical zoo.

1. *The New York Times*, 7 January 2010: '31 Places to Go'.
2. *The Times*, London, 20 May 2009: 'Photographs expose Sri Lanka's lie on civilian deaths on beaches'.
3. *The Times*, London, 21 October 2009: 'Barbed wire villages raise fears of concentration camps'.

YASMIN V. TAMBIAH

(*b.* 1961)

Yasmin V. Tambiah was born in Colombo, the child of a Tamil/Sinhala marriage, and spent several years in the US, with stints in the UK, Spain, Trinidad and India. She studied at Smith College, the University of Sussex, the State University of New York, and gained her PhD from Yale, following which she returned to Colombo to work for some years. From the late 1980s through 2000, her family moved to Australia: 'My parents and three siblings gradually dissolved their locational ties with Sri Lanka after 1983. But, with the exception of one brother, I don't know whether the rest of us (including me) have 'arrived', in a definitive way, somewhere else.' Trained as a European medievalist, and working later as a researcher into issues of gender, sexuality and postcoloniality, she writes prose-poetry (her own term for it) and won the Astraea Lesbian Writers Award in 1991 and the ZineWest competition in 2013. Her influences include Michelle Cliff, Irena Klepfisz and Adrienne Rich.

The Civil War

September 1984: Three months since I returned to Sri Lanka with an American college degree. The civil war has spilled beyond the Northern Province. Metal gates to my parents' house still bear the dents of rock-throwing mobs. There are axe marks on the wooden doors. New plaster hides a ceiling charred by a burning tyre. Embattled elsewhere I relive the horror of July 1983 through my siblings' eyes. It is difficult to articulate the deep loss within, the negation of familiar fictions, the awareness that exile in one's own country is even less bearable than at a distance. It is a loss compounded by my family's fear.

February 1985: Carrying the national ID card is mandatory. It will protect me from arbitrary arrest, they say. But the civil war has spilled beyond the Northern Province. Authorities have collapsed many identities into a Tamil last name. The card does not attest that I am also Sinhalese, speak no Tamil, and dream in English. It is silent on conflicting loyalties and the struggle to recover myself from colonialisms. I am reduced to someone else's definition, terrorised into keeping boundaries I neither constructed nor consented to.

December 1985: Exile. Four months in North America. White graduate classmates are puzzled that a twentieth-century South Asian might share the experiences of a Medieval Jew. Their imagination stops at my brown skin. There has always been a civil war beyond the Northern Province. Those at risk cannot afford ignorance. I have learnt to recognise the languages of domination and gather a community of resistance for a dangerous journey toward necessary transformations.

1988-1990

Sandalwood

As i step through the door your scent meets me, mingling intimately with incense burnt for Devis. Enclosed by your strong brown arms, bangles tinkling their welcome, i taste melted jaggery on your lips, sea salt within. In your eyes i forget time, collapse space. Your well-ordered apartment outside washington d.c. transforms into dense lush jungle heady with araliya, jasmine, magnolia, sandalwood. My fingers sink into moist soil rich with life. Rounded, like the elephant yogini we celebrate, you claim me. Familiar endearments roll off your tongue teasing nipples dark as your own. Fierce, passionate, protective, reflections dancing where our Kalis meet, you bring me home.

I am no longer cracked earth hidden between asphalt sidewalks in north america waiting for the monsoon that comes only in my dreams to drench, heal, close fissures through which i bleed. Your firm knowing touch re-members sensations grown distant... tired limbs massaged, face caressed, head stroked to lessen pain, to calm a restless spirit. That touch you cook with, food we both know, grew up on, still eat making do with american substitutes and precious imports. Tastes of jeera, koththamalli, pepper, star anise blend easily on your fingers. You name us 'rasam and rice sisters', 'ovaltine dykes', laughing, voice concepts made alien here. Dravidian warrior, friend, lover, you bring me home.

1990

(MEARY JAMES THURAIRAJAH) TAMBIMUTTU

(1915–83)

Tambimuttu's career raises still important questions about the roles writers from the Global South come to play – are forced into, or may choose to exploit – within Anglo-American literary cultures. A Tamil poet better known for his editorial work, and his networking prowess, he founded *Poetry London* in 1939 (the magazine after which today's *Poetry London* is named). As editor, he championed a style of neo-Romanticism, publishing major poets and introducing names, like that of Keith Douglas, that are now canonical. He also created two publishing houses, Editions Poetry London (1943) and Lyrebird Press (1968). But only one book of his own poetry appeared – *Out of this War* (1941) – and for Ruvani Rupasinha, he was as a poet ultimately a sham: 'Tambimuttu's anti-rationalist stance and preference for 'mystical, mantric' poems […] cohere with the stereotype of the untamed oriental he had begun to embrace.'

My Country, My Village

When I was young, the flame tree and the jasmin
Gilded my youthful eyes with tenderness
For natural things – the lotus pond and the palmyra:
The ring-dove tore the air with natural passion;
At Atchuvely, my Northern home, all else
Seemed unimportant beside a bassia star.

The carrion eagle atop the rambling lanes
Wheeled in the pastel sky, and a big owl
Dozed in a tree beside the tethered cow;
The goat coughed among the pecking hens
Of which I owned two, three; and morning's haul
Of eggs belonged to me, they said, for supper.

I had a goat too, a cow and Lakshmi,
Gentle, big-eyed mongrel of a dog;
And when she died I did not feel like supper –
And there was Aachi, wrinkled kind old Aachi.
At six, she told us stories about a frog
In a well: food slipped down like sweetened milk and guava.

Around our house the mango shoots were pink.
The big bassia dropped its blossom like snow.
The pomegranate spun its exciting wheel
Against the dropcloth of palmyra mink,

Between the oleander's and trumpet-lily's show
Pencil of grey areca nut, was wire of steel.

I was four or five, and grandfather, the poet,
In turban of gold and coat of black was a prince
Who was kind to us; he flicked the coiled whip,
And off we went down limestone white roads
Fringed with lantana eyes; from prints
He cut us paper dolls, with a clever snip.

Remember evenings in the theatre, his plays
Like Kalidasa's full of dance and song;
(My father once taking the leading role,
Great-uncle Thambar dancing with a painted face,
Agile as Nijinsky); his poems, a song,
Stung me to listen to the metrics' whirl.

All this was home, and we were self-contained.
Our fields provided grain, tobacco, shallots,
Garlic, pepper, bay leaves, ginger, saffron,
Yams, greens, herbs, fruits, famed
For delicacy and flavour. The seas filled with pots
And nets, rang in the whole sea's kingdom.

This was long ago. And there was home
Beside the Eastern harbour full of ships,
And pretty shells on the deserted lunar beach;
Goatsfoot underfoot, and a lyric poem
In the screw-pine smell. The harbour lips
Enclosed a town beyond the railroad's reach.

There was peace in Trincomalee too:
With leopard, deer and buffalo I roamed
The jungle paths with Elizam and my brothers;
And beyond were the dead cities, the clue
To ancient hubbub, now becalmed –
All the mighty dead Anuradhapuras.

Colombo. Ah, Colombo. Excrescence of Trade,
Competition, Endeavour – the pattern did not hold;
Chaos of many patterns, amorphous –
The island's harlot, and Empire's accolade
In those days; still you were home, a mould
That shaped me in the Western swirl and rush.

Colombo was home indeed. The silver lights
Etched the night's dark with fauns and delicate shapes,
The streets magical by the half-light;
And when the moon dispelled the grey nights,
Silver palms stood by elfin capes,
Proud and feminine in their lissom flight.

All this we loved, my friends, Noel, Rowan,
Tissa (a young school of friends);
All this was heaven, until we grew
And learnt the dog bit, the moon was ruin,
The gilt wore off, and all that magic lends
Is a false perspective, with the chocolate-box view.

And there was Nuwara Eliya, the new-found escape
With a trout stream in the well-kept park;
Upcut, Haputale, Maskeliya knew few rivals,
But, alas, the concrete base and rubber crepe
Brought my village, all villages to mind, from far dark.
Self-contained, these knew no rivals.

So on this festive day, with bells and bunting,
I am wondering whether the hectic pace
Will give the peace and plenty that we seek;
Whether the brash plane and limousine affronting
Shiva in the wooden cart can grace,
Or start a new tear, on the ancient cheek.

Whether it's better to adorn the top or bottom,
To increase the village round, and soul's girth,
Or roundly add to world's hue and cry –
The bazaar's cheating, and the traffic's hum;
But, this is my island, this my native earth
That bore me gently from a woman's sigh.

Her eye a blackbird among the tumbling bushes,
Her lashes, the black silk of a deep night,
Her body the pure long scarf of Laxapana,
Lights of an ocean liner in her tresses,
Black tresses, filled with dark and light;
Cry, O cry, Namo, Namo Matha.*

* Glory to thy name, O Mother (Ceylon national song).

THEEPACHELVAN

(*b*. 1983)

Theepachelvan is the pen name of Balendran Pradeepan who was born in Kilinochchi, Northern Sri Lanka; he lives and works as a teacher there. Growing up in war-torn Sri Lanka he was displaced, his schooling interrupted, his family split up: his own traumas, as well as his brother's death as an LTTE combatant, influence his writing. Theepachelvan writes about survival, tyranny and the resistance to tyranny; he strives to bring out the lilt of the voices of the land. He has published five collections of poetry in Tamil, one short story collection and several books of journalism. His first novel *Nadukal* (2019) received the Tamil Literary Garden Best Novel Award and has been translated into Sinhala. His poetry has been translated into English, Sinhala, French, Telugu and Farsi, and his work is influenced by poets such as Pichamoorthy, Pramil, Jayapalan, Puthuvai Ratnathurai, Captain Kasthuri, Malaravan and Mahmoud Darwish. Theepachelvan has stated that he has no desire to leave Sri Lanka, to move abroad: 'I only want to live in my land and write about my people.'

The Lost Kitten

The children must have
Abducted you

They have begun to point
Guns again
Turned the cannons inward
Opened the checkpoints

Where could you have gone at this time?

You posed for a selfie
With my friend who had no one else
Chased insects and centipedes
Ate with us
Stood guard
Slept like a child on my lap
But where did you go then?

The war begun over who knows what
Has us in its stranglehold again
When orders are to
Close the doors before dusk

Where will I search for you?

In a country that hunts down photographs
Arrests songs
Imprisons tears and
Interrogates memories
Why did you step out of the house?

Can a pet be lost in a country
Where someone has been disappeared
From every home?

When people disappearing in masses and masses
Is the way of war and morality
At what police station do I register a complaint?
In what court do I argue my case?

Moved by your child-like eyes
And your mischievous ways
Some child or other must have taken you
I say to console myself
As I have consoled myself over everything else

[tr. from Tamil by Nedra Rodrigo]

A Friend Stands Behind Me

It is simple
To cross the oceans
To fly the vast skies
It is easy
To carry mountains of fire
To be drenched in the winter forest
Behind me
A friend stands
Like the pen that writes
The epic of my people
And every poem yet to be written

[tr. from Tamil by Nedra Rodrigo]

An Unpublished Poem

An afternoon
Filled with an unshifting yellow light
The pattern of fallen mango leaves
Two tea tumblers
Pill boxes
Butterflies that flit and roam
Like the thoughts of my woman
Who has gone far away
My friend, all that is left
Is a house filled with books
An unpublished poem
Your friendship

[tr. from Tamil by Nedra Rodrigo]

AJITH THILAKASENA
(*b.* 1933)

Ajith Thilakasena is a Sinhala poet and short story writer, a critic and a script writer who deviated from the conventional use of language, creating his own modernist style. His short stories use the grammar of spoken Sinhala without descending into colloquialisms. Thilakasena is interested in the visual aspect of words and has published two volumes of concrete poetry. He has published more that fifteen books, with some of his more popular poetry collections being *Mal Wani Gal* (1978), *Rali Suli* (1991), *Maariyawa* (which won the State Festival of Literature in 2009) and *Mona Tharam Awulakda* (which won the Vidyodaya Literary Award in 2020).

Where

I feel the weight of shadows
Under the trees at the edge of the pool
Quivering in the sun with the whispering of the water

Where are the girls who said they would wait
The sly hidden glances, the crowing loud laughter

Where?
Are they like stars concealed in daylight?
They have wasted my morning

The fragrance of the flower floats from a twig
The grass is crushed where one was seated
The wrapper of a toffee lies in the thicket
A forgotten handkerchief on a stone

But
Where are the girls?
Have my dreams too grown old?

[tr. from Sinhala by Lakshmi de Silva]

I do not know if...

In the two years after our divorce
We came across each other often in the bazaar

You looked at me once, as you crossed the road
And once I saw you lug our son as you ran for the bus
I lifted him up, over the footboard
So that he could swiftly nestle against you.

Once as I walked along the pavement
Just to see if you were there
I peered into the drapery store
With its dresses and lace

From a bus moving swiftly
One day your smile came across to me
Like a flash of silver

I do not know if
I have begun to love you again

As my second wife –
I have no child with her –
Cooked dinner last night

I smelt an old fragrance
The kitchen came before my eyes
As it had been before
The place where the spoons hung in a reed holder
Where the stand for the water jars was kept
Where the rope was slung for the baskets to nestle
And I did not know
If I had begun
To love you again.

[tr. from Sinhala by Lakshmi de Silva]

THIRU THIRUKKUMARAN

(*b.* 1978)

Thiru Thirukkumaran is a poet, lyricist, journalist and environmentalist who was born in Jaffna, Northern Sri Lanka, and now lives in exile in Ireland. He has published four collections of poetry in Tamil: *Thirukkumaran kavithaikal* (2004), *Villungappatta vithaikal* (2011), *Thaniththiruththal* (2014) and *Vidaiperum velai* (2019). His poems have been included in the syllabus for Postgraduate Degrees in Sri Lankan and Indian universities and have been translated into English, German, Irish and Sinhala. His poems have been published in Tamil literary journals and newspapers and he has read widely at festivals in India, the UK, Germany, Switzerland, Ireland and Canada.

Resurrection

Even now, as the winter snow lies scattered
across the doorway, spilled like the brains
from a friend's shattered skull,
I cannot be rid of my memories.

Even now as the leaves fall from trees
like the dried blood of my massacred people,
the mind gives birth to a delirium
and I am bereft of all belief.

Now, as the returning birds flock
tearing open the cold wind
the days pass in silence.
I am alone in a room.

There is no one to feel for fever on my brow.
No one to unconsciously take hold of my hand.
Why does the morning dew captured in the fleck
of my pupil, drip from the side of my eye?

During this time of hardship as the saliva
gags in my throat, an angel appearing
from somewhere gathers me in his arms
and says 'Lay your burdens on me and rest'.

And like a woman reaching the heights
of pleasure, like a poem
unfolding on a page
the world resurrects in a miracle.

[tr. from Tamil by Shash Trevett]

This Is How the Buddha Disappeared

Wordlessly, Siddhartha stole away one night
from Yashodhara and his son
abandoning lives which had melted
into his own. Abandoning the springs
of devotion which had circled his heart.
As they searched for him in tears
he transformed into the Buddha
teaching the ways of love to the world.

Yet within him lay broken this irony.
When his seed bore fruit and grew
into the sacred Bodhi tree
Sanghamitta tore off a branch
and sped to Eelam.

That which travelled with her
was not a branch bearing love.
It was a branch of grief
given succour by agony,
watered by the tears of those
who waited, anticipating love.

From every leaf of that pitiless branch
rose the suffering of mothers and sons.
Unable to bear their agony
by himself, the Buddha divided it
among the people of Eelam
and disappeared into a glow of saffron.

[tr. from Tamil by Shash Trevett]

A Detached Feather

How like a cloud
you range across my sky.

How like a fragrance
you break open a flower.

Yet how as a brush
have you forgotten my colours?

How in this new language
have you disappeared my speech?

How, little feather
suspended in mid air,
did you abandon your bird
and where are you heading to today?

[tr. from Tamil by Shash Trevett]

THIRUMAVALAVAN

(1955–2015)

Thirumavalavan was the pen name of Kanagasingam Karunakaran, who was born in Varutthalaivilaan in the Northern Province. He left Jaffna and emigrated to Canada in 1990, where he continued to write, editing the literary journal *Zha'garam*. He published four collections of poetry in Tamil, and a collected edition of his poetry called *Siru pul manam* was published after his death in 2015. He received the poetry award from the Tamil Literary Garden (Canada) for his collection *Irul Yaalli* in 2010.

Mullaitivu

A pile of flesh,
the sun is lying there,
eviscerated.

And all over the sky
the blood
has spread.

Who is the boy
that pounced on the sun
this morning at daybreak
with piles of explosives?

[tr. from Tamil by Sascha Ebeling]

Living

a small tank
four glass walls
filters and disinfected water heated to an ideal temperature
floating artificial plants in a dim electric light
at regular intervals processed food
within the posh prison
the little fish sings its sorrow

[tr. from Tamil by S. Pathmanathan]

SHASH TREVETT

(*b.* 1974)

Shash Trevett (*née* Selvachandran) was born in Manipay, Northern Province, Sri Lanka. She is a poet, critic and a translator of Tamil poetry into English. Harassed by both the Sri Lankan Army and the LTTE (her father, being a prominent surgeon, was kidnapped several times and taken to operate on casualties on both sides under gunpoint), her family sought refuge in India in 1984. Returning to their home in 1987 on the signing of the Peace Accord, she was brutally caught up in the atrocities committed by the Indian Peace Keeping Force. A staunch pacifist, she lives in the UK and writes almost exclusively about the civil war and its aftermath on the lives of civilians. Shash is a winner of a Northern Writers' Award, her poetry has been widely published in the UK, her debut pamphlet *From a Borrowed Land* was published in 2021 by Smith|Doorstop, and her first collection is forthcoming in 2024 (also from Smith|Doorstop). She was a Visible Communities Translator in Residence at the National Centre for Writing, is a Ledbury Critic, reviewing for *PN Review* and the Poetry Book Society, and is a board member of *Modern Poetry in Translation*.

Uduvil, Nightfall

As the night descends quickly again,
a thick curtain drawn across the sky,

floating over the scent of jasmine
something else, a smell

my body wants to run from.
In the heavy silence sheathing the land

a weaver bird hurries to its nest.
Houses are shuttered, showing no light.

On the empty street, black tar cools.

I am like a ghost hovering over
this vacuum of non-life.

It is 6pm – curfew has begun
in this vacuum of a non-life.
I am like a ghost, hovering over

the empty street as black tar cools.
Houses are shuttered, showing no light.

A weaver bird hurries to its nest.

In the heavy silence sheathing the land
my body wants to run from

something else, a smell
floating over the scent of jasmine.

A thick curtain is drawn across the sky
as the night descends quickly, again.

The Sinhala Only Act, 1956

Tamil words that lilt, soothing as a lullaby
on a mother's breath. Their *isaioli*   melody
nourishing our *uyir*, a life force   life
marked on a stave imagined
a millennia ago. In whispers
of promises they show themselves
as *paadal* and *kathai* and *kavithai*.   songs; stories; poetry
Our generations were formed
by their fluid *naatiyam*, our voices   dance
tuned to their scripted *sangheetham*.   hymns
And when we dreamed, our dreams erupted
in அs and இs and உs: building blocks   Aaa; Eee; Uuu
of a nation now without a homeland,
a people now without a place.

And when in '56 they tried to silence
your *innisai*, gag your *uyiroli*   sweet melody; vowels
and eradicate your *meiyelluthal*   consonants
we took to the streets carrying
your *unmai* as our arms. Warriors   truth
of the Tolkaapiyam on Galle Face Green
paying with our blood for your right to be.
Oru naadillaathe aatkal, in exile,   A people without a country
bearing the music of your beauty, still.

378

My Grandfather's House

There is moss growing in the bedrooms
of my grandfather's house.
Green and sticky, staining the walls
and the floor with shades of the sea.
They climb, tracing intricate patterns, around
browned squares, where pictures used to hang.

The roof has fallen in. Water stagnates
on a cushioned floor as disturbed bats circle,
drawing the night in. The rooms are empty
of all that was him. The doors have been locked
warped and unwilling to open onto
a tomorrow which does not contain him.

It is six o'clock and the mosquitos
gather noisily in rooms that once
smelt of sweet margossa leaves.
They are the music makers, the sum total
of our dreams. The inheritors of rooms
that reek and sweat in angry dismay.

There is moss growing in the bedrooms
of my grandfather's house and raindrops
sing a lament on deserted floors.

URVASI

(*b.* 1956)

Urvasi is the pen name of Juvaneswary Tharmaratnam, who was born in
Karukampanai, Jaffna. A poet as well as an academic, she was one of the
Tamil women poets who came into prominence in the 1980s, writing about
women's place in society and the effect of the civil war on their lives. Although
appearing widely in anthologies she published only one collection (*Innum
Varaatha Sethi*, 2014) and is rumoured to have stopped writing in recent
years.

Do You Understand?

It is no use
to send this letter
to any address that I know.
Nevertheless, somehow or other
it must reach you.
That you will certainly receive it
is my unshakeable belief.

Here, in the front courtyard
the jasmine is in full bloom.
Honey birds by day
and the scent-laden breeze by night
reach as far as our room.
All sorts of people whom I do not know
walk past our house, often.
Yet, till now, no one has come
to interrogate me.

The small puppy runs in circles
around the house
without reason,
its tail raised high
as if it wants to catch someone.
At night, when I cannot sleep,
I dust your books and put them away.
I have read most of them, now.
I have never opened
your mother's letters.
The weight of her grief for her sons
I cannot endure.

And then, my love,
the thought that you have gone away
only for our people sake
is my only consolation.
Although this imprisoning sorrow is huge,
yet, since our separation,
I have learnt to bear everything.

One thing more:
it is this, most of all

I wanted to say.
I am not particularly a soft-natured woman
nor am I as naive as I once was.
Our current state of affairs
gives me no sign of hope.
It is certain
that for a long time
we must be apart.
Then,
why should I stay within this house
any longer?
Well,
do you understand what I write to you?

[tr. from Tamil by Lakshmi Holmström]

Why Must We Wait?

Why must we wait?
For the chill mist hugging the earth
and clouds covering the mountains
to dissolve?
For the golden sun of the morning
to reach its peak in the sky?

I cannot wait so long,
my love.
How many hours have gone by
like this?

The midday sun scorches
lovers' brimming eyes.
Sea waves are touched with beauty
and the wind sings against palm leaves
only at dawn, or else at dusk.

But,
when this earth, these times,
and everything that is ours is lost,

such an hour as this
may never be ours again.
In the darkness of the night to come
anything could happen.

So, my love,
in the deep silence
of this daybreak
let us be one.

[tr. from Tamil by Lakshmi Holmström]

VIVIMARIE VANDERPOORTEN
(———)

Vivimarie Vanderpoorten teaches at the Open University of Sri Lanka. Her
first book of poems, *nothing prepares you*, won the 2007 Gratiaen Prize in Sri
Lanka, and she went on to publish two more collections, *Stitch Your Eyelids
Shut* and *Borrowed Dust*, both of which won national awards. Her work has
also been published internationally in print and online journals and in India,
Pakistan and Bangladesh, and other countries, in English as well as in translation.
Most recently two Sinhala poems she translated into English were published
by the online literary magazine of the Commonwealth Foundation, Adda. Her
fourth collection of poems, *Pictures I Couldn't Take*, was longlisted for the
2021 Gratiaen Prize. Her first book of translations, *Speechless is the River*, is
forthcoming.

Cadaver

They say that holding on to the past
is like tying a corpse
to your back and taking it along
with you
wherever you go,
the stench horrible,
people around you hold their noses
and avoid you like

the proverbial plague.
(A radio DJ spouts such
words of wisdom
between Beyonce's song
about replacing her lover
and a commercial for detergents)

Driving in rush hour traffic
with a knot of grief
in my throat
I believe he's speaking
just to me.
So I'm thinking
I should let memory die
let loving you go
imagine the maggots surface
white and thick and sticky
from the depths of your eyes
I drowned in once
and try to hold in my hands
the crumbling flesh
of your once-loved body
as it falls
bit
by
bit
from
the skeleton of
your devotion
I should untie you
from the back of my heart
dig a hole in the dark deep
night of my past
and bury you,
kisses and all.

Traditional

I was seven when
I first saw my uncle

kick his pregnant wife, hard.
In the stomach.
It was Avurudu and
festive times were upon us

Dropping him at his house
because he couldn't drive on his own
Waiting in the car
until he made it through the door which
opened
and his wife came
outside
expressing disappointment
at his inebriation

My father swore
slipped out of the driver's seat
and pulled him off
my screaming aunt
and punched him in the face. He went flat
out.
Bleeding from the nose.

He had been named
for a notorious Italian dictator
and much was always blamed on that.

Inside the house,
the milk heated at the auspicious hour
had boiled over signifying abundance
and was still warm
in the pot.

Diplomatic

At a diplomatic gathering
an ambassador's wife
smiles sweetly
as I'm introduced as a poet

(a term I'll always wear
like a size 14 dress
on my size 8 frame)

I smile back
embarrassed
hoping I can talk about the weather
the cricket world cup final
which we might win
or the war
which no one will

but her next question's one of
mild surprise
'you write in English?'
and my smile turns
apologetic
for a reason that can't find its voice
in poetry or prose
so I nod a diplomatic yes
and grab a drink from
a passing tray.

S. VILVARATNAM
(1950–2006)

S. Vilvaratnam was known as 'Su. V' to his friends. Born in Pungudutheevu, Northern Province, he began writing in the 1970s. A prominent poet of protest, he wrote extensively about the hardships faced by the Tamil people. He worked in the civil service and published several collections of poetry in Tamil, including *Akangalum Mukangalum*, *Kaatruveli Kiramam* and *Kaalathuyar*; his collected works was published in 2001. He also wrote about spirituality and was vocal in his opposition of caste practices. He was a celebrated orator and singer and a committed supporter of a separate Tamil homeland of Eelam.

There Was a Time

Oh yes, there was a time
when we were kings of our own earth
when there was no one to interfere

in our affairs
when even poverty didn't hinder
the pleasant dreams of our lives.

Oh yes, there was a time.

We eked a living out of our dry soil
we protected the right to live
even of the grass edging our canals.
The harvest we gathered in,
the result of our hard labour,
we shared amongst all of us.
Like the cowbells on oxen pulling Time's cart,
our steps jingled in merriment
at that time.

Oh yes, that was the time
when our fields were our own
our streets were our own
the nights were sweet, the moon was sweet,
we enjoyed life as if it were
love's honeyed torment.

Today our earth
is like a widowed woman,
her wounds calling out in lament.

Oh yes, in this, our time,
we are slaves
held within streets steeped in blood.

[tr. from Tamil by Lakshmi Holmström]

The Echo of Moonlight

Parampu mountain.
Pari had died,
and the sun had vanished in the darkness.
Ankavai and Cankavai
were refugees.

They had fallen
to the 'royal drums beating victory'
and on the hill, on a narrow path
that seem to be filled with the sorrow
of their downcast moonlike faces
Pari's daughters walked. Coming down
from the hill, the moonlight itself seemed to walk slowly
accompanying them like Kapilar, who had grown so old.

The moonlight,
Kapilar,
Pari's daughters
and the good life of Parampu.
They all walked
growing weary
weak and pale

With reverence Kapilar entrusted
Par's daughters whose lives were broken
to Auvai and disappeared.
The journey continued.

Pari's daughters walked with Auvai
through all the villages
of the poor whose only food was gruel,
and the moon stood, hesitating, and went with them.

As if her long life
granted by Atiyaman's nelli fruit
were approaching its end,
Auvai hurried.
Sealing the marriages by pouring water,
she gave Pari's daughters
to the man who had destroyed their lives on Parampu Mountain,
Pari's daughters who, like her,
made Tamil.
If only she had given them
to the families of men so poor
that, late in giving taxes,
they have only gruel or porridge to pay,
Pari's soul would have rejoiced.

That day, in the white light of that moon,
there was Parampu mountain,
and the drums beating victory,
and Ankavai and Cankavai
who became slaves in the harem of kings
and cried in pain – and now
on this day, in the white light of this moon,
their echoes still resound.

[tr. from Tamil by George L. Hart]

VINOTHINI
(*b*. 1969)

Vinothini was born in Eelam and now lives in Miwuk territory in California. She is a Tamil poet, biophile, naturalist and visual artist, who began writing in the 1980s. Her poetry deals with love and war and her collection (*Muhamoodi Seipaval*, 2007) was published in India. In recent times Vinothini has concentrated on the symbiosis between word and image, and strives to live a life in harmony with nature.

The Mask Maker

On the walls of her house
are the masks she has made.

Using a drop of her own blood
a wisp of her breath
fragments of her ageing muscles,
she makes her masks.

Whether in the middle of the night
or at the break of first light,
wherever there is a life waning
or another beginning,
when someone is being oppressed
or another being murdered
she makes her masks.

During the heartbreak of a love affair
or when a girl is assaulted
when children forget how to cry out in fright
when explosions rattle the nests of birds
when a man, disappeared for no reason,
fears for his life
when a house is abandoned and a village deserted
when a stray dog dies of starvation
when people realise that their gods
having drunk milk and honey have gone away –
during these moments, she makes her masks.

Deceived into thinking that the lifeless masks
with their unseeing, ever open eyes
are like children
she gives them life, somehow,
and from time to time they steal her dreams.

[tr. from Tamil by Shash Trevett]

The Night

The sea draws down the sun
concealing the world in darkness.
A creeping darkness which saturates my room.
Through my window I see
a strip of sky, no moon,
and only the glitter of one or two stars.
With my fingers and my eyes I long to feel
this night. But it cannot be.
The night offers no answers to my questions.

As the marching footsteps
of the angels of death fade away,
someone, somewhere plays a lonely flute.
The drifting music saturates me.

And in a song the night speaks.

[tr. from Tamil by Shash Trevett]

NANDANA WEERASINGHE

(————)

Nandana Weerasinghe was a poet of the free verse generation and began writing in the 1980s at a time when Sinhala poetry was becoming increasingly insular. Along with Eric Illayapparachchi and Ariyawansa Ranaweera, Weerasinghe with his first collection *Gingage Vilapaya* (1984) offered some hope for the future of Sinhala verse. His poetry makes the reader think, engaging as it does with socio-political issues, form and aesthetics. Weerasinghe also worked as a journalist and published several collections of poetry. He has won the Sahitya Award several times, the Gratiaen Prize and the State Literary awards.

The Moon-shadow

What difference does it make
Whether it is a big vessel
Or a small one?
We look at so many different vessels
With clear water and see
Only the reflection of the moon
When full

[tr. from Sinhala by Manoj Ariyaratne]

Full Moon on a Dewdrop

Unwilling to listen
to the cacophony
of the rolling
angry waves
that leap high up
in pride
into the empty sky
as if they had sucked the moon's whole light
that silent dewdrop carrying the glory of
the full moon and the joy
of endless moonlight
falls on a cold leaf

and dries up
slowly, secretly

contentedly

[tr. from Sinhala by A.T. Dharmapriya]

Kalidasa and the Moon

Kalidasa!
Where was he born?
Where did he live?
And to whom does he belong?

Along with critics,
teachers and professors
gathered for a great debate that evening
to claim Kalidasa for their own country
a city and a village.

'Open *Mega Duta*
it is the country of Malawa that is described in it
so he belongs to the area of Ujjain.'

'That shows great misunderstanding
recall *Kumara Sambhawa* or *Wickramorshiwa*
with descriptions in them of the Himalayas
so it is to us in Kashmir that he belongs.'

Another learned person
getting up quickly
said firmly
'He belongs to us at Darbhanga,
for he worshipped
the old statue of the goddess Kali.'

Then the moon appeared
to soften the darkness that had grown
and an old man
by then tired by debating

asked a young poet who was there:
'Where was Kalidasa born
where did he live?
To whom should he belong?

That poet raised his hand to the sky
and pointed out the moon
spreading light and comfort
equally in all directions.

[tr. from Sinhala by Liyanage Amarakeerthi]

Something Square-shaped

The waterfall splashes down
Amidst the darkening shadows
Evoking the itinerant
Monotonous noise

I search the bottom
Of the river bed
Into which it cascades

Pebbles big and small
Nurtured moulded
Pounded into a single round shape
I collect in my palms

What use are these slavish minions
Who yielded
To the wiles of water without the murmur
I throw them back
To the stream where they belong
And search and search for
Maybe something square shaped
To take back home as a treasure

[tr. from Sinhala by Ariyawansa Ranaweera]

RUSHIKA WICK

(*b.* 1973)

Rushika Wick is a mother, poet and paediatrician based in London, with interests in social ecology and visual poetics. Her work can be found in *Magma, Ambit, Shearsman, The Poetry Review* and *Poetry Birmingham Literary Journal* amongst others. Work from her debut collection, *Afterlife as Trash* (Verve Poetry Press, 2021), was highly commended in the 2021 Forward Prizes. Rushika is an editor at *sunseekers poetry project* (Instagram) and assistant editor at *Tentacular* magazine. She is a member of the female collective, Kinara.

Hair

I had only one desire: to dismember it. To see of what it was made...
TONI MORRISON

You brushed her hair when your mother was ill,
sunlit silk, hot sand slipping through fingers by the creek,
not of burnt sugar spun in air.
You stared at it, trying to make some of the gold go into you,
she asked you what you were doing.
Body cane-straight so that when she wore dresses,
they hung like elegant washing, left to dry.
Calico and soap, Sunday milk,
the cat with golden eyes watching the
relentless washing and scrubbing until skin split
to white flesh.

Ultramarine Pink PV15

1

Can you remember that shade of Angel Delight?
It was the time of Michael Knight & pixie boots.
But I could not focus, reeling from the pink balloon
reminding me of intensive care ventilators
& a Dutch sex doll I had seen at an installation
sitting with a vase of giant peonies,
each like a face, sympathetic to her escape
from a canal-side bedroom stained with tobacco.
I remembered the school trip to Amsterdam

where I learned that sex is not a thing of beauty in itself,
but could look like a multi-pack of Salt 'n' Shake,
each packet with its own blue sachet
containing exactly 0.6g of salt.

2

Sex is not a thing of beauty in itself. It is a plastic bag caught in
the wind, seeking headlights. It is half a breath, a self-portrait. A
white porcelain heart clamped between legs. It is a machine, a salt
lick in the field – solid as animals come by, or bitter greens for
health. It is a clock, a severed oyster, a dream of Orpheus or physical
exercise. It is smeared blue make-up across the face and not looking
down. It is sleepwalking. Feigning sleep. Electrocution from a plug
socket. Turning a musty page. It is not Freud & the patriarchy. It
is biting filled candy until it leaks. Falling sequins. A sick bag. A
footnote. The beast whose face is faceless, a burning wound. A
salve. Bird entrails strung out across the lawn. It is both a whistle
& a trained dog, a cracked jug seeping water.

Yellow Phone in the Yellow House

(after Van Gogh)

A licked finger passing through a flame.

We wallow in screen-shine
tallow-faced, & marked to the bone
mind like jaundiced sailors in sun-fog
navigating a new body,
oil slicks reflecting golden moon
held in a transparent cortex of silica, like fruits in jelly
that someone else's children have died for.

A corrupt phrenology is imposed –
stop tattooing maps on our scalps,
the sulfur will turn olive over time
& eating sparrow yolks as art
is no antidote.

In Arles, Vincent ate digitalis
& everything was sunflowers,
flower begat flower & still his ear was lost.

ILLAVALAI WIJAYENDRAN

(b. 1961)

Illavalai Wijayendran is the pen name of Wijayendran Thiyagaraja, who was born in Nuwara Eliya in the hill country of Sri Lanka. A poet and a journalist, he moved to Norway from where he edited the Tamil literary journal *Suvadugal*; he was also one of the editors of the Canadian Tamil journal *Mutram*. He has published one collection of poetry (*Niramatrrup pona Kanavukal*) and is also a lyricist, some of his poems being set to song and classical Bharathanatyam dance.

To Those Who Bear Sticks

My strength lies in my words
not in my body.

To terrify the people, you pile on words
borrowed from the night.

But my words remain upright.
They beat and subdue yours.

Having lost to my words
you return bearing sticks.

What words can I use to answer
this display of your power?

[tr. from Tamil by Shash Trevett]

The Missing Children

The hanging roots of the banyan tree
like swinging ropes, promise hours of fun.
Around it, the ponnachchi flowers
laugh in the breeze.
To the East, a pond overflows
in the middle of the rainy season.

By its shore a boat made of dead palm wood
on which to voyage repeatedly.
The only thing missing from this scene
was the children.

I asked the old man climbing the coconut trees,
their heads still unbent despite the bombings,
where the children were.
They have gone to harvest
the money fields of Canada
he replied, with sadness.

[tr. from Tamil by Shash Trevett]

The Veenai and the Sword

We have received news
that several poets who lived in our land
have been lost, or are now dead.

We have heard
that their poems also
languish in the burial ground.

Who consented
to the loss of both
the Veenai and the sword?

Be fearless
we will recover
those we have lost.

[tr. from Tamil by Shash Trevett]

RATNA SRI WIJESINGHE

(*b.* 1953)

Ratna Sri Wijesinghe was born in Galle and studied at the University of Peradeniya, where he obtained a Bachelor of Arts degree in Sinhala. His award-winning career began with *Biya Nowan Ayyandi*, published in 1975, and was followed by *Wassane, Suba Udaasana, Midday Yamaya, Sandhya Theertha* and *Sandagira Pamula*. He has composed Sinhala lyrics for many famous musical artists in Sri Lanka: these songs include *Sudu Neluma Ko Sorabora Wawe, Mage Bisawune Asaapan, Maala Girawiya, Punsanda Raata, Kirula Muthu Lihee, Lenchina* and *Mage Duwe Numba Dan Awadiyen Nam*. His work is inspired by real events and encounters.

Two Teardrops

'Be quiet, I command
You, lunatic patients
Be quiet, and behold
Tread not, these steps
Do not tarnish them
With your sandals.'

Steps leading to the upper deck
Of the lunatic asylum
Were glittering,
Its worn-out cement
Soft as a cheek
Softly caressed
By the thin golden fingertips
Of the morning sun.

On the worn out cement lay
Two drops of tears
Facing each other
In dumb silence
Not murmuring a word.

'Can it be believed
That I dropped from an eye
Of a chaste and faithful wife
Who dedicated her life
At the feet of a husband
After having been tormented

With love for him
For seven years?'
So said one tear drop
After long silence.

Treetops heaved, sobbing
With the dry wind
That comes from afar.

A moment later
The other teardrop
Broke the silence.

'I know that man so well
Who despised and spat on
That love so holy and sacred –
Lament not, sister dear
Believe me
For I'll tell you the truth.

'Behold that
Unfortunate woman there
Who was his second wife
And I am a drop of tear
Born in her eye.'

[tr. from Sinhala by the author]

from The Motherless Two

Nithyakala your letter
was like a stream of tears to me
but isn't this taste of salt
from my own tears?

The thin moon
sleeping on the lap of the sky
discoloured like the clothes of a wet-nurse
– when will it fade?
Or will it die in that embrace?
Dearest, I cannot say.

In the compassionate shade
of the Sirimaha Bodhi
upon the sands
shot dead
my mother fell
carrying lotus flowers in her hands
entwining her fingers
upon her forehead

Should I come
to make her sleep
under the palmyra trees
with the dying fragrance of jasmine?
Should I come?
Nithyakala, tell me.

Two of us
motherless
in two places
washing tears with more tears
Nithyakala
you and I...

[tr. from Sinhala by Madhubhashini Ratnayake]

LAKDASA WIKKRAMASINHA
(1941–78)

Lakdasa Wikkramasinha's relentlessly original depictions of local and colonial violence, art and art history, are accompanied by metaphysical riffs on sexual desire. His author and poem notes are wickedly humorous (he announces that 'Memorial', not included here, is 'the greatest Asian poem in English') and one wonders, given the brilliance of rhythm and lineation and word-choice and imagery of his Anglophone works, what to make of his statement: 'I have come to realise that I am using the language of the most despicable and loathsome people on earth; I have no wish to extend its life and range [...] To write in English is a form of cultural treason.'

He studied law, taught at the University of Kelaniya, and released six books of poems. Vihanga Perera compares him with the Romantic poet Percy Bysshe Shelley: 'both were from socially elite backgrounds [...] Both display immense political commitment in their writing. Both Shelley and Wikkramasinha evoke violence and force – even revolution and social upheaval. Both died in their 30s. And by drowning.'

Don't Talk to Me about Matisse

Don't talk to me about Matisse, don't talk to me
about Gauguin, or even
the earless painter van Gogh,
& the woman reclining on a blood-spread...
the aboriginal shot by the great white hunter Matisse

with a gun with two nostrils, the aboriginal
crucified by Gauguin – the syphilis-spreader, the yellowed obesity.

Don't talk to me about Matisse...
the European style of 1900, the tradition of the studio
where the nude woman reclines forever
on a sheet of blood.

Talk to me instead of the culture generally –
how the murderers were sustained
by the beauty robbed of savages: to our remote
villages the painters came, and our whitewashed
mud-huts were splattered with gunfire.

The Flames, 1972

I love
sunflowers. Once, my great-grandmother
using
the true colours
of sunflowers bled
from the abraded bark of the
gokatu tree
painted a bouquet of them
standing in an 18th-century
clay vase.
Since then the leaves
have shrivelled and died. The flowers
are fallen
all over my mind –
My mind cannot contain them. I see
that my great-grandmother

had little, if any, reason
to paint sunflowers
– which, in any case, grow wild. And
my passion
to set fire to things, derives,
perhaps, from this sad
history…

Luis de Camoes

Luis de Camoes, spitting in the sea –
slanting – the sea off Galle,
singing of frost over the Mondego: a Lusitanian breeze:
Mondego; frost (you will remember);
a very cold wind, you remember, was flapping about –
you thought there were two winds –
you thought it was like an eel, bleeding –
but really, the wind was very still
that year.

And then
the gaiety of the kafferinha,
& the fledgling gull
dead on the topmast…: so the tragedy
begat! O LUSIADS

Sand. Weed. Water. & the sailors as you know
know nothing. My grandfather was a sailor
at 16; a soldier
in the Latin wilderness,
& then he became
a priest. Such ruminations, such memories, however
have now exploded
in my face. 42 'chieftains'
in my distaff
died in the fighting between 1505 &
1630. Luis

de Camoes! A poem contains nothing
but the bones of the dead.
& the bones of the dead, my friend,
do not last forever.

Middle

The middle of the night
Was built for two people:
For myself, and for myself.

But the middle of the day is called noon:
Taking in memories of the hot air,
Dreaming in the siesta,

Sleeping alone, with a long knife.

RICHARD DE ZOYSA
(1958–90)

A journalist, activist and actor as well as a poet, Richard de Zoysa was asso-
ciated with the Janatha Vimukthi Peramuna – a Marxist, militant organisation
– and during the government crackdown on their activities he was abducted
and murdered (his body was dumped on the beach, shot in the head and throat).
His father was Sinhalese, his mother Tamil. Rajiva Wijesinha wrote a novel
about him, controversial for suggesting he was gay. His poems aren't all well-
wrought – the direct, prosaic, anecdotal stuff isn't featured here – but he writes
with allusive urgency, mischief, and never complacently, shaping agitation into
nonplussing forms. He challenged norms of sexuality and gender, and also pub-
lished verse under the pseudonym of Angela de Silva, supposedly a schoolteacher.

Animal Crackers
(for Dimitri, when he is old enough to understand)

'Draw me a lion.'
So I set my pen
To work. Produce a lazy, kindly beast…
Colour it yellow
'Does it bite?'
'Sometimes,
but only when it's angry –
if you pull its tail
or say that it is just another cat…'
But for the most part indolent, biddable
basking in the sun of ancient pride.

(Outside, the sunlight seems a trifle dulled
and there's a distant roaring, like a pride
of lions, cross at being awakened
from long, deep sleep).

Then
'Draw me a tiger.'
Vision of a beast
compounded of Jim Corbett yarns
and Blake
stalks through my mind, blazing Nature's warning,
black bars on gold.

'Draw!'
You turn and draw the gun
on me, as if to show
that three-years-old understands force majeure
and as you pull the silly plastic trigger
all hell breaks loose: quite suddenly the sky
is full of smoke and orange stripes of flame.

BUT HERE THERE ARE NO TIGERS   HERE THERE ARE ONLY LIONS

And their jackals
run panting, rabid in the roaring's wake,
infecting all with madness as they pass
while My Lord
the Elephant sways in his shaded arbour,
wrinkles his ancient brows and wonders –
if, did he venture out to quell this jungle-tide
of rising flame, he'd burn his tender feet.

'Put down that gun. If you do, and you're good,
I'll draw a picture of an elephant.
A curious beast that you must understand …

DON'T LOOK OUT OF THE WINDOW –

Just a party down the lane
A bonfire, and some fireworks, and they're burning –
No, not a tiger – just some silly cat.'

Colombo, 25 July 1983

Author's note: The Lion is the heraldic emblem of the Sinhala or the Lion Race. The principal Tamil terrorist group in the north of Sri Lanka is known as the Tigers. The Elephant is the party symbol of the ruling United National party. Jim Corbett has written a good deal about the Indian jungles, particularly about his pursuits of several man-eating tigers.

Corporation Love Song (I)

Look!
One can actually see a patch of sky
One can see it from the balcony
(Only to call it 'balcony' would be to glorify it
Far beyond its function)
Just a corridor with a view
Not much – just a little patch
Of not-so-blue
Sky …

And even that not-so-blue is darkening, now,
darkening into grey, and your face is thundering, now,
thundering, and inside me it has already started, the hard rain.

You talk of pain.
I have nothing to say. For me
There has not been a moment without it
These past five years or more
And so it only pours inside from what probably seems to be
A perfectly calm blue sky.

A bureaucrat
Goes ambling past
Favours us with a jaded glance.
He's seen too many of these things
These desperate couples clinging onto corners
Of each other …
The affairs don't stand a chance.
They never last.

Still, it's turning into quite a grand storm
That last flash of lightning was far too close
For comfort.
Funny! you're saying that for me
These things must be the norm

404

But I …
Funny! –
I can feel a raindrop growing
At the corner of my eye.

Gajagavannama

(published under the pseudonym, Angela de Silva)

February 1983 – Gangaramaya Perahere

The elephants are out. Last night they marched
Gorgeous through streets, caparisoned like kings,
Electric radiance shattering the night,
Laden with relics, talismans and things.

Dawn came. And they were tethered in their stalls
(the back garages of an Institute of Education)
Where they swayed and chafed,
Had time for thought. A notion then took root

In the huge cerebellum that uncoils
Behind the great, domed skull. 'We are the lords
Of open spaces. Great bucolic monarchs
Of the land.' The city's teeming hordes

Hooted and jangled by beyond the walls
That prisoned and demanded patience from them.
With one accord they snapped their ankle chains
And lumbered forth towards the gates to storm them.

The city froze. Then birds sprang to the air
And men to trees. Vehicles clambered walls.
All order vanished as the blind grey surge
Swept down the arcades and the trumpet calls

Drowned klaxons, sirens, bells, horns, engines – swamped
The roaring of the bloodstream of Colombo.
Quite suddenly it ended. Having made
His point, the pachyderm returned to Jumbo

And plodded meekly home. The city now
Knows behemoths, aroused, will rule by riot.
We bow the head and bend a loyal knee
To jungle law, in hope of peace and quiet.

Note: Gajaga Vannama – Elephant Dance (a traditional dance form). In February 1983, some elephants brought to Colombo for the Navam Perhera held by the Gangarama Temple broke free from the makeshift stalls where they were tethered and ran through the streets of Colombo. The elephant is the symbol of the UNP, the ruling party of Sri Lanka (from 1977 to 1994). UNP thugs are believed to have been heavily involved in organised anti-Tamil violence in July 1983.

The Poet

i
am the eye of the camera
can only reflect, never reject,
never deflect

i
am the eye
of the camera
silent recorder of life
and death
eye that can only reflect
never conjure up images
probe the reality
never reject

i am the eye
of the camera
i reflect nothing
but truth

the external reality
cannot deflect
the mind of the viewer
from picture to passion

i let them all fashion
their truths through my magic
i cannot reject
the external reality
that passes for truth

and what is rejected
by natural selection
has nothing to do with me
when i am impotent
robbed of my power
my eyes in the dark at the moment of crisis
see nothing but well favoured men of the hour

i
am the storm's eye
ceaselessly turning
around me the burning the death the destruction
the clichés that govern the world of the words
of the prophets and preachers, and maybe the saviours
are lost to my peering
blind eye in the dark

TRANSLATORS

Notes on translators who are also poets represented in this anthology appear with the selections of their poems.

Janani Ambikapathy was born and raised in Chennai. She was awarded a PhD in English at the University of Cambridge. Her essays and poems have been published in *Modernism/Modernity, Modern Poetry in Translation, Lana Turner, Datableed, The Rialto* and *Visual Verse* amongst other magazines. Her pamphlet *If Not Theirs* was published by Veer2 in 2022. She is currently working on translations of *Akkananuru*, an anthology of classical Tamil poems from the 3rd century CE.

Liyanage Amarakeerthi: see page 46.

Manoj Ariyaratne is an academic in the Department of Languages at the Sabaragamuwa University of Sri Lanka. His research interests include the comparative study of syntax in Sinhala and English, and translation studies.

A.J. Canagaratna was an editor, journalist, scholar and translator, who translated the Sinhala poetry of Siri Gunasinghe as well as various Tamil poets. His translations were published widely in journals and anthologies. He died in 2006.

Sascha Ebeling is Deputy Dean of the Humanities and Associate Professor in the Department of South Asian Languages and Civilisations and Comparative Literature at the University of Chicago. Partnering with Lakshmi Holmström, he has translated: *A Second Sunrise: Poems by Cheran* (2012) and *Lost Evening, Lost Lives* (2016), a translation of Tamil poetry from the Sri Lankan civil war. He is the recipient of the 2007 Research Award of the German Oriental Society for his work on 19th-century Tamil literature, and in July 2010, he was honoured with the award for Outstanding Achievement in Tamil Studies by the Tamil literary Garden, Toronto.

A.T. Dharmapriya was a trained English teacher, and later in his life, he took to translating Sinhala literature into English. He has translated numerous Sinhala novels, short stories, and poems during his career.

Wimal Dissanayake: see page 101.

E.M.G. Edirisinghe was a translator of poetry, fiction and film scripts from Sinhala into English, as well as a critic and social commentator. He chaired various award-giving bodies in Sri Lanka including the Presidential and the Sarasaviya and died in 2012.

Garrett Field is Associate Professor of Ethnomusicology/Musicology at Ohio University, specialising in the history of Sinhala song and poetry in 20th-century Sri Lanka. He is the author of *Modernising Composition: Sinhala Song, Poetry, and Politics in Twentieth-Century Sri Lanka* (University of California Press, 2017).

Malini Govinnage was a journalist, literary critic and translator from Sinhala to English and vice versa. Her translations of Sinhala poetry were published widely in journals and anthologies. She died in 2021.

George L. Hart is Professor Emeritus at University of California, Berkeley, where he founded the Tamil Department. He specialises in early Sangam Tamil poetry, has translated several important works from Tamil to English including an annotated translation of *The 400 Poems of Wisdom and War (The Purananuru)*.

Lakshmi Holmström was an India-born British writer, critic and translator who for over 30 years translated short stories, novels and poetry by major contemporary Tamil writers into English. Her most recent translations were: *Lost Evening, Lost Lives* (2016), a translation of Tamil poetry from the Sri Lankan civil war; *Wild Girls, Wicked Words* (2014), poetry by four Indian Tamil writers; *In a Time of Burning* (2013), a translation of the poetry of Cheran, which won an English PEN award; *The Hour Past Midnight* (2009), a translation of a novel by Salma. She received many awards for her translations including, in 2008, the Iyal award from the Tamil Literary Garden, Canada. In 2011, she was awarded an MBE for her services to literature. She died in 2016.

Chelva Kanaganayakam was Professor of English at the University of Toronto, Canada, and a distinguished scholar of postcolonial literature and South Asian Studies. One of the foremost translators of Sri Lankan Tamil poetry and prose, he edited and published several anthologies including *Lutesong and Lament* (2001), *Wilting Laughter* (2009) and *Uprooting the Pumpkin* (2016), and was instrumental in providing a platform from which Tamil poetry could be heard outside Sri Lanka. He was a Fellow of the Royal Society of Canada and died in 2014.

Meena Kandasamy is an anti-caste activist, poet, novelist and translator from Tamil Nadu, southern India. An acclaimed poet and novelist, her work has been translated into eighteen languages and she was elected a Fellow of the Royal Society of Literature in 2022. Activism is at the heart of her literary work and she has translated several political texts from Tamil to English: *Talisman: Extreme Emotions of Dalit Liberation* (2003); *Uproot Hindutva: The Fiery Voice of the Liberation Panthers* (2004); *Why Were Women Enslaved?* (2007). She received a PEN Translates award for her translation of Salma's *Manamiyangal /Women, Dreaming* (2020) and has co-translated *Waking is Another*

Dream (2010), a volume of poetry from the Sri Lankan civil war. She holds a PhD in sociolinguistics.

Chamini Kulathunga is a Sri Lankan translator currently based in the US and Sri Lanka. She is a graduate of the Iowa Translation Workshop and a former visiting fellow at Cornell University's South Asia Program. She is a recent recipient of The Global South Translation Fellowship awarded by Cornell University's Institute for Comparative Modernities. Chamini is currently working as *Asymptote*'s Editor-at-Large for Sri Lanka and as an Associate Editor at The Song Bridge Project, a non-profit publisher of literary translations based in Iowa City. She was the former blog editor and a staff editor at *Exchanges: Journal of Literary Translation*. During her time in Sri Lanka, she has worked in the corporate sector as an editor-in-chief in a news platform and as a visiting scholar at three Sri Lankan universities.

Fran Lock is the author of many poetry collections, most recently *Hyena! Jackal! Dog!* (Pamenar Press, 2021). She obtained her PhD from Birkbeck College, University of London. Lock has co-translated with Hari Rajaledchumy a selection of Tamil poet Anar's work, *Leaving* (Poetry Translation Centre, 2021).

R. Murugaiyan: see page 234.

Gaya Nagahawatta lives in Colombo. She works with languages (Sinhala and English) and with audio-visual media (photography, theatre, film, and also sculpture). She enjoys conceptualising and organising events, is passionate about open-source software, and believes in people's collective power to bring about meaningful change.

M.A. Nuhman: see page 248.

Ranjini Obeyesekere is a prominent translator into English, of both medieval and contemporary Sinhala poetry and prose. She has taught in the Department of Literature at the University of Peradeniya, the University of California, San Diego, and in the last ten years in the Department of Anthropology, Princeton University. Her publications include *An Anthology of Modern Writing from Sri Lanka* (1981), *Jewels of the Doctrine: from the Saddharmaratnavaliya* (1991) *Yasodhara, Wife of the Bodhisattva* (2009) and *Sinhala Poetry in Translation* (2017). At present she is engaged in editing a three-volume translation of the 14th-century Sinhala Book of Jataka Stories. Retired now she lives in Kandy, Sri Lanka.

S. Pathmanathan: see page 258.

Hari Rajaledchumy is an artist/writer originally from Sri Lanka and currently based in London. Her writings have appeared in *Manalveedu* (India) and *Aakkaddi* (France). She worked as a translator on Kim Longinotto's 2013 documentary film *Salma*, about the life and works of the Indian Tamil poet. In 2021, she co-curated 'Queer/trans Collaborations: Sri Lanka' – a study programme that strengthens queer cultural productions within Sri Lanka. She co-translated a selection of Tamil poet Anar's work with Fran Lock, *Leaving* (Poetry Translation Centre, 2021).

Shirani Rajapakse: see page 270.

S. Rajasingham: see page 272.

Ariyawansa Ranaweera: see page 279.

Madhubhashini Disanayaka Ratnayake is the former head and a senior lecturer in the Department of English Language Teaching, University of Sri Jayewardenepura. Her anthology of translations, *The Routledge Companion to Sinhala Fiction from Postwar Sri Lanka*, was published in 2022. She won the Gratiaen Prize for her novel *There is Something I Have to Tell You* (2011), the State Literary Award for her short story collection *Driftwood* (1991), and for the Best Translation of a Novel from Sinhala to English for *The Sowing Festival* (2020), a translation of Somaratne Balasuriya's *Vap Magula*.

Nedra Rodrigo is a translator, academic, curator of multi-arts events, the founder of the Tamil Studies Symposium at York University, Canada, and The Tam Fam Lit Jam. Rodrigo's published translations include Thamilini's *In the Shadow of the Sword* (2020). She is in the process of translating the *Prison of Dreams* quintet by B. Devakanthan, the first two volumes of which, *His Sacred Army* and *A Time of Questions*, were published in 2021. Her translations of Tamil poetry from Sri Lanka have been included in anthologies and journals.

Ra Sh (the pseudonym of Ravi Shanker N) is a poet and translator based in Kerala, India. He has published four collections of poetry and a play. Ra Sh translates from Malayalam and Tamil into English. He has several publications from Malayalam into English; from Tamil he has translated Bama's *The Ichi Tree Monkey* (2021); and co-translated a volume of Sri Lankan poems, *Waking is Another Dream* (2010). He has also translated the Tamil poems of Leena Manimekalai into Malayalam. A book of 142 translations, in Malayalam, and other Indian and international languages, of his poem 'Silent Farewells' was published in 2022 by Fabian Books.

Lakshmi de Silva: see page 333.

412

Prathap de Silva: We have been unable to obtain a biographical note for this translator who died a few years ago.

Sumathy Sivamohan: see page 344.

S. Sivasegaram: see page 350.

Geetha Sukumaran is a Tamil poet and a bilingual translator from India, who works between English and Tamil. She has published a translation of Sylvia Plath's poems into Tamil (2013) and a collection of her own poems, *Otrai Pakadaiyil Enchum Nampikkai* (2014). Her translations have been widely published in anthologies and journals, and her translation of P. Ahilan's poetry, *Then There Were No Witnesses*, was published by Mawenzi House in 2018. She is the recipient of a SPARROW R. Thyagarajan award for her poetry in Tamil. She is pursuing doctoral research on culinary narratives from Sri Lanka, at York University, Toronto.

Shash Trevett: see page 377.

Viviemarie Vanderpoorten: see page 382.

Pramila Venkateswaran is a poet and translator and co-director of Matwaala: South Asian Diaspora Poetry Festival. She has published eight collections of poetry, most recently, *We Are Not a Museum* (2022). She teaches English and Women's Studies at Nassau Community College, New York.

Rebecca Whittington won the Sardar Patel award in 2019 for her PhD dissertation from the Department of South and Southeast Asian Studies at the University of California, Berkeley. She has translated work from Tamil, Bengali, and Hindi and has a working knowledge of Persian, Arabic, Spanish, Italian and Icelandic. Her publications include *Time Will Write a Song for You* (2014), an anthology of contemporary Sri Lankan Tamil writing; and 'Patni (Wife)', a translation of a Hindi poem by Gopal Prasad.

Ratna Sri Wijesinghe: see page 397.

ACKNOWLEDGEMENTS

The poems in this anthology are reprinted from the following sources, all by permission of the copyright holders cited below. New translations cited as such are likewise printed with the permission of the translators. Thanks are due to the poets, translators and other copyright holders for their kind permission to include the work noted here. References to *Lost Evenings, Lost Lives: Tamil Poems of the Sri Lankan Civil War*, ed. Lakshmi Holmström & Sascha Ebeling (Arc, 2016) are abbreviated to *Lost Evenings, Lost Lives*; references to *Mirrored Images: An Anthology of Sri Lankan Poetry*, ed. Rajiva Wijesinha (National Book Trust, India, 2013) to *Mirrored Images*; references to *Time Will Write a Song for You*, ed. Kannan M., Rebecca Whittington, D. Senthil Babu, David C. Buck (French Institute of Pondicherry/Penguin Books India, 2014) to *Time Will Write a Song for You*; reference to *Uprooting the Pumpkin: Selections from Tamil Literature in Sri Lanka*, ed. Chelva Kanaganayagam (OUP India, 2016) to *Uprooting the Pumpkin*.

Aazhiyaal: 'Unheeded Sights' and 'Mannamperis', translated by Lakshmi Holmström from *Lost Evenings*. **Bashana Abeywardane:** 'The Window of the Present', translated by Prathap de Silva, from *Journalists for Democracy Sri Lanka*, 30 July 2013. **Packiyanathan Ahilan:** 'Days of the Bunker III', 'A Poem about Your Village and My Village', 'Corpse no. 182' and 'Corpse no. 183. Newborn no. 2', translated by Sascha Ebeling from *Lost Evenings*. **Alari:** 'When Someone is Killed', new translation by Shash Trevett; 'A Lifeless Sea' and 'The Sun Wanders, Searching for Shade', translated by Shash Trevett from *Adda Stories: Translations South and South-East Asia* (Issue 4: 2021). **Liyanage Amarakeerthi:** 'Once Upon a Foreign Country' and 'Will We Find the Strings of the Veena?', translated by Liyanage Amarakeethi from *Mirrored Images*; 'A Poem's Plea', new translation by Vivimarie Vanderpoorten. **Premini Amerasinghe:** 'The Matrimonial Column' and 'A Rustic Scene' from *Tapestry of Verse* (Sarasavi, 2019). **Indran Amirthanayagam:** 'The Death Tree' and 'Not Much Art' from *Ceylon, R.I.P.* (International Centre of Ethnic Studies, 2001). **Anar:** 'Killing a Woman', 'Woman' and 'Zulaikha', translated by Hari Rajaledchumy with Fran Lock from *Leaving* (The Poetry Translation Centre, 2021). **Jean Arasanayagam:** 'Wasp' from *The Pomegranate Flower* (University of Michigan, 2005); 'The Poet' from *Shooting the Floricans* (Samjna, 1993); 'A Country at War' from *Trial By Terror* (Rimu, 1987); 'Ancestors' from *Reddened Water Flows Clear* (Forest Books, 1991). **Parvathi Solomons Arasanayagam:** 'Identity' from *Identities* (Godage, 2007); 'A Familiar Terrain', 'Human Driftwood' from *Humantide* (Godage, 2015). **Thiyagarajah Arasanayagam:** 'Kappal Matha – Kayts' from *White Lanterns Wesak* (Godage, 2011). **Ki. Pi. Aravindan:** 'Look at the Sky', 'Directions' and 'The Night

Approaches'; new translations by Shash Trevett. **Upekala Athukorala:** 'Snaggle Tooth', 'Some Yashodara's' and 'Crazy Woman' from *Speechless is the River*, a translation by Viviemarie Vanderpoorten of Upekala Athukorala's *Irthu Aga Shesha Path* (Sarasavi Publishers, Colombo, 2023). **Avvai:** 'The Homecoming', translated by Lakshmi Holmström from *Lost Evenings*; 'The Return', translated by Lakshmi Holmström from *The Rapids of a Great River: The Penguin Book of Tamil Poetry*, ed. Lakshmi Holmstöm, Subashree Krishnaswamy and K. Srilata (Penguin, 2009).

Thilakarathna Kuruvita Bandara: 'The Gods Alarmed, Descend to Earth' and 'A Child's Pestering', translated by Ranjini Obeyesekere from *Sinhala Poetry in Translation* (Vijitha Yapa, 2017). **Ruwan Bandujeewa:** 'Earthworms', 'A Tree to its Flowers' and 'A Joy – A Bliss', translated by Chamini Kulathunga from *Doublespeak: Literary Translation Journal* (University of Pennsylvania, Spring 2020); 'What Answers from the Common Crows?', new translation by Gaya Nagahawatta. **Biriyanthi:** 'Sorrow Created and Sorrows Relieved', translated by Nedra Rodrigo from *Still We Sing: Voices on Violence Against Women*, ed. Sarita Jenamani (Dhauli Books, India, 2021). **S. Bose:** 'My Life in Books', from 'The Veenai' and 'Now', new translations by Shash Trevett.

Suresh Canagarajah: 'Lavannya's Twilight Bike Ride', by permission of the author. **Cheliyan:** 'Those Who Enter the Pit' and 'Untitled', new translations by Shash Trevett; 'Merciless Ones', translated by Rebecca Whittington from *Time Will Write a Song for You*; 'On a Rainy Day', translated by S. Pathmanathan from *Uprooting the Pumpkin*. **Cheran:** 'I Could Forget All This', 'My Land' and 'Nandikadal', translated by Lakshmi Holmström from *In a Time of Burning*, tr. Lakshmi Holmström (Arc, 2013); 'Grave Song', translated by Shash Trevett from *From a Borrowed Land* (Smith|Doorstop, 2021). **Rienzi Crusz:** 'Song of the Immigrant', 'Leaving – Michael-style' and 'The Elephant Who Would Be a Poet' from *Insurgent Rain: Selected Poems 1974-1996* (TSAR, 1997).

A.P. David: 'Fishermen' by permission of the author. **Megan Dhakshini:** 'In Lockdown' and '21' by permission of the author. **Wimal Dissanayake:** 'Anuradhapura', translated by A.T. Dharmapriya from *Mirrored Images*; 'Strange Flowering', translated by Lakshmi de Silva from *Mirrored Images*; 'Homecoming', translated by Wimal Dissanayake from *Journal of South Asian Literature* (Spring 1987); 'Anjali', translated by Wimal Dissanayake from *The Toronto South Asian Review* (Vol 3: 2, Fall 1984). **Dushyanthan:** 'They Do Not Know', translated by Sascha Ebeling from *Lost Evenings*.

Patrick Fernando: 'The Fire Dance', 'Aeneas and Dido', 'Ballad of a River' from *Selected Poems* (OUP India, 1984). **Sandra Fernando:** '…and in the middle', 'Setting the Table for Dinner' and 'Shirt' from *Candle And Other Poems* (Vijitha Yapa, 2003). **Ru Freeman:** 'In Your Hour of Need, God' from *Narrative*; 'Loose Change' from *Adirondack Review*; 'Erasure' by permission of the author.

Buddhadasa Galappathy: 'I Am Not Sita', translated by Ranjini Obeyesekere from *Sinhala Poetry in Translation* (2017); 'Alms for King Vessantara', translated by Malini Govinnage from *Mirrored Images*. **Kapila M. Gamage:** 'Teriyum Kokila' and 'Prayers to Konesvaran', translated by Chamini Kulathunga. **V.V. Ganeshananthan:** 'the faithful scholar dreams of being exact' and from 'The Five-year Tongue Twisters' from *Groundviews* and *Michigan Quarterly Review*. **Yasmine Gooneratne:** 'Horoscope', 'Peradeniya Landscape', 'The Brave Man Who Keeps Snakes as His Pets' from *Celebrations and Departures* (Pennsylvania State University, 1991). **Sunil Govinnage:** 'The City of Light', 'My English Verse' and 'On Becoming an Intellectual' from *White Mask* (2004). **Amali Gunasekera:** 'How to Watch a Solar Eclipse in a Bowl of Water' and 'Peace' from *Lotus Gatherers* (Bloodaxe Books, 2016); from 'Beloved' from *The Golden Thread* (Bloodaxe Books, 2022), by permission of the publisher. **Dayasena Gunasinghe:** 'The Blue of My Eyes', translated by Ranjini Obeyesekere from *An Anthology of Modern Writing from Sri Lanka*, eds. Ranjini Obeyesekere & C. Fernando (University of Arizona Press, 1981). **Siri Gunasinghe:** 'A Memorial', 'The Water Buffalo' and 'Renunciation', translated by Ranjini Obeyesekere from *Sinhala Poetry in Translation* (2017). **Yvonne Gunawardena:** 'Homecoming', 'Ancestral Voices', 'Thoughts on a Train Journey' and 'Letter to England' from *Harbour Lights: More Collected Poems* (Bay Owl, 2011). **Romesh Gunesekara:** 'The Big Wave' and 'Circled by Circe' by permission of the author. **Rohitha Gunetilleke:** 'Eventually' and 'Cowboys' by permission of the author.

Aparna Halpé: 'Poson' and '5.45 at St George' from *Precarious* (Bay Owl, 2013). **Ashley Halpé:** 'the tale of Divnuhamy', 'all our Aprils' and 'The Second Reading' from *Waiting for the Bells: Collected Poems* (Gunasena, 2013). **Tashyana Handy:** 'C189' by permission of the author. **Lal Hegoda:** 'I'm a Man Because You Are a River', translated by A.T. Dharmapriya from *Mirrored Images*; 'Bhikku at the Ferry', translated by Manoj Ariyaratne from *Mirrored Images*. **Ajith C. Herath:** 'Last Station', translated by Prathap de Silva from *Journalists for Democracy Sri Lanka*, 26 December 2014; from 'Seven Dreams', translated by Ajith C. Herath, Dawson Preethi and Karin Clark from *Journalists for Democracy Sri Lanka*, 18 June 2012. **Vipuli Hettiarachchi:** 'We are Women', translated by Liyanage Amarakeerthi from *Mirrored Images*; 'Balachandran' and 'Iron Lady' from *Vipuli Hettiarachchi Rukavya Rupavalia* (A Chain of Poetic Images), translated by Shirani Rajapakse (Godage, 2015).

Eric Illyaparachchi: 'The Bomb at the Rooftop Restaurant', translated by Gaya Nagahawatta from *adda online magazine* (August 2021); 'Against Colombo', new translation by Gaya Nagahawatta.

Faheema Jahan: 'The Sea's Waters', translated by Lakshmi Holmström from *Lost Evenings*; 'After Catastrophe', translated by Rebecca Whittington from *Time Will Write a Song for You*. **V.I.S. Jayapalan:** 'One Night in Frankfurt' and 'Blue', new translations by

417

Shash Trevett; 'Hope', translated by Rebecca Whittington from *Time Will Write a Song for You*; 'Songs of the Defeated 1,4 & 11', translated by Meena Kandasamy from *Waking is Another Dream: Poems on the Genocide in Eelam*, ed. Ravikumar (Navayana Publishing, 2010). **Ramya Jegatheesan**: from 'The Ariel Collection, or Colonise my tongue and laugh at the irony', by permission of the author. **A. Jesurasa**: 'Under New Shoes', translated by Lakshmi Holmström from *Lost Evenings*; 'In Memory of the Nameless', 'Afterwards' and 'Yet, Time Remains', new translations by Shash Trevett. **Ramya Chamalie Jirasinghe**: 'Food for My Daughter', 'On Waiting with a Friend Getting His Heart Tested', by permission of the author.

Madri Kalugala: 'Last night I dreamed your horse had died' and 'Sundowning' from *Exulansis* (Wachana, 2021). **Karunakaran**: 'Along That Very Road', translated by Lakshmi Holmström from *Lost Evenings*; 'Burning Nests' and 'The Warrior Who Could Not Part from His Shadow', translated by Rebecca Whittington from *Time Will Write a Song for You*. **U. Karunatilake**: 'Letter from Boralanda' and 'Hometown' from *Testament in Autumn* (Nugegoda: Sarasavi Publishers, 2004). **Timran Keerthi**: 'The Forgotten Book', translated by Ranjini Obeyesekere from *Sinhala Poetry in Translation* (2017). **George Keyt**: 'Kandyan Village' from Collected Poems, ed. H.A.I. Goonetilleke (The George Keyt Foundation, 1991). **Parakrama Kodituwakku**: 'Court Inquiry of a Revolutionary', 'An Unfinished Lesson' and 'Little Brother', translated by Ranjini Obeyesekere from *Sinhala Poetry in Translation* (2017). **Senerath Gonsal Korala**: 'The Song of a New Shawl', translated by A.T. Dharmapriya from *Poems from the SAARC Region* (2011). **Sita Kulatunga**: 'Pitu padam namamaham (I worship at the feet of my father)' and 'Why' from *A Godé Person and Other Poems* (Godage, 2003). **Neetha Kunaratnam**: 'The Afterlife', 'Poppy' and 'Beeline' from *Just Because* (Smokestack, 2018).

Latha: from 'Untitled', sections 1, 3 & 4, translated by Ra Sh from *Waking is Another Dream* (2010). **Sundra Lawrence**: 'Gold' and 'Rassam' from *Warriors* (Fly On The Wall, 2021). **Mahakavi**: 'Ahalikai', translated by Chelva Kanaganayakam from *Uprooting the Pumpkin*; from 'Birth' and from 'Excellence', new translations by Shash Trevett. **Sunanada Mahendra**: 'The Mountain', translated by A.T. Dharmapriya from *Poems from the SAARC Region* (2011). **Imaad Majeed**: 'arma christi' and 'keppetipola mawatha' published online, by permission of the author. **Sharanya Manivannan**: 'The Mothers' from *Rattle* (April 2019); 'River' from *The Altar of the Only World* (HarperCollins India, 2017). **Arji Manuelpillai**: 'credit card', 'after the Sri Lankan bombing that kills 360 (after the 20-year war that killed significantly more)' and 'after being called a paki', from *Mutton Rolls* (Out-Spoken Press, 2020). **Mishal Mazin**: 'Rajagiriya' and 'Té Kadé' from *The Slick Mongoose* (self-published, 2018), by permission of the author. **Ciara Mandulee Mendis**: 'The Dancing Woman at Embekke' and 'SWOT Analysis on Marriage', by permission of the author. **Tyrrell**

Mendis: 'Pivot' and 'Spring Morning' from *Broken Petals* (The Mitre Press, 1965). **Carl Muller:** 'Deiyyo Saakki!' from *A Bedlam of Persuasions* (Vijitha Yapa, 2005); 'Que sera, sera' from *Propitiations* (Vijitha Yapa, 2004). **R. Murugaiyan:** 'Variations' and 'Toil', translated by R. Murugaiyan from *Uprooting the Pumpkin*; 'Aboard a Van', translated by S. Rajasingham from *The Toronto South Asian Review* (Vol 3: 2, Fall 1984).

Neelaavanan: 'Sleep', translated by R. Murugaiyan from *Uprooting the Pumpkin*; 'Murungaikaai', new translation by Shash Trevett; 'Faster, Faster', translated by A.J. Canagaratna from *Lutesong and Lament: Tamil Writing from Sri Lanka*, ed. Chelva Kanaganayakam (TSAR publications, 2001). **Nilanthan:** 'End of an Age 2' and 'Kanji Song 1', new translations by Geetha Sukumaran and Shash Trevett; 'The Mother of Two Martyrs', translated by Geetha Sukumaran and Shash Trevett from *Poetry London* (Issue 100, Autumn 2021); 'Pina Koorai', translated by Geetha Sukumaran and Shash Trevett from *Modern Poetry in Translation* (fourth series, no.2, 2021). **S. Niroshini:** 'Neruda's Last Word(s)', 'Period Party / புண்ணியதானம் ', and 'Girl, Ceylon' from *Darling Girl* (Bad Betty Press, 2021). **M.A. Nuhman:** from 'Saluting Heroic Vietnam from the Corners of Our Little Village', new translation by Sumathy Sivamohan; 'Last Evening, This Morning' and 'Buddha Murdered', translated by Lakshmi Holmström from *Lost Evenings*.

Michael Ondaatje: 'Letters & Other Worlds', 'The Cinnamon Peeler' from *The Cinnamon Peeler: Selected Poems* (Vintage, 1997); 'House on a Red Cliff' from *Handwriting* (Vintage, 2000).

S. Pathmanathan: 'See Through', translated by S. Pathmanathan from *Sri Lankan Tamil Poetry*, ed. S. Pathmanathan (Sivasothy Pathmanathan, 2014); 'A Thorn in My Flesh', translated by S. Pathmanathan from *Down Memory Lane* (English Association of Jaffna, 2021). **Vihanga Perera:** 'The Playwright' from *Busted Intellectual* (Creative Prints, 2010); 'The Memory of Fragrance' originally published online, by permission of the author. **Kasro Ponnuthurai:** 'Amir's Lover', new translation by Nedra Rodrigo. **S. Porawagamage:** 'My Kinda Name', 'The Wings' and 'The First Name' by permission of the author. **Pramil:** 'The Desert', translated by the author, and 'The Great Wind Tamer', by permission of the author; '(your) Name', new translation by Janani Ambikapathy.

Shirani Rajapakse: 'Unwanted' and 'Chant of a Million Women' from *Chant of a Million Women* (self-published, 2017), by permission of the author. **S. Rajasingham:** 'Lizards', translated by S. Rajasingham from *The Toronto South Asian Review* (Vol 3: 2, Fall 1984). **T. Ramalingam:** 'The Future', translated by Lakshmi Holmström from *Uprooting the Pumpkin*. **Anne Ranasinghe:** 'Judgement', 'At What Dark Point' from *Poems* (Lake House, 1971); 'July 1983' from *At What Dark Point* (English Writers Co-operative of Sri Lanka, 1991). **Ariyawansa Ranaweera:** 'Today's Lion', 'The Giraffe' and 'Paintings at Gothami Vihara', translated by E.M.G. Edirisinghe from *Mirrored Images*; 'The

Intersection', translated by Liyanage Amarakeerthi from *Mirrored Images*. **Eva Ranaweera:** 'In the Street of the Pearl Tree' *from What will you do do do Clara what will you do?* (Godage, 1994). **Chalani Ranwala:** 'The in-betweeners' by permission of the author. **A.M. Rashmy:** 'Songs in a Time of Confinement' 1 & 3, new translations by Nedra Rodrigo; 'Songs in a Time of Confinement 2', translated by Nedra Rodrigo from *Words and Worlds* (PEN Austria, Winter 2020). **Sahanika Ratnayake:** 'Murmur', 'Case Study #1: Vocabulary Lesson', 'Case Study #3: Chariot' by permission of the author. **Vidyan Ravinthiran:** 'Uncanny Valley' from *Grun-tu-molani* (Bloodaxe Books, 2014); 'Ceylon' from *The Million-petalled Flower of Being Here* (Bloodaxe Books, 2019), by permission the publisher; 'The Annupoorunyamal', originally published in the *London Review of Books*, reprinted by permission of the author. **Monica Ruwanpathirana:** 'My Grief' and 'Your Friend She is a Woman', translated by Ranjini Obeyesekere from *Sinhala Poetry in Translation* (2017); 'Wife Lamenting', translated by Ranjini Obeyesekere from *Mirrored Images*. **Pubudu Sachithanandan:** 'Anthem: The war is over' by permission of the author. **Minoli Salgado:** 'Blood Witness' and 'Telegraph' by permission of the author. **A. Sankari:** 'Living and Dying', translated by Lakshmi Holmström from *Lost Evenings*; 'In Their Eyes', translated by Sumathy Sivamohan. **Dipti Saravanamuttu:** 'Among the Icons' and 'Landscape Art' from *Language of the Icons* (Angus & Robertson, 1993); 'Line Drawing' and 'Flying North in Winter' from *The Colosseum* (Five Islands Press, 2004). **Peter Scharen:** 'Landscape', 'Winter Lines' and 'Transitory' from Signs and Seas (Angus & Robertson, 1980). **Mahagama Sekera:** 'The Moon and New York City', 'No. 16' and 'No. 24', translated by Ranjini Obeyesekere from *Sinhala Poetry in Translation* (2017); 'See Yourself in My Poetry', new translation by Garrett Field. **Selvi:** 'Summertime', 'Raman, like Raavanan' and 'Within Me', new translations by Shash Trevett. **G.B. Senanayake:** 'Philosophers and Pundits', translated by A.T. Dharmapriya from *Mirrored Images*. **Dishani Senaratne:** 'Dreams' and 'Lament' by permission of the author. **Gamini Seneviratne:** 'Tune for Ariel', 'Nangi' and 'Arjuna' from *New Ceylon Writing* (1970). **Malinda Seneviratne:** 'Nangi', 'Oil-bullets' and 'Mitsi' from *open words are for love-letting* (SANASA 2012). **Seni Seneviratne:** 'Dear Mum' from *Unknown Soldier* (Peepal Tree Press, 2019); 'Opus Tesselatum' from *Wild Cinnamon and Winter Skin* (Peepal Tree Press, 2007); 'Slave Lodge, Cape Town' from *Her Wings of Glass* (Second Light Publications, 2014). **Natchathiran Sevvinthiyan:** 'Until My Wineglass Was Empty', new translation by Shash Trevett; from 'Kokkatticholai 166', translated by Sumathy Sivamohan. **Sharmilla Seyyid** 'Three Dreams' and 'Keys to an Empty Home', translated by Lakshmi Holmström from *Lost Evenings*; 'Fire', new translation by Pramila Venkateswaran. **Alfreda de Silva:** 'Grassfields in Sunlight' and 'Cormorants and Children' from *Out of the dark the sun* (Sarvodaya, 1977); 'The End of Something' and 'Kotmale' from *The Unpredictable Blood* (Samayawardhana, 1988).

Lakshmi de Silva: 'Tangalla, 9th April 1971', from *New Ceylon Writing* (1971); 'Addition and Subtraction' from *New Ceylon Writing* (1979). **S.J. Sindu:** 'Gods in the Surf', 'For Sale: 1997 Christmas Barbie, $600' from *Dominant Genes.* **Regi Siriwardena:** 'Birthday Apology and Apologia', 'Colonial Cameo' and 'To the Muse of Insomnia', from *Selected Writings*, ed. A.J. Canagaratna (Colombo: International Centre for Ethnic Studies, 2005). **Shirani Situnayake:** 'Beginnings' by permission of the author. **Shanmugam Sivalingam:** 'Nowadays', 'Unsung Songs' and 'In Memory of Our Songs', new translations by Shash Trevett. **Sumathy Sivamohan:** 'on reading the astonishing novel "mm" by shoba shakthi' from *like myth and mother: a political autobiography in poetry and prose* (Sirahununi, 2008). **S. Sivaramani:** 'Oppressed by Night of War', translated by Lakshmi Holmström from *Lost Evenings*; 'Untitled', translated by Lakshmi Holmström from *The Rapids of a Great River* (2009). **S. Sivasegaram:** from 'Faces of War', translated by the author; from S. Sivasegaram, *About Another Matter: Poems in Translation* (Dhesiya Kalai Ilakkiyap Peravai, 2004). **Solaikili:** 'The Story of a Golden River', translated by Lakshmi Holmström from *Uprooting the Pumpkin*; 'A Refugee Poet Talking to the Moon', translated by M.A. Nuhman from *Mirrored Images.* **Isuru Chamara Somaweera:** 'The Little Fellow', 'My Pillow Is Wet', 'Mother's Actress Friend' and 'The Meaning of Life', translated by Ranjini Obeyesekere from *Sinhala Poetry in Translation* (2017). **Sandaresee Sudusinghe:** from *Gini Wadunu Piyapath*, '105', '27' and '30', new translations by Chamini Kulathunga. **Pireeni Sundaralingam:** 'Lot's Wife' from *Ploughshares* (2004); 'Fugue' from *American Poetry Review* (2016); 'Times Two' from *Postcolonial Text* (2015).

Yasmin V. Tambiah: 'The Civil War' and 'Sandalwood' from *The Vintage Book of International Lesbian Fiction*, ed. Holoch and Nestle (Vintage, 1999). **M.J.T. Tambimuttu:** 'My Country, My Village' from *Bridge Between Two Worlds* (Peter Owen, 1989). **Theepachelvan:** 'The Lost Kitten', 'A Friend Stands Behind Me' and 'An Unpublished Poem', new translations by Nedra Rodrigo. **Ajith Thilakasena:** 'Where' and 'I Do Not Know If…', translated by Lakshmi de Silva from *Mirrored Images.* **Thiru Thirukumaran:** 'Resurrection', 'This Is How the Buddha Disappeared' and 'A Detached Feather', new translations by Shash Trevett. **Thirumavalavan:** 'Mullaitivu', translated by Sascha Ebeling from *Lost Evenings*; 'Living', translated by S. Pathmanathan from *Mirrored Images.* **Shash Trevett:** 'Uduvil, Nightfall' by permission of the author; 'The Sinhala Only Act, 1956' and 'My Grandfather's House' from *From a Borrowed Land* (Smith|Doorstop, 2021).

Urvasi: 'Do You Understand?' translated by Lakshmi Holmström from *Lost Evenings*; 'Why Must We Wait?' translated by Lakshmi Holmström from *The Rapids of a Great River* (2009).

Vivimarie Vanderpoorten: 'Cadaver' and 'Diplomatic' from *Stitch Your Eyelids Shut* (Akna, 2010); 'Traditional' from *Borrowed Dust* (Sarasavi, 2017). **S. Vilvaratnam:** 'There Was a Time', translated by

Lakshmi Holmström from *Lost Evenings*; 'The Echo of Moonlight', translated by George L. Hart from *Time Will Write a Song for You*. **S. Vinothini**: 'The Mask Maker' and 'The Night', new translations by Shash Trevett. **Nandana Weerasinghe**: 'The Moon-shadow', translated by Manoj Ariyaratne from *Mirrored Images*; 'Full Moon on a Dewdrop', translated by A.T. Dharmapriya from *Mirrored Images*; 'Kalidasa and the Moon', translated by Liyanage Amarakeerthi from *Mirrored Images*; 'Something Square-shaped', translated by Ariyawansa Ranaweera from *Poems from the SAARC Region* (2013). **Rushika Wick**: 'Hair', 'Ultramarine Pink PV15' and 'Yellow Phone in the Yellow House' from *Afterlife as Trash* (Verve, 2021). **Illavalai Wijayendran**: 'To Those Who Bear Sticks', 'The Missing Children' and 'The Veenai and the Sword', new translations by Shash Trevett. **Ratna Sri Wijesinghe**: 'Two Teardrops', translated by Ratna Sri Wijesinghe from *The Toronto South Asian Review* (Vol 3: 2, Fall 1984); 'The Motherless Two', translated by M. Ratnayake from *Mirrored Images*. **Lakdasa Wikkramasinha**: 'Don't Talk to Me about Matisse' and 'The Flames, 1972' from *O Regal Blood* (Praja Prakasakayo, 1975); 'Luis de Camoes' from *The Grasshopper Gleaming* (Felix Press, 1976); 'Middle' from *Lustre Poems* (Ariya, 1965).

Richard de Zoysa: 'Animal Crackers', 'Corporation Love Song' (I), 'Gajagavannama' and 'The Poet' from *This Other Eden: The Collected Poems of Richard de Zoysa* (English Association of Sri Lanka, 1990).

The editors wish to record their immense gratitude to Harvard University, for helping fund this anthology, and to Neil Astley at Bloodaxe Books for taking it on.

Our thanks to the following people who helped us source poems, contact details for various poets and translators, and the details of the estates of those deceased: Ahilan, Liyanage Amarakeerthi, Cheran, Malathi de Alwis, Sulochana Dissanayake, Garrett Field, Aparna Halpé, Radhika Holmström, Pathmanabar Iyer, Karunakaran, Chamini Kulathunga, Gaya Nagahawatta, Nilanthan, The Noolaham Foundation, S. Pathmanathan, Vihanga Perera, Menika van der Poorten, Samodh Porawagamage, A.M. Rashmy, Nedra Rodrigo, Shyam Selvadurai, Sumathy Sivamohan, Kaala Subramaniam, Geetha Sukumaran, Vivimarie Vanderpoorten, Senaka Weeraman, Rajiva Wijesinha.

Every effort has been made to secure permissions for the works reprinted here, either from the poets and translators themselves, their publishers, or their estates. There are however some writers for whom no contact information was available. If you feel that any of the poems have appeared without permission, please contact the editors through Bloodaxe Books.